Ramakrishna and Christ

THE SUPERMYSTICS

New  *Interpretations*

PAUL HOURIHAN

Vedantic Shores Press

Published by Vedantic Shores Press
P.O. Box 493100
Redding, CA   96049-3100 U.S.A.

ACKNOWLEDGEMENTS:
We gratefully acknowledge permission to use excerpts from the following:
Sri Ramakrishna The Great Master trans. Swami Jagadananda. Copyright © 1952
by the President, Sri Ramakrishna Math, Mylapore, Madras.
The Upanishads, Breath of the Eternal, trans. Swami Prabhavananda and Frederick
Manchester. Copyright © 1947, 1957 by the Vedanta Society of Southern
California; *The Song of God: Bhagavad-Gita*, trans. Swami Prabhavananda and
Christopher Isherwood, Vedanta Press, Copyright © 1944, 1951 by the Vedanta
Society of Southern California.

Christian scriptural texts used in this work are taken from the King James version
of the Holy Bible.

Cover photos courtesy of and available from The Vedanta Society of Southern
California.

Cover and book design by Angela Underwood www.booksindesign.com

Publisher's Cataloging-in-Publication
(Provided by Quality Books, Inc.)
Hourihan, Paul.
    Ramakrishna and Christ : The Supermystics : new
interpretations / by Paul Hourihan. – 1st ed.
    p. cm.
    Includes bibliographic references and index.
    LCCN 2001097125
    ISBN 1-931816-00-X
    1. Ramakrishna, 1836-1886. 2. Hindus–India–
Biography. 3. Jesus Christ–Hindu interpretations.
4. Jesus Christ–Biography. I. Title.

BL1280.292.R36H68 2002   294.5'55'0922
    QBI01-201384

DEDICATED
To the Memory of
SHIRLEY THÉRÈSE LEWIS
(1936-81)

A devotee of both the great souls treated here,
who in life ceaselessly urged that this work be written.

CONTENTS

The dictum about power tending to corrupt applies to power *per se*, like what each of us habitually exercises over the soul, evident in the way we live, in our inability to sustain higher values: a power so rooted, so extensive, that it becomes identified as the source of our corruption, making it almost impossible for us to gain any comprehension of a personality as *un*-corrupted as Ramakrishna or his predecessor in Nazareth. But we must make the attempt before our slide back to something like unregeneration becomes irreversible. We must take action quickly and apply to our heated brains the balm of understanding, even to the slightest degree, the life of an *avatar*.

A PREFATORY NOTE

Few ever recover from the reflex of awe that fixates the mind upon studying Ramakrishna, India's nonpareil mystic. Skeptics aside, others, whether or not they become partisan, rarely recapture a sense of balance when appraising his life. His unprecedented spiritual career and unique personality leave the minds of the sympathetic in a prolonged state of arrest. Which helps not at all large numbers of souls who might benefit from an introduction to his life but are estranged by hagiographical passion, the euphoria of the converted. *Analyze everything* was one of his characteristic sayings, although in the case of the man who spoke it no analysis has been made that will provide much interest for the Westerner who comes to the legend without benefit of faith, but who yet might sincerely wish to know where to lodge his spiritual hungers.

The present work attempts to remedy this lack and so differs from the several biographical studies in existence. It also avowedly makes its appeal to the Western mind, and possibly to Hindus capable, with one of their own mystics, of that searching analysis of all things which not only Ramakrishna but their other illustrious names from Buddha to Gandhi have enjoined upon them. For biographical particulars it depends upon two massive works, the chief pillars of the extensive Ramakrishna literature: *Sri Ramakrishna, the Great Master* by a direct disciple, Swami Saradananda; and *The Gospel of Sri Ramakrishna* in the complete and literate translation of Swami Nikhilananda.

But a saint's mind is so unlike every other that in hazarding a psychological study one is risking a great presumption. Perhaps the author can only reveal himself—his own psychology, not the mystic's: the saint's life a mirror in which are reflected the shadows of the author's psyche. Fortunate, at least, if he is able to correlate them sufficiently with the reader's to suggest something universally relevant in the picture he draws.

Although this work in its original intent was to be a concentrated analysis of Ramakrishna alone, there were so many cross-references to Christ in the early chapters that subliminal intuitions were plainly overruling the promptings of the conscious will. The result was a book about Ramakrishna *and* Christ, mystics supreme, who over the last twenty-five centuries—their last peer, Gautama Buddha—stand preeminent for spirituality. Just as a new Ramakrishna is presented here, so there is much that is unexpected in the portrayal of the Galilean; in both cases the orthodox devotee will doubtless suffer unavoidable chagrin not only from the nature of the material but from the realization that minds exist which approach the object of his reverence from standpoints that have never occurred to him. We are less offended by heretical sentiments than by the discovery that heretical minds, after the truth has been thoroughly revealed to us, go on existing.

If more of the book has been devoted to Ramakrishna it is because many pages had to be spent establishing the facts of his life before that life could be properly assessed—a condition obviously not applicable to the founder of Christianity.

Ramakrishna and Christ

THE SUPERMYSTICS

1

 Early Life: Kamarpukur

BOTH OF RAMAKRISHNA'S PARENTS declared they had received messages from the gods Vishnu and Shiva, with a special communication from the household deity Rama (considered an early avatar by Hindus), to the effect that because of their virtuous lives they would become parents to a divine child—that, indeed, Rama himself, an incarnation of Vishnu, would be born as their son. At this birth,[*] in awe-struck gratitude, they named him after Rama—Gadadhar, or *Gadai* as he became known: affectionate epithets for the god.

Whether the supernal messages were received or imagined, in a very short time life in Gadai's family proceeded in ordinary, mundane channels and the theophanies later alleged were as quickly forgotten.

The birthplace, Kamarpukur, a rural Bengal village some sixty miles northwest of Calcutta, was situated near a highroad which pilgrims and itinerant monks took to the venerable shrine at Puri, where was

---

[*] His birth-date may have relevance for Americans, the people—an enlightened stratum of them—who discovered and made famous his chief disciple, Vivekananda, giving him as a revelation to his own homeland, and who therefore, as well, brought Ramakrishna to the world's notice. He was born early in the morning of February 18, 1836, midway through the ten-day interval separating nativities of the two most celebrated Americans, Washington and Lincoln. Vivekananda himself often expressed fondness for America, and his impassioned poem of admiration, "The Fourth of July," marks the day in 1902 when, after careful planning, he took a yogi's leave of earthly life. In these dates there may be, or there may not be, some special significance.

observed the cult of Krishna as Jagannath. Hence there were usually holy men in the environs of the village throughout Gadai's boyhood and religious festivals of various kinds going on. While still of tender age he loved to sit among the sadhus as they rested on their journey and listen to their stories of old-time saints and their well-rehearsed mythology of Hindu gods. And his father, Kshudiram, a pious brahmin, further nourished his religious imagination out of his own stock of inherited caste tradition.

Kshudiram was sixty-one and his wife Chandra (or Chandramani) forty-five when Gadai, fourth among five children was born. The eldest son, Ramkumar, fated for a critical role in the drama, was thirty-one years older than Gadai; the next son, Rameswar, ten years older. There were two sisters, Katyayani, twenty-six years older, and Sarvamangala, three years younger.

He went a few years to school, but listlessly attended. He could write a little, read perhaps less, but as he failed afterwards to make use of what schooling he did have he lost most of even that and later was, essentially, what we would call illiterate. All his knowledge of the Hindu scriptures, for which his memory was prodigious, was communicated orally.

After tales about gods and religious heroes he liked drawing and music best and excelled in both.

Those who profess to see in his life a register of divine commentary on human endeavor, manifesting even in his early affinities, would find in his boyish enthusiasm an affirmation of three major arts: poetic literature, music, painting—while mathematics repelled him. From which they might conclude that mathematicians, like rich men, cannot gain the kingdom. The reason is not far to seek: just as great wealth leads the mind to believe in the reality of riches, so mathematics leads it to believe in the reality of numbers. The arts awaken the power of the imagination and feeling—empathy, sensibility—and at least point the mind toward that which is shimmering through them. Through the word, first. In the beginning was the Word. Then music, the divine Sound—the harmony of the spheres as the word becomes creation, manifests as form. The arts stir the mind to its depths—to some of its depths—and lead us expectantly on. Mathematics deifies abstraction, encloses itself in a cocoon, cuts the mind off from vital flow, organic response, living principle.

The drama is salutary also—providing noble or religious themes are enacted. He loved to watch plays commemorating ancient spiritual glories or dramatizing the lives of famous sages, loved even more to participate in them, memorizing all the roles and performing with a talent, including a special gift for mimicry, that amazed and delighted everyone. He formed his own theatrical company of teenagers, which staged ambitious dramas like those they had been watching, drawn from the ancient Hindu epics.*

Nature, too, is glorified in Gadai's boyhood. His first supersensuous rapture was inspired directly by Nature in one of her rare, bewitching moods. It was the experience in the paddy field just as a storm was gathering. He was walking home eating a handful of puffed rice, felt the electric atmosphere generated by the imminent summer storm, gazed up at a black spreading cloud that completely filled the sky, when suddenly a flock of milk-white cranes flew overhead. The exquisite, dramatic contrast enchanted a mind already quivering with joyous tension in the overcharged atmosphere; with a cry of ecstasy he fainted and fell to the ground. Later his friends found him and carried him home.

So the beauty of Nature may also be a source of truth, may stimulate the mind to receive influences borne to it from transcendental realms: Nature being the mask through which shimmers the light from beyond.

Both his parents, forgetting their visionary experiences of long ago, worried about the incident; Chandra thought evil influences were at work on him. A brahmin (and his wife) believes his way of life unparagoned, the standard of all excellence, the object of all envy. He may have a divine child born to him but the child's way of life, his values and experiences, must essentially conform with one's own: otherwise the evil eye may be at work. At the very least one has cause for anxiety.

The epiphany in the paddy-field made it obvious that Gadai's sensibilities were not only more acute than most but unique. Still, this first

---

* Years later he would enjoy being taken into Calcutta to watch religious dramas in the Star Theatre. Sometimes visiting backstage, he would counsel the actors to perform only the roles depicting heroic or elevated characters. Not only would such dramas inspire the audience but the minds of the actors would benefit directly: it being a basic mystic doctrine that whatever you dwell on persistently, you become. By playing a villain we tend to become one—stirring into psychic manifestation the villain-potential latent in everyone. By playing noble characters we awaken the opposite tendency—also universally latent.

ecstasy came unaccompanied by wisdom. Afterwards he was as carefree, innocent, unsuspecting as ever—a dreamer in Eden. But the experience demonstrated he was ready for something more advanced. Let him be made serious—*introspective*. Let the darker hues of Existence, and of his own constitution, emerge—as suddenly as possible, the better to strike his mind with lasting impact; and from a cherished, unanticipated corner. Let him begin his real Life. Let him discover Death—the death of his father.

Kshudiram had once refused to bear false witness against a neighbor despite the plaintiff being a powerful landlord who, in revenge, succeeded in wresting from him ancestral property. He was also a man who wouldn't accept gifts from members of a lower caste and shunned fellow brahmins who offered them religious services; on various similar grounds he rejected brahmins who did not share his rigid caste philosophy, regarding them as unclean. This blend of moral probity, caste exclusiveness, and total obedience to the letter of Vedic injunction, made him a Hindu version of the Hebrew pharisee, Muslim *mullah*, and Christian puritan: self-reliant, self-righteous, dogmatic, orthodox *in extremis*, unimaginative.

His children followed his example, especially the first-born, Ramkumar, and Gadai imbibed from both of them tendencies to unexamined, hereditary brahmin behavior which only spiritual experience later displaced. Had Kshudiram, now sixty-eight, continued to live, these tribal, ethnic patterns of response would doubtless have taken root in his son, which neither he nor the world needed more of. Therefore, to assist the process of his budding new consciousness, foreshadowed by the rapture in the field, Kshudiram, pious, respected, and dogmatic to the end, was, in the same year, taken from the scene.

At seven, Gadai was just old enough to experience grief for the first time. That Kshudiram was mourned by Chandra, and by other family members and the villagers who had held him in repute, only added to the shock of the boy's sudden bereavement. The bitter lesson told him: life was more than running in the fields, living free as a bird. What *was* life, anyway? What was death? Did anyone speak from beyond to the living? How could anyone be sure of these things? If his father could die, anything might be possible.

His mind gradually turned in upon itself, deepened its perception of outer events. Spiritual reality began to tug at his consciousness. He found it difficult to interest himself in school and spent most of his time away from it, despite the efforts of everyone to get him to change his ways. Nature he still loved but there was something he was beginning to love more, even in its rudimentary state: his own mind, his inner world, the movement of his own thoughts.

He began to frequent, in the Kamarpukur environs, the two cremation-grounds and other solitary places. He grew more quiet, though retaining his boyish amiability. He was noticed to observe others with an extraordinary attention to the details of their speech and behavior. He continued to go to school but with no interest in any subject except what pertained to spiritual themes. His preternatural memory exhibited its powers in his memorization of hymns, religious tales, dramas taken from the ancient epics and *Puranas*. He began to fall into abstracted moods which, more than before, came upon him spontaneously. Sometimes they took the form of trances, when his limbs would go numb and motionless, his mind lost to consciousness. At least one of the village women, Prasanna by name, recognized his spiritual nature acting upon his mind as the cause of these conditions, but Chandra, having given birth only to his flesh and therefore never attuned to his inward life, worried always that they had something to do with his health. When Gadai told her and other family members that he experienced intense joy at such times, describing some of his visions to them, they remained long in a state of alarm.

On one of these occasions he fell to the ground in the midst of certain village women bound for a nearby shrine to a Hindu goddess, his body rigid, his unconsciousness deep. Nothing succeeded in waking him until Prasanna suggested that the spirit of the goddess may have taken possession of him and therefore they should call on her by name. Which they then did. Almost at once, we are told, the boy's face relaxed, brightened, and slowly external consciousness returned.

More dramatic yet, and reported by many witnesses, was the ecstasy during the Shivaratri, the night-of-Shiva celebration. The adult actor scheduled for the role of the great male god fell ill at the last moment, and Gadai, though only about twelve at this time, was prevailed upon to replace him because of his well-known mastery of the play. After the action began he made his first appearance on the stage with matted hair and body smeared with ashes, traditional accessories to the role of Shiva, the god of renunciation, pacing slowly, rhythmically

to the center of the stage, the audience marveling at the life-likeness of
his performance. As time passed he did not move; it was evident he had
fallen into an ecstatic trance, his body completely motionless, his eyes
transfixed inward. Nothing could rouse him even after he was bodily carried off the stage; the play abruptly ended as the audience dispersed in
confusion and wonder. The trance lasted until early the next morning.

His fondness for the village women and their love for him has
been widely reported; in view of the unique role of the feminine in his
life afterwards we are not surprised. They doted on his boyish singing
of traditional hymns, his flawless rendering of lengthy passages from
ancient epics, his remarkable talent for impersonation, his artless and
guileless nature. They would call for him at his house and sometimes
keep him for hours, particularly after Ramkumar had settled in
Calcutta, leaving Gadai with no guardian, free to spend his time after
his fourteenth year in any way he pleased. He was especially fond of
dressing as a woman and playing the role of female characters in religious dramas, or imitating some well-known woman of the district
with humorous effect. It was said that at such times no one could tell
he was not a woman.

But he was not effeminate—which is weakness, softness, lack of
will. Gadai, and in his later flowering as Ramakrishna, was in texture
essentially masculine—a rigorous male being, a young Shiva. The feminine nature that was highly developed in him, and would become still
more so, was always under the sway of his masculine will: whereas in
the effeminate youth his feminine instincts are at the mercy of themselves, his maleness functioning only as a mask for its opposite reality
within. The ideal, which Gadai even now was heralding, is a maximum
development of both masculine and feminine principles in the psyche—
in the soul—but with the more sensitive, vulnerable feminine girded
and controlled by the rigor of an austere, enlightened masculine.

The women's gravitational attraction toward Gadai, in his
mid-teens and suggesting manhood, itself implied a strong masculine
nature in him. They would not have been drawn so powerfully to a
merely feminine youth, would have sensed the disproportion, the
imbalance, the cross-development. Though their love was pure and
maternal, the erotic, being the life-principle, could not be completely
absent.

Ramkumar's departure for Calcutta was motivated to help the financially pressed household. He planned to set up a school there and as soon as possible to send back funds to Rameswar, who was twenty-six at the time. But Rameswar himself had to bend all his energies to find work and thus had little incentive, or inclination, to function as guardian to the irrepressible Gadai, whom he secretly thought might do better if left unsuperintended anyway. Gadai as a result was more free than ever. Those last two or three years, until his sixteenth, when Ramkumar summoned him to Calcutta, were consequently the freest, happiest he had known, the last such before the unearthly drama began. The enveloping embrace of the village women was a token of what the divine powers intended to communicate to him and of what he in turn would communicate to modern man struggling to cope with the enormous implications and unnerving complexities of the Age of the Woman.

From this standpoint his adolescent challenge to purdah—the concealment of women from men—may be seen as the first blow his life would register against traditional attitudes toward females: those, at least, which prevented the spiritual growth of men and women alike. Purdah, a product, like so much in India, of Hindu folk religion—part of the rank ethnic forest of custom and prejudice which had also produced the pariah, the caste system, suttee, and animal sacrifice—symbolized the long epoch when the dominant masculine element in society kept hidden and undeveloped the feminine power of its own psyche. East and West, pursuing each's idiosyncrasies, had both practiced this segregation. The result had been, in the East, the stultification of the female; in the West, the disintegration of the male.

A certain Durgadas Pyne, having many females in his Kamarpukur household, often boasted that male strangers had never seen his women nor could ever imagine what their inner, secluded apartments looked like, and scorned other householder males who failed to enforce purdah as strictly as he did. According to village tradition—which we may accept as true, in view of all we know about him at this stage—Gadai is presented, even at fourteen or fifteen, as lecturing Durgadas on what alone could protect women, namely, devotion to God and a well-developed moral life.

Shortly afterwards he disguised himself as a poor young weaver woman with a basket on his arm, his face veiled, his well-rehearsed

movements suiting the action to the word, the word to the action, in
the feminine manner, begging Durgadas at sundown for a night's shelter since "she" had become separated from her friends and had nowhere
to stay. Durgadas directed her forthwith to the women of the house,
who questioned and then readily accepted her, providing a bed for the
night. During an interval of several hours she observed the ways of the
sequestered women, studied the inner apartments, joined in their general talk, and only got up abruptly at the sound of Rameswar's voice
calling out loudly (it having grown dark long since): "Gadai! Gadai!
Where are you?" To which the poor young weaver woman, running
out of the inner apartments toward the front of the house replied: "I
am coming, brother!"—to the astonishment of all the women and of
Durgadas Pyne, who, it is said, took the trick played on him in good
humor and, perhaps, with food for private reflection as a result of
Gadai's subtle instruction.

Throughout his life he was critical of those who had "crazes" of
any kind. Purdah crazes, food crazes,[*] cleanliness crazes, ritual crazes.
And all the rest. Such people, he taught later, would have great difficulty realizing God. Any extremism rendered you ineligible.

Thus these halcyon years, up to the sixteenth, drew to a close:
more beloved by women than most men ever hope to be in a lifetime.
Freely, eagerly, with some gentle sublimated eroticism, they had
opened to him the wells of their affection. The universal Feminine,
which later he would invoke as Mother Kali, had given him during this
time a preview of her later favors by the love and adulation showered
on him by her human manifestations, so that already his psyche was
conditioned to a softened, deferent, and at the same time highly comfortable and assured mood toward the feminine principle in life.

It seems that everything that had happened to him had come from
a realm of purpose, and even though still a boy his freedom was clearly circumscribed. Or we might say: he was completely free—to follow
the promptings of the divine, which would not be slow in announcing
themselves at each turn in the road.

That road veered sharply when Ramkumar, struggling to cope with
his school and other activities in Calcutta, summoned the

---

* But nobody was perfect. He himself, as we shall see, was afflicted for some years with
undeviating adherence to the brahmin caste standard of food purity—"the religion of the
kitchen" as Vivekananda would call it.

sixteen-year-old Gadai to assist him and to try to continue with an education that had been all but abandoned during Ramkumar's stay in the metropolis. He hoped to act as tutor to his brother while engaging Gadai to serve him as an apprentice in various ways. Without the slightest hesitation Gadai, taking leave forever of the pastoral life he had been enjoying, readily agreed to his request.

2
The Phenomenon of the Family

IT APPEARS TO BE the divine intention that families, parents most of all, always oppose our spiritual interests, and it was so with Gadai, with Christ, Buddha, St. Francis, and in every instance where soul is seeking to emerge from the toils of matter that entrap it. "A man's foes," Christ reminds us (Matthew 10: 36), "shall be those of his own household"—a *spiritual* man's (for whom alone his words were spoken). An ordinary man finds his family a mirror of his needs, desires, and aspirations; not foes at all. A spiritual man copes with it as with beasts of prey.

Though Gadai's father had died when he was seven, his mother, Chandramani, provided the traditional anti-spiritual values we come to expect in parents, and particularly those involved in the advent of great saints. The more potent the spirituality about to be developed the more contrary will we find the family, and especially the parents, to be. Indeed, the bosom of a family that has produced a potential saint is the very last place where spirituality is to be looked for, but where materiality, the operations of nature, of creatureliness, will dominate instead. The higher his potential for God-realization the more they will be rooted in earthliness, in the once-born mentality, in the thrall of *Maya*.

In time the burning fervor of his budding holiness, even as it does not yet know itself, gradually consumes the creature-virtues around it; like an absolute flame it glows in the midst of their dimmer gropings; the moths of their minds, sensing his light, are drawn to it in spite of themselves, become magnetized, and by stages slowly disappear in its orbit or revolve wanly around it like satellite fires.

There is a legend in the Ramakrishna tradition that his mother was saintly, a vessel of grace, as there is in the Christian tradition about Mary. The reality is something else. We recall the visions she and her husband said they had, but when she was not reflecting conventional parental attitudes toward a strange and complex son, she was making efforts to discourage his single-minded spiritual dedication. When she heard, a few years later, that he was spending all his time in prayer and meditation, she felt he was wasting his life, and when false rumors of his madness reached her she at once credited them as confirming her worst fears. Her solution to his intense solitary practices was the same that millions of other mothers have reached at similar junctures: he should get married as soon as possible.

Nature is more powerful than any visions or dreams of gods, however genuine, except when the receiving heart is that of a potential saint.

This is not to suggest she was not a pious woman: a state far from holiness, and the divine consciousness. It is to remind ourselves that the knowledge of God is won only through years and decades and, indubitably, lifetimes of effort. Love of God is not easily *given* to any individual by the Supreme; it is to be attained through innumerable years of ego-sacrifice and unremitting toils of devotion. *Then* it is given, *then* the grace is shown. Neither Chandra nor Mary met these requirements. They were pious *by nature*.

In a spiritual reckoning, what we have by nature does not count. What we mine out of the inner depths, what we make our own by struggle, discipline, consecration, and grace—*that* counts. Indeed, what we have by nature, in a spiritual sense, impedes our growth. Nature is the foe, within and without. The family in the early stages is the enemy because nature—as well as society—is embodied in the family as nowhere else.

Modern followers of Ramakrishna are as superstitious in this matter as ancient followers of Jesus; in both cases the mothers of the God-men were assumed to be channels of perfection, ever-supportive of the greatness of their offspring, remembering the special destiny that had marked them off from other women. The *opposite*, we are sobered to discover, is true.

The image that we have of Mary is purely conjecture without any scriptural foundation. The few places where she appears in the Gospels suggest no special bond between her and her son.

When he was twelve, on the threshold of young manhood, she lost him for a few days during the Passover festival in Jerusalem. After searching everywhere she and her husband finally found him, as Luke reports (2: 48), conversing animatedly with learned men in the Temple, astonishing everyone with his wisdom and responsiveness. "Son," she exclaimed, in the identical accents of parental complaint that any other mother might have registered at that moment, "Why hast thou dealt with us thus? Behold, thy father and I have sought thee sorrowing." No awareness of his divine nature is evident, no remembrance of the angelic visitation thirteen years before, no suggestion that she herself in a moment of tension was capable of anything but the conventional response. And no relief to find *him*—rather, the need to express maternal complaint: *my* troubles, *my* anxieties—why have you done this to *me?* It is true, any normal mother would have had the same creaturely, nature-dominated, instinctive reaction, and that is what we find Mary to be, neither more nor less.

"How is it that ye sought me?" he asks them. Did you not imagine I was under divine protection all the time? Have you forgotten so completely the vision and the dream that came to you thirteen years ago? Did ye not know that I must be about my Father's business? On the basis of her automatic, self-centered reaction upon finding him at the Temple, we can believe Luke when he writes: "And they understood not the saying which he spake unto them." Nature cannot understand Spirit. Flesh cannot hear the voice of the soul when it speaks, as it spoke then. No mother can recognize the genius of her son—least of all when it is spiritual genius. Everyone will discover his greatness before her—and, indeed, she *never* discovers it. She is in thralldom to the immense sway of Nature over her entire life.

At the marriage of Cana, eighteen years later, we see them together for the second time, and no sense of intimacy or mutual rapport arises from their brief but significant exchange. When she urges him to assist the hosts in their embarrassment (the supply of wine having been exhausted), he demurs: *Woman, what have I to do with thee?* (John 2: 4), speaking thus for the benefit of his disciples with him—not, certainly, for hers, since the statement itself makes clear that she will not be able to understand him. But his disciples—eventually—will, and it is for them he is living, for them he is making all his mysterious utterances, for them, also, he will die: they alone who will carry the message of his life to posterity. "Woman, what have I to do with thee?" You who represent nature, what can you receive from me, who represents the soul? And, since she has suggested that he employ his supernatural powers to assist the embarrassed hosts, he adds quickly: "My hour is not yet come." That is, you—living in a realm of consciousness entirely different from mine—cannot possibly know when my time will come, cannot advise me in any way.

Christ's use of "I" in this brief encounter prefigures his similar usage throughout the gospels, where "I" represents the spiritual consciousness, the soul, the God within, not the man, the ego-consciousness, the individual. Here, the spiritual consciousness in his own life has already emerged triumphant over the "woman" in him: woman representing the world of nature, of the senses, and his mother epitomizing womanhood. Hence, what has "he" to do with "her"? The exchange reaffirms the truth contained in his "a [spiritual] man's foes shall be those of his own household"—namely, that spirit, embodied in the spiritual man, and matter, embodied in the family members, and particularly in the parents, engage in mortal struggle within the household.

The only other time we observe them together, except in the symbolic appearance at Calvary, occurs in Mark 3: 31-35. Surrounded by his disciples, he is addressing what Mark calls a "multitude"—although, as we have seen, all his words will be spoken for the benefit of his disciples, who alone can understand, or partly understand, what he is saying. In these gatherings we never get the impression that Jesus' mother is there, or any member of his family—leading to the inescapable conclusion that Mary had no chance to hear her son teach, and probably had little idea of what his message was, as she had no idea of what his nature was: again, the mother being the last person to truly know the character of a spiritual child for whom she has provided an earthly womb. In this scene she and some of her other children—Jesus' "brethren"—appear on the edge of the crowd wishing to speak to him: "Standing without, they sent unto him, calling him. And the multitude sat about him, and they said unto him, Behold, thy mother and thy brethren without seek for thee." If there was any vital bond between Jesus and Mary here was a simple, unambiguous opportunity to indicate it: he could have turned quickly, reverently, and made his way to where she was standing, giving his disciples *that* impression of their relationship. Instead he pauses and gives them quite another impression by dramatically answering:

Who is my mother, or my brethren? And he looked round about on them who sat about him, and said, Behold my mother and my brethren! For whosoever shall do the will of God, the same is my brother, and my sister, and mother.

As a boy in the Temple, with his earthly father before him, he had reminded his parents of "my Father" and the work he had to do. Here, with his mother and brothers awaiting him, he reinforces upon the minds of his auditors, his disciples most of all, that his earthly family meant little to him. Only those who served the Lord were his family.

Mary does not appear with Jesus *anywhere else*. The source of her veneration, in Catholicism and in portions of Protestantism, as a peerless queen of saints is folklore and mythology. Clearly we see that she has been created down the centuries out of pure imagination, like a primitive goddess moulded and changed by the simple earth-yearnings of primitive men. We are not surprised when *they* do such; we imagine we do not. This psychic, mythic yearning is the source of Mary as we know her. Which does not mean the image is "false," "groundless," and the like—anything produced out of men's necessity is not false or artificial. But let us recognize the phenomenon for what it is, and the role—uniquely rooted in sense-consciousness—for which she is cast.

Buddha's mother died a week after giving birth to him. Her name was *Maya*—a fitting appellation for Woman, particularly a Mother, whose primary occupation with men is to make the world of the senses seem real to them, just as the power of Maya is dedicated to the same seducing end.

Let us acknowledge that the source of Mary the immortal queen of heaven is in Western man's own need to worship an image of the divine female, of the feminine principle itself—so completely lacking in the male-dominated scheme of the Christian Trinity.[*] This is a profound and urgent need, but we should see it in its true light and seek to fulfill it in more psychologically realistic ways. To choose fulfillment of so spiritually imperative an urge through the ordinary Jewish girl who served merely as the physical channel for Christ's advent and who manifested no understanding of it is strange in the extreme.[**]

---

[*] And lacking even more in Islam and Judaism.

[**] There is another, paradoxical possibility. The veneration accorded her may be precisely because she *is* ordinary—Everywoman herself. By such veneration (cont.)

But what of the other members of Christ's family? His brothers, according to John (7: 3-7), had no interest in his mission, ridiculed what they saw as his pretensions, and in general acted as families behave when a light-bringer appears in their bosom. Buddha's father, even after he had been told his son was a divine personality, tried to frustrate his destiny in innumerable ways, as any other father would have done, and had to do. They "did not believe in him," John says simply. To which we might add, in the light of our analysis: they *cannot* believe in him. "Because the carnal mind is enmity against God," says St. Paul. "For it is not subject to the law of God, neither indeed can it be" (Rom. 8: 7).

To his brothers' scoffing insinuations Jesus replied: "My time is not yet come, but your time is always ready. The world cannot hate you, but me it hateth." The world—that is, the spirit of the world—cannot hate itself, which is what the family represents. The family's time, like Nature's, is always ready, immediate. The time of the spiritual man is geared to invisible reckonings, must abide in itself, must slowly flourish, must appear only according to the higher design.

Family, in short, represents Nature functioning in society, parents being the flywheel in this mechanism. It is true of all families, rich and poor, in India and elsewhere, true of the families of saints and avatars. It was true in Ramakrishna's case.

Even if parents are relatively enlightened, truth cannot be transmitted except by implication. Truth, the precious meed of life, can only be attained by rare, *individual* effort maintained over vast periods. It is creature-conceit that persuades some parents that what they think is their enlightenment can be passed on. If it could, it would be worth little. Only peripheral or rudimentary principles can be transmitted but nothing connected with the spiritual path. Diet can be taught, manners, a healthy way of life, morality, for these are creature-oriented, unconcerned with the soul, the inner self, the still-to-be-awakened individuality. Where individual perception is required for mastery, there can be no transmission of values, even if the parents are saints.

Catholics, Anglicans, and others are demonstrating that *anyone* may become a saint by acclamation and goddess by an act of will. Earth-mother she may be, she is still representative of a humanity created in the divine image and likeness and therefore undeniably adorable. The adulation the British give their plain, undistinguished Queen—herself another Everywoman—offers something of a parallel to this deep-rooted psychic process of which, of course, the worshippers of Mary are entirely unaware and which *may*, in some obscure, mythic sense, be responsible for her elevation.

This mortal combat between matter and spirit, externalized in the life of the family, will of course find expression in the individual psyche most of all. And it is when spirit is about to stamp some indelible impress upon the surface of time that the resistance of matter, of nature, will be most desperate. When Ramakrishna's personally moulded messenger, the still unknown Vivekananda, was about to address his first audience in the West, in September 1893, at the famous World Parliament of Religions in Chicago, he nearly collapsed because of the strain which the weight of the moment imposed upon him: the moment when, as some believe, the future of the modern mind began. Great yogi though he was, the powers of darkness nearly quenched his light before his mission could begin. The most dramatic illustration of this principle was, as the world knows, Christ's fateful hesitation in the Garden of Gethsemane, on the eve of a day when an earlier future was launched on the ocean of history.

Who was Jesus' father? Was it Joseph the carpenter? If so, he is an enigmatic figure, almost nonexistent in the testament narratives. Perhaps he is deliberately reduced by the gospel writers—Matthew and Luke, at least—to impress upon posterity the legend of the virgin birth. It could also be that he simply disappears from Jesus' life after the early years, or he may have been a source of difficulty to the young seer to such an extent that he had to be removed from the scene by superintending powers. Not close to his mother, though respecting her as the source of his physical life (as his invocation to her from Calvary makes clear), he was less close to his father, whoever his father was.

In our choice of religious devotions, no less surely than in our choice of spouses, we are motivated by need and insufficiency. We will yearn for what our personalities lack or for what life has failed to provide us with. The image of God as Father occurs in the Old Testament, at times, but with nothing of the profound and original impact it makes in the New, where, in the love of the Father, Jesus gives the Western world a revolutionary mode of worship. A prophet blessed with a congenial and loving earth-parent would have lacked the requisite ardor to seek a transcendental replacement, and we must assume that the Christian concept of God the Father issued from a personality denied the warmth and reassurance of a loving male parent who protected him and was always there when he needed him.

So with Ramakrishna and the divine mother-love to transcend and perfect the too-ordinary relationship he experienced with his earth-mother, and his worship of an absolute Mother to replace the all-too-human Indian mother who in her old age became stubborn and senile. God as Mother (God as Father, too) was an ancient theme in the complex heterogeneity of Indian devotion but no one ever gave it quite such an individual significance as Ramakrishna: it has once again, because of his influence, become a popular mode of worship in India—and in the Orientalized West. If the worship of God as Mother was overdue in the world—and if the West needed to discover this power-ful means to self-transcendence—then the prophet to promulgate it would *a priori* be denied the comfort of an ideal earthly mother-love.

Inevitably, then, the family life will be antagonistic to the spiritual seeker—by the will of God. Mothers will abrade, fathers will discourage, siblings will scoff—by the divine design. Parents will eternally misun-derstand their offspring with a radical, universal ignorance, will be the last to comprehend the nature that has flowered in their midst, through no individual fault but through the overpowering influence of the role cast for them in the destiny of a potential saint, will drive him from the hearth into the arms of another Love, to the warmth of another Bosom ... and thus, even as the spell of ignorance overhangs them to the end, will be serving the Divine in a special and indispensable way.

3

The Stage: Dakshineswar

GADAI'S DEPARTURE FROM HIS home village at the tender age of sixteen to assist Ramkumar at his Calcutta school clearly marks a vital division in his life and suggests that his sympathies were now directed more to him than to his mother and the rest of the family. Ramkumar loved his intense and affectionate younger brother and shared their mother's con-cern that the boy find some kind of worldly occupation to counteract his precocious spirituality, that being the chief reason why the family had urged him to join Ramkumar. Still, since Gadai (and later Ramakrishna) never in his life did anything whatever unless he wanted to, or unless he saw a valid reason for doing it, it is equally clear that he *wished* to join his talented surrogate father in the metropolis, despite its sinful repute.

The family also hoped that under Ramkumar's guidance he might be persuaded to resume his oft-interrupted village schooling. Reflecting the spirit of a practicing father, Ramkumar of course had strongly urged upon him the necessity of a traditional, worldly education suitable to one of the hereditary brahmin caste. While he had great affection for Gadai he showed no more spiritual insight into his character than their mother had. The hoped-for schooling failed to materialize, partly because Ramkumar (despite his rather self-righteous brahminism) was, in reality, complaisant with his difficult-to-fathom youngest brother, and partly because Gadai had made it plain to everyone, including Ramkumar himself finally, that he had no intention of pursuing a merely "bread-winning" education: he had been told it did not lead to God-realization (about which he had heard so much from the wandering sadhus), and therefore he wanted nothing to do with it.

Gadai's stubbornness was not actually a negative trait, to be passed over in silence when contemplating a life otherwise so saintly. It is one of the keys to the saintliness. The mystic has such a difficult and lonely road to tread that a greater-than-ordinary measure of self-reliance is absolutely necessary if the new life is to flourish. So many forces will play upon him to test his inner strength, so many people will try to discourage him from taking his eagle-flight above their tribal perimeters (beginning with his family), that if he possess not an exceptional stubbornness, an essential self-belief, from the beginning, he will never be able to rise from the ground in quest of distant eyries.

Ramkumar was gifted with psychic powers: he could predict coming events, foretell your death-day. India is full of such, but within his own family Gadai had close familiarity with one: a serious, well-meaning, essentially ordinary man. He saw that his brother's psychic faculty was congenital, had nothing to do with character or intelligence, much less with spirituality. Like most of the people in his story, his brother was once-born, afflicted throughout his days with his original personality— like their mother. His psychism was only an aberration from the norm, like the ability to remember hundreds of digits or to see auras. There

was no link between any of these gifts and spiritual development, not
to speak of the knowledge of God, as he himself would later declare.

Ramkumar's Calcutta school enabled him to send a little money
home but to make a success of the venture he needed the income from
extra work, which consisted of religious instruction he offered, as part
of his brahmin inheritance, to various Calcutta families, and often
meant his functioning as private priest in their homes. With Gadai
assisting him in every way he could, three years passed. The boy's happiest times were experienced when he served as priest himself in
Ramkumar's absence, spending hours in devotional fervors beyond the
call of duty, impressing the families he was serving with his hieratic
ardor and youthful purity.

His work with Ramkumar was absorbing but all around him was
a strange, new world he could scarcely have dreamed of—the teeming
life of Calcutta. How utterly unlike the life of Kamarpukur, how
worldly and driven the people were, how different they looked from
the villagers, how much less religion meant to them, how cut off they
seemed from ancient spiritual traditions, how much given up to sense
pleasure and the pursuit of gain! How powerful the spirit of the world
when millions, living close together, could be caught up by its influence
and virtually made over into its image and likeness. How deluded and
ensnared they were by that spirit which, his brother explained, was
known as *Maya*. How tragic that so many had come to believe in the
reality of the senses, of the world around them, and had lost touch with
the only reality that endured. He thanked God that he had his priestly
work with Ramkumar, which protected him from worldly intoxication—and, no doubt, from much more that he had no wish to know of.

Thus, these three years in Calcutta—then suffering the worst
effects of its exposure to British and Western materialism in all its viti-
ating forms—gave the future mystic invaluable experience of what life
in the world actually was like, and what it does to the minds and hearts
of those who live that life. It would be the only time he would ever live
in Calcutta (except at the end when his disciples brought his dying
body there for several months), the only opportunity he would ever
have for gaining so vital a part of his incarnational experience. His life
from the age of twenty moves so rapidly, in momentous stages, that it
was no coincidence that he was given this chance of prolonged exposure
to the cross-currents of a vast city while his inner life was gathering its

forces for the first of its attempts to scale the heights of spiritual vision.

Meanwhile one of Ramkumar's religious contacts had led, by a natural sequence, to a certain wealthy widow named Rani Rasmani who, on twenty acres of property on the east bank of the Ganges four miles north of the seething metropolis, at the village of Dakshineswar, had built an impressive temple garden compound honoring Shiva and Krishna and for its centerpiece a great temple to Kali the Divine Mother, monumentalizing her own religious preference. Though born into the low sudra caste, she was a shrewd businesswoman with a generously liberal nature and sincere spiritual aspirations, which had to cohabit in a head filled with financial schemes that occupied most of her time. Ramkumar, in the course of things, had come to her attention by virtue of a written opinion he had provided her on some vexing caste question that no one had been able to solve, and she had been pleased by his astuteness. When, soon after, an opening for priest of the Kali Temple appeared (and as the day of its commemoration approached), Ramkumar, who badly needed the job, was invited to take it, which he did. Rani and her favorite son-in-law, Mathur Babu, a capable ally, had spent many weeks unsuccessfully trying to find a brahmin priest to accept their offer. Since she was from a low caste herself, caste-mania was the reason for her difficulty. Hindu brahmins had considered this rich, benevolent, able, humanitarian, widely-respected woman to be not only inferior but unclean.

Ramkumar brought Gadai with him as assistant to Dakshineswar and a year later he who could foretell other people's death was dead himself. By easy stages Gadai was, at the age of twenty, the temple priest.

Through no fault of his own Ramkumar's life had been conjoined with the ascending momentum of a divine destiny—one of purer carat than that of other men—and when the time was right for Gadai—for Ramakrishna—to begin in earnest to enter into the world within, Ramkumar, his closest friend, his brother-and-father in one, and the bridge to his past twenty years of life, was without any delay removed from the scene. In the unfoldment of supernatural design we can discern several reasons for this.

First, it was evidently vital that Ramakrishna, as soon as possible, have his virgin mind exposed to the atmosphere of an orthodox temple where daily religious services would be conducted; he was supposed to play an appointed role in such observances but that was less important for his inner growth than to have his mind steadily immersed in a spiritual ambience—to fortify devotional tendencies already awakened. Officiating as priest was but a job for the worldly Ramkumar. For the unworldly Ramakrishna it was the adoration of a votary.

Symbolically, also, he had to occupy the post almost immediately once he had appeared on the Dakshineswar scene, for the feminine principle in the universe—personified for Hindu *bhaktas* as Kali—would find in him its supreme devotee, which it must have long waited for. Now that he was in the field of destiny at last, the stand-in priest, Ramkumar, must be removed quickly—to impress upon the mind of the young aspirant the significance of what had happened to him and perhaps to satisfy the yearnings of the goddess herself. Just as the most womanly of women—her beauty inward, her virtue unsuspected, her divine femininity largely unguessed by her acquaintance—will yearn for her lover, her worshipper, with elemental passion, with a need much greater than even the need he will feel when at last he discovers her, so the Personal God—what we might term the Feminine Power in the Godhead—will yearn for a lover with a need indescribable. When she glimpses his arrival on the earthly scene, she hastily removes all impediments to the launching of his career of devotion. [*]

Finally, the scorching heat of sorrow was introduced to Ramakrishna's soul to reinforce what he already felt about the transiency of life and the impermanence of human affections. He must know these things at the deepest psychic level so that the call of the divine contemplation and communion with the *permanent* Love, the *non*-transient Friend, would be irresistible ... would also become the only *logical* object of one's ardor.

He is made to feel what it is to be alone in the world: the recognition of man's real state. It is true, there was his family, but he seems to have forgotten them, makes no references to them, has to be reminded of them by others. He faces the universe alone for the first time, but chooses to personalize the new, terrifying relationship to the maximum by thinking of the power behind this antagonist as a being—as his Mother, in fact, and he as its son.

We are not surprised that in this same year—when he was still only

---

[*] She becomes the Word, which moveth fast, cutting like a sword, burning like a conflagration.

twenty—would come his first genuine (though limited) realization of God. But human psychology had played a necessary role in his ascent.

Whatever desolates us will make us divine. Even Ramakrishna needed help from human despair to bring him to the Absolute, and the arid nakedness of spirit that would long be his portion, beginning now, was itself the prime condition making for spiritual triumph. We take his spirituality for granted and assume *it* was the chief factor. No doubt, in one sense, it was; but the state of desolate loneliness to which his grief had brought him, the Dark Night of Soul and Senses alike, which for so long he would know, beginning in this year, was the psychological *sine qua non* that, desert though it was, paradoxically fructified—*fulfilled*—his unsurpassed spirituality.

We should not only accept our loneliness, our desert period, we should rejoice in it, embrace it with the full strength of our being, in the knowledge that without it we cannot come to a knowledge of God, cannot ever depart from the kingdom of darkness. *The years of happiness are that kingdom.* Just as St. Francis married poverty as a bride, so we should marry emptiness, barrenness, sorrow. The progeny of this wedding will light us to the banquet-hall of the Secret King.

While we are in the house of sorrow, Jacob Boehme reminds us, we are not in the house of sin. While we are in the house of desolation, we are supremely favored by the Shy Lover, as Ramakrishna will later describe the eternal, who prefers his beloved's purity of embrace unmixed with worldly joys, and the eclipsing complacence they breed.

Sorrow is more rewarding than poverty. For sorrow can make even a rich man worthy of grace—nay, his sorrow, his repentance, *is* grace, *is* illumination: he has but a short way before the fields of asphodel open. Loss of the beloved is evil, Buddha warned in the *Dhammapada*. But if one endure the loss? Endure, with grace, and gathering insight? The result is strength, humility, *change*—a profitable sorrow. So the experience of feeling the beloved to *be* lost is the evil, but priceless the experience of enduring it.

In a very short period, then, his well-beloved Ramkumar dies without warning, he becomes temple priest, and Mathur Babu, the Rani's indispensable son-in-law and now the temple compound manager, gives Ramakrishna his personal protection as a result of a strong, mysterious attraction he feels toward the twenty-year-old solitary. Almost simultaneous with these critical developments occurred another: the unannounced arrival at Dakshineswar of one Hriday, three or four years younger than Ramakrishna, who was, through intricacies of kinship, his "uncle" and cousin alike, with whom Hriday had been long acquainted (since their childhood days in Kamarpukur indeed) and to whom he had been long devoted. Mathur readily gave Hriday permission to stay on the grounds as a kind of body-guard to the dreamy young mystic, whose absent-mindedness and moods of utter withdrawal and indifference to the world around him had begun to perplex everyone. Hriday, a nonspiritual youth but strong, intelligent, quick, fearless, and utterly loyal to his boy-hood friend, accepted the offer with joy—and filled the role painstakingly for the next twenty years.

Thus the stage was set in a dramatically short time, everything being brought into position with a provocative directness whose source was unmistakable.

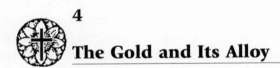

4

The Gold and Its Alloy

NOW BEGAN LONG ABSENCES from the temple compound. For hours, then all night, he would conceal himself in a thick jungle north of the temple, formerly used as a Muslim burial ground and even in daylight shunned by everyone for fear of ghosts, and pass the hours in deep blind meditative yearning, praying, calling, crying out, beseeching, demanding a vision of deity, of Kali—the eternal feminine. He chose the burial ground because with the death of the person closest to him the world itself had become a graveyard. (His mother, we recall, could not have been that one, since he was agonizing so relentlessly for the embrace of another Mother.) To Ramakrishna, even as a boy, what his mind believed was reality. For him there was no horror—as there was to those who discovered it—in meditating naked all night in a dense jungle brush over the buried skeletons of unknown men: the place was an exact metaphor of his view of the world. The gloom of the scene reflected back the emptiness of his heart—of him who once had fainted at the sight of natural beauty. Craving an absolute relationship with the Godhead through its feminine mode, he found the jungle desolation an appropriate setting for his hunger.

There is something a Hindu brahmin never dreams of doing—removing the sacred thread that symbolizes his brahmin estate, his life's hereditary vocation as priest. But this is what he did. The simple Hriday was thunderstruck when he heard of his action and the explanation he gave: that from his birth man labors under the "eight fetters"—pride of noble descent and obsession with the show of good conduct being two of these. The sacred thread also is a bondage, he said, a sign of the egoism, "I am a brahmin and superior to all." For the rest of his life he held the same view and afterwards passed it onto those of his disciples inclined to ascetic obsessions. "Give up this craze for outer cleanliness," he would say. "People with a craze do not attain the Knowledge of God."

With respect to food, however, as we have noted, he did not follow his own counsel. For years it would remain a stone of stumbling in the unfoldment of his higher consciousness. He genuinely felt compromised and shamed for having to eat food cooked—and *provided*—for him by someone not of his caste. He felt this even at Dakshineswar where Rani Rasmani was exceptionally generous and kind-hearted to him from beginning to end.[*]

Later he conceded that certain imperfections, this one chiefly, attached to his character. He never made an effort to present himself as flawless. "The shape of an ornament cannot be given to gold if it does not contain some alloy," he said. That is, when the soul of an avatar assumes a human form, he must accept imperfections of the mind as

---

[*] "Sri Ramakrishna," says Swami Nikhilananda, "did not at first approve of Ramkumar's working for the sudra Rasmani. The example of their orthodox father was still fresh in his mind—" [Kshudiram had refused gifts offered him by sudras] "—He objected also to the eating of the cooked offerings of the temple, since, according to orthodox Hindu custom, such food can be offered to the Deity only in the house of a brahmin"—intro. *The Gospel of Sri Ramakrishna* (New York: 1942), 10.

well as body. While most of these, as we shall see, were steadfastly uprooted, not all were, not all could be. He, too, was swayed, to some degree, by the limitations of mortality, the gold partly subject to the nature of its necessary alloy. If the incarnational principle be true and the divine capable of an earthly vehicle, it would have to abide by the innate restrictions of matter, and though its light would shine through the material form it could not transcend it totally.

Matter is unconscious but derives its power from the creative energy behind it and from the divinity inhabiting it. Ultimately it may be seen as spirit in a *manifested* dimension, or as spirit assuming a phenomenal reality—for the purpose of creation, of evolution: to provide experience of phenomena to spiritual essences, namely, souls. Bodies are matter, like the earth of which they are composed. Society is matter, is nature, is blind force—lit through by gleams of truth, but only transiently. Society is matter organized, nature made purposeful, instinct harnessed.

The oldest societies are the most indurated, mineralized, like the Jewish, the Hindu. To be born into a Jewish body two thousand years ago (for already that culture was ancient, desiccated with law and custom) meant that you would assume the powerful tendencies of Jewishness to begin with, the habit of baiting your adversaries, for example (as Jesus did with the Pharisees). To be born into a Hindu womb, and especially a brahmin's, in the nineteenth century (the culture-environment being four to five thousand years old) meant that even the saintliest man could never completely free himself of the bondages of this closed society; he would perform rites and observances of his upbringing—taught him in his boyhood as not only traditional duties but as divine mandates—still thinking they were, to some extent, somehow divine.

So we find Ramakrishna all his life, after his most devastating realizations, unable to eat food offered to him by non-brahmins, at least thinking he was unable to. After it had been revealed to him that all such practices, and the attitudes that sustained them, were fetters to the soul, he was able to implement the insight only in meditation and while speaking to others under its influence.

Socrates, a man of mystic realizations, perhaps the most enlightened soul in the Hellenic world, acknowledged the wisdom of the Delphic oracle, observed religious rites in propitiation of the Greek

gods, and on his deathbed asked that a cock be paid to the god
Asclepius. He apparently did these things in no spirit of irony, just as
the syllogisms of dialectic, the preferred mode of Athenian discourse,
became the manner of his habitual speech, as though verified by truth
itself.

Krishna, the hero of Hinduism, declared in the *Bhagavad-Gita* that
women were unfit for enlightenment; Buddha would not allow women
to be ordained in the order he founded, citing their unsuitability.

Which does not signify that their spiritual experiences were not as
genuine as we have believed. It simply enforces upon us the necessity
of revising our conceptions of them and of the character of the saint
itself.

Even a divine incarnation must struggle, for some years, to pierce
the last veil of *Maya*, the power of delusion that afflicts all living things.
In the necessity of his struggle *he accentuates the tendencies of his embodiment.* After his emancipation this creature-personality is rendered
harmless, is purified by the light that has broken, is turned permanently inward. Nevertheless it is by this outward man, purified though it
now is, that he communicates with others. Selfishness has been purged
out of it, but some of its original, culturally ignorant and conditioned
tendencies remain fairly intact: especially those unargued, implicit, pervasive in his education from the outset—attitudes, habits, rituals, about
which he has never, in the immediate circle of his upbringing, heard
discussion. *Whatever* these were are likely to remain intact after the blaze
of illumination to his *inward* mind. The outward man continues as
before, only more mildly, selflessly—pursuing the original tracks in the
mind-stuff where, long ago, Nature traced its pattern. The inward man
alone receives the fire of vision, as being like unto it: the outward man,
in saint or sinner, being a foreigner to that vision. The power of the light
in passage, however, robs the outward man of his characteristic traits,
leaving the mould intact, the inner substance changed to tranquil love
and compassionate serenity. But the mould is the habit pattern. If he has
been a food fanatic before the enlightenment he will be so afterwards,
only more lovingly, wonderingly: the fetish will persist. On his deathbed
he may ask that only brahmins wait on him, or urge his disciples not to
forget the cock owed to Asclepius. Nature, or matter, has been overcome; but to the end her voice, though muted, will still be heard.

A thoroughgoing perfection, in other words, is not possible in this body for anyone.

If it were otherwise, if by a nature aboriginally divine or by divine *fiat* a man were to attain immunity from such a process, he would be immune to human tragedy—of human reality itself. He would be escaping experience of the *mysterium tremendum* of human incarnation. His advent would be insufficiently involved with the stuff of humanity's characteristic, irreparable limitation.

When Jesus, on hearing news of the death of Lazarus, wept, despite his cosmic vision (experienced in the spiritual, not the human dimension) of the omnipresence of the divine and the will of his Father behind all events—he revealed a measure of the ordinary, nature-rooted consciousness which, in Gethsemane, would manifest as transient inability completely to embrace his Father's will, as it had been vouchsafed in contemplative insight. The tears and hesitation were both portions of the same eternal Nature and its individualization in man in the form of self-will or creature-consciousness.

Thus admirers who discover in Ramakrishna manifestations of the same Nature need not be ashamed of reverence once they identify their source, rationale, and inevitability. Like his lifelong food-fetishism.

Moses, Muhammad, and St. Paul retained their vehemence of personality to the end—Nature rioting in them as powerfully, sometimes, as spirit elevated them. St. Catherine of Siena bore the stigmata of Jesus on her body and at the same time was able to recommend to the Pope that the quarrelling sects of the Church could be reconciled by warring against Muslim infidels in the Holy Land. Ramakrishna's spouse, Sarada, systematically ignored his advice concerning food and other domestic matters, which suggests that there were aspects of his personality—his domestic advice, for example—where not God but man spoke, and her awareness of this lesser part, and her readiness to ignore it, suggests that the same division was evident in her own.

Nature, or Matter, and its individual human form, egoism, is always subdued in the saint, but its activity shows through indirection. There was never, thus far, a Christian mystic who did not feel Christianity was the only way to Truth. They liberate themselves from the arrant superstitions of their age, and of course conquer the grosser thrusting of self-will, but remain heir to other shibboleths. A leading Sufi mystic and guru, reflecting a universal Sufi outlook, told his disciples there was only one unique path to illumination: Sufism. Buddha is alleged to have made a like remark but identified the path as the one he himself was teaching.

Zen Buddhists take comfort in the fact that they have transcended Buddha and all forms and names, but the psychological process found among theists is clearly operative among them also. Like the Sufis, they venerate their path as Truth itself. So profound is it that no scripture—including that of Buddhism—can contain it, Zen being a "special transmission outside the scriptures."[*]

The minds of men, including the very greatest, are formed ready to believe in exclusivism, as we all are tending to do at every moment of our lives: a temptation we must consciously and unnaturally resist to the end. In this respect—as in many others—Ramakrishna was unique. Every religion, he said, was a path to the Truth; each had produced its genuine saints and prophets; none was completely true—all being mixed with human error; each was divinely inspired.

He said that when God becomes man he behaves exactly like a man. Or, in the vein we have been pursuing, if he becomes Hindu he must, first of all, reflect the Hindu fanaticism with the kitchen as the sanctuary of the Hindu faith, as Vivekananda complained. And the fixation of the Hindu mind on ritual: in order to be believed on a wide scale Ramakrishna must practice rituals faithfully. Of course he might come as a reformer, like Keshab Sen, his friend of later years, and denounce rituals, but this role would convert only a few and soon would be swallowed up in the all-devouring maw of Hindu traditionalism: the fate of Keshab and his reform movement, in fact. Hindus consult astrology seriously, and so Ramakrishna to some extent must do so. Throughout his life he is aware of favorable days of the week, auspicious lunar periods and planetary conjunctions. It is not a dominant theme in his life and plays no role in his teaching, as his food-fetishism does not; but it is present as a nature-given element in his ethnic and psychic makeup.

Krishna-worship is another facet of his personality illustrating the Hinduism that had dyed his mind so deeply. The emancipated modern Hindu upholds the Vedantic ideal of the universality of truth, believes that avatars have appeared in almost every religious mainstream, that many more will appear in times to come. But Krishna was special. The others were divine, Krishna was God Himself. This was also, or seemed

---

[*] See Appendix for amplification of these ideas.

to be, Ramakrishna's view. (It is like the liberal modern Christian conceding that God has spoken through every major religious leader but that only Christ was God on earth.) It was the Hinduism in Ramakrishna that held this belief, that avoided doing certain things on certain days of the week and regarded most hands that offered him food as unclean. The Hinduism of the caste system, of the dense and trackless mythology.

In previous incarnations, he would have manifested different tastes, habits, prejudices; in future ones it will be still different. The prejudices will shift, the compulsions will interchange. Underneath them all will be the nonpareil spiritual man, the mystic gently discarding the accident and quirky, the hereditary, the culturally induced, seeking only the universality which his life, despite these environmental blurrings, so remarkably mirrored; seeking the gold beneath the dross of the creaturely embodiment; seeking beneath the thick underbrush of Indian custom the God-intoxicant unparalleled.

His gigantic yearning for God, which we observe clearly about the time of his advent at Dakshineswar, seems to have had hardly an equal, at least among lives sufficiently familiar to make comparisons possible. Buddha's passion for Truth (as he termed the Infinite) was equal to it, admittedly, but scarcely any other. So intense was his craving that he renounced the best of this world's joys in order to satisfy it, gaining only years of terrible privation and failure in response to his hunger to aid a lost humanity. His desperation brought him to the point of death and to an utter indifference as to whether he lived or died. It was this desperate resolve, his noninterest in a life devoid of truth realized, this excruciating, karma-dissolving detachment, that brought him the victory. Ramakrishna would come to his goal through a similar psychological process.

Buddha's enlightenment appears to have been total, since his mission henceforth would be to demonstrate beyond any doubt, through his own testimony, that the mystically divine character was man's true nature and all the rest his shadow-life, his mere karma-nature. To questing minds, to seeking hearts, over a period of half a century, he had to manifest a degree of conviction regarding the Truth, and insights into its nature, of a profundity not to be discovered elsewhere. Full enlightenment was required.

Ramakrishna was to be the teacher of a more complex age. He was to tread every path, assume every religious attitude, experience every spiritual mode, he was to incarnate all the major psychic dimensions of modern man in search of a soul so as to be able to speak to his condition in a unique fashion, with unrivaled directness and aptness. Each was greater than the other in certain respects. In this regard, just noted, Ramakrishna's task was more formidable, and hence the period of his sadhana* lasted some years longer. Buddha was essentially to give to the world a religion for the nondevotional, the rationalistic, the skeptical, the unorthodox, and similar types unhappy with traditional religion and with theism even of the metaphysical variety. He was to be the salvation of millions who, but for him, would have no place to direct their aspirations to higher truth.

Ramakrishna, for this epoch, was to provide a potential message for everyone else discontented with their received creed.

5

First Vision

HIS FIRST EXPERIENCE OF Kali, whom he was addressing simply as Mother, unaware of those near enough to witness his devotional intimacies, would be much less intense than Buddha's world-eclipsing conquest under the historic Tree. Ramakrishna, a wooing lover, needed—at this germinal stage—far less to satisfy him. A putting aside of one or two veils, a glimpse or two of the bliss-giving form, a touch of the beloved's hand, a glance of her eyes—was enough. He had chiefly wanted to know that she was real, that her love was true, and—like any other lover—that his ardor was returned. Possession, union—is not yet required. The lover lives content in the contemplation of the new reality and the undeniable existence of his ideal. He is transformed by intuitive certainty.

To get that first glimpse he had to prove himself worthy of it. He proved his worth by becoming unfit for life. The more fit we are for worldly life, the less we deserve the otherworldly—the less, in truth,

---

* Spiritual practice.

do we *need* it. So we do not get it. Which should not invite us to cultivate ineffectuality. It must be a genuine unfitness, springing from indifference, not from neurosis; grounded in spiritual longing, not egoistic disappointment with an unappreciating world.

For hours at a time he would lie motionless on the ground, his chest red with the strain of devotional fervor. He lost sleep altogether, day and night went sleepless—for weeks, months on end—forgot to take food, rubbed his cheek against rocks until the blood came, cried out for the Mother like a child forsaken, day after day; meanwhile meditating hour after hour, blindly, desperately, ignorantly, with no effective channeling of his voracity, all through the night, in the abandoned burial-ground, the silent jungle hushed around him in the darkness.

With difficulty he made efforts to carry out the prescribed duties of temple priest as he lost himself in trances of rapture performing actions not expected to be more than symbolic: in the symbol, the idol, the ritual he saw the hidden meaning, felt the divine presence, became increasingly abstracted, drawing upon his head at first derision and then reverence from temple visitors.

He said he felt as though someone was wringing out his heart like a wet towel. Life did not seem worth living. Despair filled him. When it became prolonged for many weeks, and seemed endless, he resolved to put an end to his existence.

He had not felt this way prior to the death of Ramkumar, we should remember. Human psychology and divine insight are inseparably fused in the life of the spiritual seeker, even one like Ramakrishna.

There was a ceremonial sword hanging in the Kali temple. He did not hesitate. He rushed and seized it, and just before he plunged the weapon into his heart the vision came. A vision of pure Energy, infinite Life, pouring into him in continuous, effulgent waves of boundless consciousness. Everything else vanished—all material objects—as this vast and blissful sea of light engulfed him. Overwhelmed, he collapsed into unconsciousness at the feet of Kali.

This experience established him in mysticism, gave him the insight and power to become a saint, would have made holy anyone else who had it. For Ramakrishna it was only the beginning, an overture to what was to come, memorable primarily because it was the first. He was twenty years old. The *Sturm und Drang* of his struggles would last another decade. But unlike the first, now successfully past, he would not wage them half in fear, half in doubt, of the reality he was hungering for. Never again would he have to threaten the deity.

We should not try to imitate him. He is not like us, we are not like him. It would be fatal to assume we have his longing, his renunciation, his devotion.

Even reading about his spiritual travails persuades us he was unique. Only when we reflect that a divine incarnation may have taken place in him does his struggle become less disquieting. If we think of him as a man only, the intensity of his labor intimidates us; if we think of him as a God-man, we are left to conclude to what lengths the divine Love may go—and has undoubtedly gone—to coax men into the paths of new life.

That first experience was memorable in another way. It revealed to him the nature of the Mother. She was the Power of the Absolute, its Unquenchable Creativity, its Eternal Energy, its Shoreless Bliss. Further, *She was he.* In all spiritual encounters—and this was the revelation—it is the Absolute alone being experienced. Significantly, no forms appeared on the first occasion. They would come, in rich abundance, later. But they are still the Absolute. Just as Humanity takes the forms of men and women. *But the essence of Humanity is not contained in any one,* and indeed is not containable in any or all. It remains apart.

Truth, said the greatest nondevotional avatar, is imageless. It is the Pure Light of the Void. Ramakrishna, after his first supernal experience, would have had to agree. More powerful splendors awaited him but the archetypal truth revealed in the first ecstasy could never be lost. The forms seen in visions, he said later, were real too—at least real enough: the Absolute, capable of everything, was also capable of assuming forms close to the hearts of devotional worshippers. Buddha never taught this, had no mystical experience of it, so far as we know: for his mission was to teach something else for those who preferred not to know about the mysteries of devotion.

The actual image of Mother Kali as it appeared in the Dakshineswar temple was thus an allegorical, multidimensional icon symbolizing the nature of phenomenal reality rather than a reality to be itself experienced. Life has pain as well as joy, beauty as well as ugliness, harmony as well as disharmony, and since life is only the projected will of the power behind it obviously that Power sanctions the existence of these pairs of opposites: the world's evil seems as necessary, in an ultimate sense, as its good. Both belong to the realm of divine activity, divine play; both lead to the higher Good, the absolute Good, beyond the opposites, transcending forms, free from modifications. Life must be *undergone*, said Keats. Experience, knowledge, truth are the purpose of life: not the happiness we have been taught to crave. Life is a sentence. If we serve it well, liberation dawns. If otherwise, greater bondage. Life—or rather the sentencing, superintending power *behind* Life (which Ramakrishna saw as the Divine Mother)—gives us the options. The evil, however, issues from the divine matrix as purposefully as the good, and must not be hated, must not (as Christ warned) be "resisted,"* must be respected. This does not mean we embrace it. We simply decline to hate, fear, resist, condemn any part of the divine design.

Thus the destructive and benign aspects, alike, of the Kali icon.

Ramakrishna as a twenty-year-old devotee wanted to face life's possibilities, to fear nothing, to embrace the universe, to affirm everything, and to do so he knew he had to worship and adore, love and propitiate the "Mother"—that is, the Creative Womb—responsible for that vast outpouring of life, that divine totality of all that was and is and will be. As he said later, he wanted the "full weight" of the universe, which he felt one did not gain by contemplation on the Absolute alone. He wanted the Absolute *and* its creation. Or, rather, since the Absolute itself was still beyond him (and would remain so for some years), he wanted the Absolute *through* its creation. He wanted the Father (so to speak) *through* the Mother. He wanted the Ocean through its waves; the Source through its fruits.

Because of his extreme power of spiritual imagination, the image became a reality to him and he tended to forget that it was, and could only be, a symbol of that which he sought: pure Spirit, Consciousness itself.

Although this first *ecstasis* could not match the later deluges of spirit that poured into him, it was potent enough to overwhelm him into unconsciousness, his mind not yet strong enough to contain its surging currents. It lacked the degree of concentration required now. In itself, by virtue of his spiritual passion, his single-hearted consecration to his ideal,

---

* He was speaking to his disciples, we should remember, who were being taught the deeper truths of life. Those who "see" the evil and believe it *is* evil, must "resist" it. Not to do so, for them, would be a kind of madness.

it was more concentrated than almost any other. But higher vision is not produced without collecting *all* the mind's scattered forces, and that is why yoga has been instituted. Of which he knew nothing. He knew one thing: *yearning.* Monumental, it had brought him to the saint's consciousness. But the truth was on the mountain-top, he was in the foothills. He badly needed someone to guide and instruct him, show him how to harness all his spiritual potential and direct it to his goal with undeterred, one-pointed effectiveness. But that was not to be for several long years.

Meanwhile, in the aftermath of the first intoxication he prayed for more vision, more power, and it began to come, as what has been traditionally interpreted as the divine play of disclosure and concealment, between lover and Beloved, went on ... though in reality it was the process of his mind becoming habituated to ever clearer glimpses of Truth, ever stronger infusions of light. As it attempted to assimilate a particular insight arising from the divine world, it closed itself temporarily from further illumination the better to absorb and comprehend what it had received, and during these reactive, gestating periods there was, emotionally, a sensation of being cut off from the Light itself: in devotional terms, of the Mother deliberately withdrawing from her favorite. *It is the mind, not God,* that withdraws, partly out of self-protection as it feels itself being annihilated by blasts of excess light, partly out of need of time to understand the unprecedented mysteries being showered on it.

His nerves grew more strained, the state of high fever which had become so frequent was now his habitual condition, his chest was flushed red much of the time from the convulsions of his ardor, his body afflicted every day with strange heat.

Heat from love—devotion turned within and without. The devotee admittedly seeks the Divine within; but unlike the yogi or the *jnani* (the follower of the path of Knowledge—the philosophic or intellectual mystic), he believes in the world around him and, though it is evanescent, loves it as a mirror, if often a distorted one, of the benign reality he seeks. The yogi and the *jnani* believe only in the inner world: the mind, the spirit. The individual self that searches for Truth, in their cases, is restricted to the secret, inward-moving psyche; the individual self of the devotee includes the emotional life, which in turn means the nervous system, the sense-organs, the body itself. As emotions peak in longing and urgency, nerve and tissue are affected, the inner heat is felt on the pulses, in the flesh, and becomes visible.

For this reason the Christian stigmata experience is unknown to the analytical, discriminating type of personality; only the devotional, the passionate, the self-convinced, the wholly trusting temperament impresses upon its outer form (the temperament itself being the inner form) the stigmatic wounds, which are outlets of emotions felt more acutely by the worshipper than by any other. That is why so many more women than men have been stigmatic. For them, the heart is the center of their religious as it is of their worldly life. When the longing fuses the beloved image intensely enough in the brain, the nerves respond and duplicate—eventually—the same image in glands and tissues. If one has tirelessly contemplated the passion and death of Christ this drama is emotionally, visibly reproduced in the theater of the body. It is internally generated. The divine is not directly involved, we might say. If it were, the stigmatic would be blessed, singled out above other seekers. But some of the greatest Christian figures were deprived of the stigmata not because of spiritual limitations but because of the nature of their temperament and the focus of their devotions. The renowned mystic Eckhart was thus cut off from the experience because of his nondevotional nature. St. Thérèse of Lisieux, as devotional as Catherine of Siena, chose not to dwell on the Cross but on the child Jesus—hence not the wounds of Christ but his child-like joys were her experience. St. John of the Cross was as devotional as any but his power of psychological self-analysis prevented him from giving full unsophisticated rein to his devotional urges; part of the center of his being was in his intellect. The emotional center must receive *all* one's energy, one's power of imagining, one's loyalty, for the body to be transfigured by the holy wounds. Again, God does not have to enter in: the experience is self-validating, self-caused, self-willed.

To treat Ramakrishna's various physical symptoms a doctor was called from Calcutta, but no medicine was found to remove them and no mind to comprehend them. Attendants and visitors at the large temple grounds generally regarded him as deranged, though unaccountably (for a merely deranged man) the source of a powerful awe they felt whenever they came near him, a holiness not to be denied. It was perceptible in the Kali temple especially, even when he was not there. He

himself remained uniformly mild, gentle, amiable toward one and all—
when he was not totally abstracted into his inner world. When a temple official warned Mathur Babu of his dangerous state, Mathur visited
the Kali temple to observe him performing the services. Though his
performance was more erratic than ever, Mathur was struck by the
communion he held with the stone goddess—that is, with the presence
evoked by the stone idol—by his child-like devotion, his utter absorption in the simplest prayer. He went away, told Rani Rasmani (who
lived in Calcutta) the news that the goddess had undoubtedly blessed
the temple, as well as Ramakrishna, and would soon reveal herself.
Rani shared his delight and gratitude. Mathur gave orders that
Ramakrishna was to be left alone, no matter how he acted.

What are we to think of Ramakrishna's claim that Kali came to life
for him in the basalt icon, that he felt her breathing, heard her step as
she passed from temple to Ganges rattling her ankle-bracelets, saw
incense rising from her nostrils? If we think of her as Consciousness, as
Divine Presence, which was her essential reality, it will be possible at
least to intuit his experience. For Consciousness, we are told in the
Upanishads and in all the major mystical documents, is One; in
Buddhism we are told that Truth is One, Spirit is One, and the
Buddha-Mind is everywhere: not only in men but in animals, in trees
and plants, in stone and earth, in water. If the awakened spirit-con-
sciousness of a living man, a saint, be strong enough, it can magnetize
into manifestation—as yogis have been able to do with fierce animals—
the dormant consciousness sleeping in a stone. We do not have any
record of a saint with spirituality so potent that this could happen but
there is no doubt of its possibility if such a magnetic force could appear.

Ramakrishna, in fact, was such a force, composed of spirituality
and faith in what he had heard about the goddess: namely, that she
would reward the worshipper's devotion by appearing to him and
speaking directly to him. Such a faith, though, was an aspect of the spirituality, the power, itself. The power brings about a transformation in
the stone, causes water to gush from the rock—and his faith believes it
is taking place. Here, faith is the grace of his own mind: faith in what
the grace of his soul has first accomplished. Both are necessary.

If one studies the miracles of the Old Testament, and of the New,
weighs the implications of Patanjali's astounding report in his *Yoga
Sutras* (where the scope of yogic omnipotence is memorably sketched),

and includes the testimony of Tibetan and other mystical and mystery traditions, not to speak of the prodigies of such as St. Francis and Apollonius of Tyana, one encounters so many descriptions of thaumaturgic wonders that, allowing for hagiolatrous exaggerations, so much still remains that one is forced to be reconciled with the long history of the marvelous that presses on us in the guileless Ramakrishna's career. One has to accept that it is *possible*, at least—such a fantasy as the basalt image becoming animate with divine life and a breathing goddess discovered behind the granitic, forbidding face.

That was why he could feed to a cat food that had been prepared as a sacred offering to Kali, an action that shocked the pious. He explained that the Mother had revealed to him that She had become everything—and everything, therefore, was full of divine consciousness. When this was *seen* with sufficient verity by the worshipper, from the standpoint of their identical inner content, the cat could not be distinguished from a man. In such exalted states the differences in form were negligible. All were seen to be made of the same substance. As Ramakrishna himself put it: a clay man, a clay elephant, a clay mouse, a clay cat.

We must remember: goddess means spirit or consciousness, and the stone form is only a vehicle more opaque than usual for that spirit to enter. A divine worshipper makes the idol divine. The Mother he is worshipping is within himself. The power suddenly arisen outside him is projected out of the soul-power awakened within. As within, so without: the prime mystic law. A saint can awaken divinity in a wild animal and, says Patanjali, cause him instantly to lose his savagery. A prophet may sanctify a tree—Moses and the burning bush on Sinai: burning with the fire of spirit. A Ramakrishna discovers in a carved stone—his own holiness. The Divine Mother of Ramakrishna, like the Father in Heaven of Jesus—both were in the hearts of these supreme devotees. Testifying to the complexity of man's nature—his actual nature: the enormous gulfs that make it up.

But isn't the whole process unreal, then—a mere projection from the mind of the individual? A solipsistic phantom? On the contrary: whatever is *not* a projection from within is unreal. *The real is within*— as all the prophets have told us over and over. Unless the real is *first* known, experienced, and become the source of a new faith, the outer world invariably has dominance over us, mesmerizes us, causes us to estimate it in accordance with the *ignorance* we have known, not the truth.

Other psychosomatic phenomena were added during the period just after the first experience of divine consciousness. Whenever he sat for meditation, in the usual cross-legged, half-lotus position, he heard the joints in his legs locking, preventing him from any motion whatever until the full term of meditation was completed; when it was, his joints unlocked and he was free to rise. Another time, while meditating, he saw a red-eyed man, black of color, reeling drunkenly, emerge from his body—this, during a period when a persistent painful sensation had gripped his chest—and soon after, a serene, orange-robed figure followed, bearing in his hand a trident with which he attacked the first and killed him; after this, his chest pain departed.

Again, his extremely sensitized psyche is drawing allegorical portraits of its own internal drama. The dark, red-eyed man is the lower self, the ego, which, though limited in Ramakrishna, was still there, and whose continuing presence, in a life hungering not only for unbroken divine realization but for the personal consciousness, the unified will, which alone would make such a state possible, was afflicting him with severe chest pain: localized in the chest because that was the area he had instinctively chosen as the focal point for meditation—the region of the "heart" recommended by devotional teachers, the yogic center of one's spiritual being, connecting-link between the physical and subtle bodies, the solar plexus chakra. And the feeling of the presence of an alien element within, a criminal interloper in the holy mansion he had already created, would be pain indeed—for a Ramakrishna, shuddering, humiliating pain. If, consciously, he did not comprehend the psychological reason for his physical distress, the visualizing of the two contrasted figures and their struggle to the death—being an inner struggle, as it always is—would have made it clear.

The benign, trident-wielding figure in the monk's robe obviously represents his higher nature, which he likens to a monk's because of his own life of utter renunciation and love of solitude. In the conflict between the two opposed forces within, his higher self emerges triumphant. This was the inner reality, but the sensations of his mind were so potent and concentrated that his equally sensitive body, as we have seen, acted as a reciprocal register, passive to the impress of his every thought: as evil is expelled from his mind, it is also "seen" to emerge from his body.

We recall his boyish veneration of monks and wandering *sadhus*, his eagerness for their company as they drifted through his native village. When he had renounced the acquisition of an education because of its worldly mindset he inevitably identified himself, in that conflict of ideals, with the monk. With worldly people all around him, even in a religious temple atmosphere (including Mathur and the Rani), he took refuge in the image of the monk—the ochre-clad *sannyasin*—as one symbolic of his own deepest desires and tendencies. Indeed the monk-figure, beginning at this period, became his guru, teaching him everything, in the first years, that he was ever to learn from living teachers later. (Sometimes his instruction assumed a severe aspect. The trident which had slain the ego—at least temporarily—was also seen poised over his own head if he allowed his mind to waver from its one-pointed focus during meditation.)   It was only after the living teachers began to appear that this fantasy-guru vanished—again testifying to its psychic reality.

In the locking of his limbs to prevent an end to meditation before its time was due we see his body being made to play the role of humble servant to his God-oriented mind. The servant might be tempted to follow its own impulses from time to time, but to a Ramakrishna no exceptions were allowed: his higher self imposes its reality by an act of will upon the body, locking it in place, and, when it chooses, unlocking it again.

No outside force did these things, no God in heaven, no Mother Kali. He did them to himself. He may interpret them in another way; we are not bound to agree.

But if he could visualize an internal monk teaching and threatening him, perhaps he could imagine that he had realized God. Was this a hallucination? A merely psychic experience?

The question might be asked at almost any stage of his life and could be answered the same way each time. Hallucinations do not transform the character spiritually—though they may do so downwards. And already the amiable, impulsive village youth had been transformed into a character that struck awe and reverence in his critics: only a revelation of *spirit* can accomplish this. Psychic experiences on the other hand are phenomena of the *mind*, though an unfamiliar dimension of it; spiritual experiences are of spirit—that is, of the divine. As a result of the latter, we receive infusions of grace, intelligence, and personality-change that are beyond the reach of human effort. We cannot, by willpower, however continued and profound, *displace* our character. Ramakrishna already had done that—and this was only the beginning of what the process would do to him.

Further, no one has struggled as he did who simply had received, or had hopes of further, psychic awakenings; no one has manifested so much world-indifference motivated by hallucination or by the expectation of one. Only someone who had glimpsed the divine itself would so effortlessly trample under foot all the joys and tender relations of worldly life, all the traditional values that bind men and women together as an ongoing social whole.

Finally, the teachings that would emerge from these experiences, the coherent body of thought which he afterwards articulated to disciple and curiosity-seeker alike, restated—often in a homely, original style inimitable for illustration and memorable for instruction—the ancient doctrines of upanishadic sage, of Persian Sufi, of medieval hermit, confirmed these venerable traditions and was in turn confirmed by them. He who has gone to the Mount—where Buddha and Jesus and Krishna communed with absolute existence—will emerge with the same teachings and cast of mind as they. For the Teaching—the universal Teaching and the Ancient Path—issue from the Experience, not from the Experiencer, who is changed by the light *into* the light, whose humanity is possessed *by* the experience and out of the fused center of that oneness he now speaks, and of course thinks and acts too. It is *the Experience* that says: "I am the Way, the Truth, and the Life," and he who unites with That, no longer to be a visitor to it only, but a son of it, must speak in the same accent, his "I" thereafter being the Experience itself, the Reality that will persist as it is, long after his form has departed.

This explains Ramakrishna's identification of himself with Kali. In the temple he would often feed himself before the goddess, place flowers to be offered to her on his own head first. "Fix your mind on Me and you will get everything," he once told a disciple who asked him upon what aspect of the divine he should concentrate during meditation.

Already, in the early, unguided period, the Reality had been achieved, though he was articulating it to himself only.

None of this, needless to say, is applicable to the hallucinatory or psychic state, where sensations of the subconscious mind substitute for revelations from beyond.

A saint he might be, and none more protective of his saintliness than proprietor Mathur Babu. But the strange youth's behavior disturbed him—and Rani Rasmani, who, though not resident in the temple compound most of the time, was informed of all developments by her trusted and efficient son-in-law. On one memorable occasion she was herself a victim of Ramakrishna's unpredictable behavior. During a solemn festival day in honor of Kali, when she had made a special trip from her Calcutta home to grace the occasion, Ramakrishna, preternaturally alert to any slights to the goddess, found her transgressing. Privately, her mind was preoccupied with thoughts about a difficult litigation in Calcutta and the thoughts had pursued her to Dakshineswar. Detecting this, Ramakrishna, in the midst of the large company, suddenly slapped her and delivered a verbal rebuke along with it, which horrified everyone, Mathur included; but the Rani, to her credit, accepted the reprimand in good spirit, declaring she had deserved it. Mathur, nevertheless, found this action additional reason to doubt the young mystic's sanity, which led him to summon another physician to examine him.

Between themselves, Mathur and the Rani concluded that Ramakrishna's firm rule of continence was very likely responsible for his oddities and peculiar habits; the strain of total self-denial was confusing his mind, oppressing his nerves, rendering him unfit for ordinary, wholesome ways of life. They made an arrangement with two attractive prostitutes in Calcutta to come to Dakshineswar and alleviate his state of nervous tension.

Mathur and the Rani were moral and religious people. That they had given Ramakrishna all the protection and encouragement he needed to enable him to continue his spiritual practices in an auspicious setting alone identified them as no ordinary Hindus, and their veneration for Kali, the great goddess, was unquestionably sincere. Moreover, in their individual characters they were not only virtuous but accommodating and congenial. They were, in other words, of a high type of personal influence in the community. Their choice of lustful women to help Ramakrishna solve the problem of excessive holiness exposes, like a lightning-flash, the nature of the human mind and its utter inability to understand the regenerated mind of saintliness.

They are the once-born religious mentality, incorrigibly worldly in their values and orientation. They are the pharisees and scribes of all religions. They are righteous but in their own eyes, virtuous but through man-made conceptions of virtue. Over the raw impulses of worldliness their religion is a painted veil, having nothing whatever to do with spirituality, with truth, with holiness. And they are the *best of men* in society, not the worst. The pharisees who slew Christ were not wicked but virtuous men, their virtue, however, centered on *this* world, on merely *human* motivations. But, "except the Lord build the house they labor in vain that build it" (*Psalms* 127: 1). Vain is the virtue of brahmin and puritan and *mullah* and scribe. A gulf, wide as the sky, deep as the ocean, yawns between them and the spiritually awakened soul—not to speak of a Ramakrishna, a soul spiritually *realized*. Their admiration of him, their appreciation of his spiritual genius and of his taking shelter with them, seems genuine. But in a moment of stress, or anxiety, their true color shines through instantly. Yet they dominate the religious tradition of every nation and set the standard by which religious truth is measured. When conduct is not answerable to their preconceptions of what virtue is, and what it is not, they will do anything whatsoever, and throughout history have done so, to bring the errant member into line. "They will kill you," Christ tells his disciples upon leaving them, "and think they are doing God's service." Just as the pharisees, the best of the Jews, who killed Christ, were unambiguously convinced that they were doing God's service. So were Mathur and the Rani, the best of the Hindus, convinced the Lord was being served when they called in the prostitutes.[*]

Just as St. Francis by involuntary yoga power robbed the Umbrian wolf of its savagery, so Ramakrishna by the same means robbed the Calcutta women of their lust. Years later he told his disciples that he saw in every woman, even harlots, the image of the bliss-giving goddess, and this was his first baptism of fire in testing so lofty an ideal. The result was foregone. With the name of Kali on his lips he mentally genuflected to the spirit behind the forms of the enemy, then went into *samadhi*, which already had become his habitat: the superconscious

---

[*] And repeated the attempt some time later when he visited the house of a friend of theirs in Calcutta.

state. Shamed, humiliated, possibly made wiser, the two Magdalenes retreated in confusion and fear, assailing Mathur with their reproaches.

During this temptation, when Ramakrishna, to check the senses and intensify his self-awareness, drew his mind within, it entered the domain of spirit immediately and thus *abandoned* the temptation rather than resisted it. Other men, at best, in such a crisis, could restrain the senses from thrusting outward toward their object of desire, like the precarious control exercised over wild horses. With Ramakrishna it was not a matter of control but of passing at once to a spiritual realm where temptation no longer existed.

6

End of Initial Phase

HIS PRIESTLY DUTIES MEANWHILE had become impossible to carry out, and no further pretense was made to do so. About this time a cousin from Kamarpukur, one Haladhari, arrived at Dakshineswar and was promptly appointed temple priest in his place. Haladhari, a highly orthodox brahmin fixated on scriptural injunction and caste regulation, was shocked at his cousin's aberrant behavior but was able sufficiently to recognize his qualities of holiness to make a tolerable relationship possible between them. He was to remain at Dakshineswar from 1858 to 1865, years when he was the astonished witness of much of Ramakrishna's sadhana. He plays no major role in the story but is one more pious Hindu convinced of his righteousness who furnished Ramakrishna with another face of orthodoxy with which he had to cope and with a potent example of religious hypocrisy presenting itself to the world as religion and to itself as the very servant of God. As with the deceased Ramkumar, there was in him a marked manifestation of the usual psychic powers, including one beyond Ramkumar: the gift of cursing people and making the curse come true.

With Ramakrishna and his life as a litmus test, a touchstone whereby every category of spiritual aspirant might be assessed, Haladhari, seen against this steady light, becomes an object lesson of what *not* to be, his character a moral—teaching us what to avoid. An unusual degree of psychic development, an erudite conversance with scriptures, a deep brahmin-knowledge of religious tradition, left him marooned on the island of the once-born, unable to discern spiritual truth directly, to act with genuine spontaneity regarding the questions of religion, or to accept his cousin's unparalleled spirituality because he did not comply with scriptural injunctions to the letter and followed no man's guidance but his own.

Appointed to conduct the service in the Kali temple, he had tried to do so, though with little heart for the task, since he suspected that Kali was one of the lesser deities, lacking the purity of his gods. There is a report, though from a none-too-reliable source, that one day the goddess, assuming her fearsome aspect, ordered him from the temple because of his negative attitude and promised that as a result of his irreverent worship his son would die: a curse—like some of his own—which, it is said, came true a few days later.[*]

Rumors of Ramakrishna's madness, breaking of caste rules, and other worrisome developments sifted back to Kamarpukur. There were many besides Haladhari to do this work of the Lord in informing family and townsmen of the deterioration of his character. Chandramani accepted the reports at face value and repeatedly urged him to return home for a visit, particularly as it had been six years since his departure. Finally, at the end of 1858, he went back. He stayed, surprisingly, for a year and a half, perhaps two years, before returning to Dakshineswar.

The long sojourn at home, in his native village, among familiar scenes, slowly brought respite to his troubled spirit. He somewhat moderated his spiritual practices out of deference to family anxiety over his unhealthy love of solitude and long hours of meditation in places shunned by everyone else: the village crematoriums. Like the burial ground at Dakshineswar, a crematorium is a place unsurpassed for reminding one of the impermanence of all things and especially of the body, which, he will observe later, "is so dear to a man." They were the bleakest locales he could find and served as an ideal antidote to the

---

* The incident recalls the endless fiery imprecations of Jehovah, testifying to a God not worth knowing. Was Kali like that? We conclude the story was apocryphal, the source being the superstitious Hriday's probably equally superstitious brother, one of the many—Hindu or Hebrew or Christian alike—who have given religion a bad name.

benign but enervating airs of hearth and kin.

Chandra shared the view of many that her son was possessed by a ghost and arranged for an exorcist to liberate him. By now she had completely forgotten the supernal visions alleged to have come to her and her husband prior to her pregnancy announcing the advent in her womb of a divine messenger, and credited her own worst fears and the gossip of unlettered villagers feeding them. She acted this way, as Mathur and Rani had acted as *they* had, because all of her religious observances, fasts, rites and rituals, enjoined on her simple soul by an ancient tradition and never for a moment examined much less questioned by her, had not in any way changed her from the person she had been at puberty, had not touched her spiritual self in the slightest, had not in any respect whatever awakened the divine potential in her. She continued to be what for years she had been, Nature in the garb of a pious middle-aged lady. The mother of a saint, as we have sadly noted, is the very last one to understand him or to practice what he practices.

Ramakrishna had returned home to propitiate this power in the world, the power that had given him a body, enabling him to materialize on the earth-plane. Hence he must worship it. Further, his mother, like all women, is a form of the Universal Mother, and he must give her additional, special worship. He must practice in secret, worshipping his own mother as a manifestation of Kali, and he must do this until he has perfected the discipline—and it has perfected him. And he must cope charitably with the spiritual mediocrity of the villagers, their age-old superstitions and race taboos, their blind obedience to forces within and without that used them wholly as pawns in a social organism that had no connection whatsoever (although they assumed it did) with the divine, with the soul. He had to come to see them in a new and milder light, to accept them, to understand the role they, too, played in the order of things. Most of all, he had to analyze within himself the representative of those rural villagers and kinfolk, acknowledge its presence, and slowly, while still in their chafing midst, pluck it out of him and watch the ochre-clad monk emerge from his subconscious and commit another slaying.

If we can love our family we can love anybody. If we can maintain our spiritual balance with relatives it is established—is real. Relatives refuse—and are unable—to see in us anything save the creature, and we are conditioned, by reflex, by karma, by reciprocal response, to see naught save the creature in them. Hence the vital discipline in close periodic association.

Ramakrishna was not exempt from this. Had he been, it would have deprived him of one of the supreme purgatories of human existence. His transcendental experiences tend to blind his followers to the truth of his mortality as well. He became immortal—on condition that he master the creaturely elements of his being: the same challenge given to us.

The particular mastery enjoined on him at this juncture would take many months—that is why, after more than six years away and with little thought given to family or village during that time, we find him content to remain at home for nearly two years. There is another reason. By now, everything he was doing was actuated by divine permission or divine will. At Dakshineswar, after the first breakthrough in the year of Ramkumar's death with the vision of "Mother" as pure Consciousness, he had attained a continuing level of spiritual realization enabling him to experience the divine presence constantly: moments apart from it caused intolerable anxiety. To maintain this level of unity he had to control his thinking to an absolute degree, could not undertake or *consider* anything that did not reflect divine sanction. Since the perishable nature of human life had been made clear to him for all time in the period following Ramkumar's demise, and the jungle graveyard been made available (by that same providence) as a fitting corollary to this knowledge, it was natural that the thought of Kamarpukur and his family and relatives should occupy so little of his mental time.

By remaining as long as he did on this first visit home it was evident that he could only have received the divine command to do so. The talk about regaining his health was the human interpretation of another, entirely different process going on. Not that his health was not on its own level a factor. The human element being resolved where a difficulty exists is not neglected, is always a humble partner in the overall design, and indeed is often the means through which the greater *raison d'etre* is accomplished.

The divine behest to remain so long at home would have included the necessity of disciplining his mind into utter acceptance of even relatives as children of God and to love them as freely and truly as he could do with neutral strangers. But the *exemplary* aspect of his life was another, perhaps more telling motive. No one on the spiritual path wishes to have more to do with his family than he absolutely must—at least in the first years of sadhana, when an emergent, new sensitivity is not yet matched with a comparable self-restraint and authenticated compassion. Traditionally, to escape them, we have become nuns and monks, have been able to disappear into religious orders, or, if laity, to fashion solitudes of independence from our ancestral past—to create, like Thoreau, Walden huts of self-renewal wherein to pursue our spiritual dream: what Ramakrishna himself had been doing during his six years away from home. But with his example before us we cannot do this any longer without anxiety. We, too, must make an effort to bring family into the orbit of our spiritual career.

"A nest of vipers" was his description of relatives; family members he had regarded, he said, as a "deep well"—sentiments that find in every regenerate heart a somber echo. Nevertheless these people have produced our bodies and shaped our childhood environment; though spirit later stirred in us, the early design of our lives was fated to be what in fact it was, including the *dramatis personae*. Their role—mysterious, inexorable, parasitical as it is—was foreseen by the same power that foresaw our awakening. Our salvation depends on our willingness to save *them*, our enlightenment on our readiness to share with them at least *some* of our spirituality. Through symbiotic transference of spiritual vibration the hidden centers of their unregenerate personalities are touched—truth touching the organ of truth within—and they are permanently affected. (Because of the blood-closeness of family members they are every moment, all unwittingly, vulnerable to the influence of the meditative being in their midst and may not resist it.) Though they do not reap the harvest of that seeding in this lifetime, their spiritual journey commences in another life on the basis, largely, of the divine implantation to which we consent during periods when called into closer unity with them.

With Ramakrishna's example we can do this with more heart and a keener sense of duty than we would otherwise have. And he stayed so long to make it clear that such renewals of association, may have to be prolonged on occasion: until the purpose that called them forth is accomplished.

He stayed for his own sake too, we should not forget—his soul's sake.

• • •

One other vital matter contributed to the long sojourn—stunning, numbing for the mind to contemplate: the search for a wife and the arrangements for the betrothal.

Chandramani's hope (and of many around her) that her son, sent to earth with a divine mission though he may have been, might be betrothed while still in Kamarpukur and married as soon as reasonably possible, dramatically betrayed her conventional views and her inability to comprehend her son. She frankly believed, and certainly hoped, that the responsibilities of married life would bring his mind down to earth and help him once and for all regain a normal health and mental outlook!

Ramakrishna did not object to this dream-like undertaking. We surmise that he already had a prescience of what would follow and, foreseeing the extraordinary role his spouse would play in his life, consented to the plan. Forthwith a long search was made for a suitable girl but for a variety of reasons none was found acceptable. Then he said they should go to Jayrambati, a village a few miles away: she would be waiting. The girl that was found was five years old, as compared to Ramakrishna's twenty-three; her name was Saradamani. The two families were known to each other and, except for her age, she was felt to be appropriate in all ways. Since it would be some eight years before her puberty (Chandra herself had married at thirteen, borne her first child the next year), Chandra and the other relatives thought that was too long to wait. Ramakrishna's problem was urgent and not likely to solve itself. But he insisted that she was the appointed girl; and so the arrangements were made and the betrothal formalized. At the time of the ceremony he cast eyes on his future wife and, before he left again for Calcutta, visited for a few days at her house. He was not to see her again for eight years.

With Kamarpukur behind, it disappeared from his mind completely as he returned to Dakshineswar and to the round of devotional practices which two years before had given rise to the rumors of insanity. The months of sleeplessness returned. His eyes refused to blink. "I went for six years without sleep," he said later. Separation for an instant from the divine consciousness—which, as we know, he had implicitly, constantly identified with the Divine Mother—plunged him into inconsolable anxiety, uncontrollable agitation. His body, the tissued, transparent garment of his mind, rejected the idea of sleep lest he be cut off from conscious apprehension of the divine presence. He would roll on the ground as one possessed, his body once again seized by its painful burning sensation, his cries day and night carried to every corner of the temple compound.

He was demanding from the "goddess"— that is, from the source of all being—*a continuous vision* of the divine: not only during meditation but during waking hours, and not in a general, euphoric way, but vividly, palpably, as real and living as his pulse or his breathing. Once before he had threatened to take his life if this demand was not met, and very nearly carried it out; again he was in a state that seemed to point in that direction, though in fact he never attempted so drastic a solution a second time, for previously the closeness between the Supreme Soul and his own was far less than it now was, in 1861, in his twenty-fifth year. Suffer though he might, the reality of the goddess was too overwhelming, too intimate, too established in his heart, for him to risk an action so unfeeling, so unlike a lover or a son. Also, much more of his will had been broken. She had subdued him to the extent of compelling him to ignore and conquer his body but not to attempt to destroy it. In short he was in a state of helpless surrender.

There was certainly *egoism* involved in his impulse that day when he had seized the sword, an impatient self-will quite as much as his love for the deity. The humility grounded deep in his nature forbade such dramatics. Even he would have to endure the apparent withdrawal of the beloved, as others have had to—though such withdrawal, as we have noted, is only apparent, the result of the mind's modifications on a remote level as it attempts to cope with the tremendous pressures the will imposes on it during the course of spiritual longing. In finding himself brought again and again to the state of seeming separation from the universal consciousness, and being forced to bear it at least for a few minutes or a few hours at a time, the self-will was ground down further, the state of being utterly poor in spirit tested over and over.

Analogous was Gautama's seven years of yoga and personality mortification prior to that full-moon night under the Tree. He, too, had to be melted down to a shape appropriate for the divine sculptor, the inward artist of the soul, before the purest, strongest rays from the Light could enter without turbulence the mind of the receiver. Similar, though less intense, are the impressive austerities of ascetics, many of them misguided to be sure. There is so much self-will, so large an egoism, so pervasive a state of delusion in our normal creaturely selves, that to purify it takes lifetimes, not years, and in that lifetime when the breakthrough into *genuine* knowledge is made, or may be made, at last, the struggle continues, in most cases, for decades, and even an avatar must spend a full decade before the tumult of his uncertainty is stilled and the light not only illumines but remains thereafter unbroken.

All of this austerity may be useless unless guided by the soul, the divine witness. We must not proceed self-directed, *scheduling our own enlightenment;* otherwise we must later undo what we have, in vain, erected. Ramakrishna of course was driven and seized by the inner goddess, entirely, throughout this period, was made to do what he did do; and made to live with it.

Feeling the ego's presence himself (the dark, red-eyed man within), he surpassed his previous mortifications with actions particularly offensive to a Hindu. To eradicate any lingering brahmin-assumption that he was better than anyone whosoever, including the outcasts, he visited the quarters of pariahs, ate the leavings of their food, cleaned the area of their cooking with his own hands, and with his hair carefully washed their latrines.

Meditation, the heart of his sadhana, grew longer, more desperate. He knew nothing of yoga but by the power of his longing alone achieved the outer and inner motionlessness, the *stillness*, of pure yoga practice. The thought of the divine, alone, transfixed his mind, gathered all his nerve force, accomplished *pratyahara,* that sense-withdrawal which the yogi by dint of protracted labor tensely achieves, precariously sustains. The vehemence of his world-indifference powered the intensity of his internal drive ever more inward, his will a blade cutting through the forest of thought ever more subtle in the subconscious world, the body meanwhile stiff, motionless as a tree, on which birds alighted, resting, pecking in his matted hair for crumbs of food, snakes curled over his limbs and slept there, each unaware of the other, as the process advanced toward ripeness: the transmutation of lower into higher self, of ego into egolessness, of the last tincture of separativeness into oneness.

Once again rumors of his madness wound their way to Kamarpukur, again the anxious Mathur called in doctors, again no medicine was found. A Calcutta physician this time concluded that not disease, not derangement, but the excessive practice of yoga—his sadhana, that is to say—had brought about the symptoms that had alarmed everyone. This diagnosis, obviously imaginative, was rejected by Mathur and the others.

Despite the organic frustration he experienced—or because of it—the gap between his soul and the goddess was closing, the supernal presence almost continuous, within, without, in the unmanifested realm, in the manifested. Earlier there had been the blazing moment that had established him in the bosom of the Absolute. The new flame was incremental, by slower degrees fixing his mind permanently in the mystical consciousness—that is, awakening to an inordinate degree (though still far from completely so) the same consciousness native to all minds but which in his had been, almost from childhood, the dominant tendency: the indigenous mystic power by which the mind perceives unity rather than multiplicity, resemblances than distinctions, unperishing rather than perishing forms, spirit than matter, truth than untruth, the One and not the Many. Do not judge according to appearances, Christ urges us, but judge righteous judgment, which only the mystic, the saint may do, though the power lay intrinsic to every mind, because in them alone the righteous *perception* has flowered.

Around this time the worldly but benevolent Mathur was rewarded for his loyalty to the former temple priest—from heaven or from his own subconscious depths—with a rare vision of the divine manifesting, as he told of it, in Ramakrishna, in which both masculine and feminine attributes—Shiva and Kali alike—shone forth in him as he strolled one day beneath Mathur's window. The perception, he said, was so powerful, unlike a flight of the imagination, that quickly he rose, rushed outside, and threw himself at the saint's feet, crying out to him what he had seen. Whether the vision was real or an hallucination, it convinced him, at least, that Ramakrishna was all that (much of the time) he had suspected he was: a special manifestation of divinity. More than a yogi, or a saint—something else. Thereafter his protection of the young mystic, his support for him, his providing for all his wants, became complete. It was to achieve this, it seems, that the vision came, as a kind of unmerited grace—to serve Ramakrishna's life directly and in so doing to serve the divine will. He became indispensable to Ramakrishna as, in a completely different way, Hriday was.[*]

* It may have been about this time, as well (that is, on the strength of his unusual epiphany) that Mathur—as many claim—gave Gadai the name by which he became known immediately and thereafter, combining in one appellation the names of the two great avatars of ancient days, perhaps to suggest by this (cont.)

His insight wavered in the months to follow, as it always does, except where the experience was earned. As it was not with the walrus-mustached Mathur. The experience was *overlaid* upon his helpful, but always worldly character, and hence we cannot be surprised to find him questioning Ramakrishna's sanity—with anxious solicitude— only a few days later. And then *remembering* the vision and thinking that perhaps he *was* a God-man, after all. Not like Krishna, of course. The modern age could not produce such great souls. And not like Rama. But someone special in some way... So it went, oscillating between viewpoints depending upon mood and *Maya*, since the center of his being, untouched, unknown, could not be turned to or relied upon as a source of truth.

Four, nearly five years had passed since the beginning of Ramakrishna's sustained effort to take by the force of his yearning the guarded sanctuary where, it is said, the gods have not penetrated. In less time than Buddha or Christ had needed he had achieved unbroken Nirvana, conquered the kingdom, and every breath of his life was a whisper from the goddess. But unlike Buddha, and according to the ancient hermetic tradition, unlike Christ, both of whom had had several teachers in their ascent to illumination, Ramakrishna had had no one.

Then one appeared, a woman, fulfilling a mysterious purpose. Rani Rasmani's death at that time, the day after his twenty-fifth birthday in February 1861, signified the onset of another pattern, of something beginning and ending such as we observed five years before with the death of Ramkumar. And as we shall observe again.

Death is prelude to the new growth, the waiting life, the gift budding. The parent, the loved one, the supportive friend, a way of living— whatever has seemed necessary or vital in an ongoing scheme may abruptly be removed: often for the others' sakes as much as for ours, since the animation of a common Soul is responsible for both. But just as often others are sacrificed that a particular life should burgeon toward spiritual ripeness.

The Rani's demise, so soon before the coming of the Brahmani, as the teacher was known (that is, the lady brahmin), suggests that she would have had difficulty assimilating the thought of her protégé (as to some extent she would have conceived him) entering into an

---

that Ramakrishna was the modern avatar.

extraordinary relationship, and at once, with a strange, beautiful woman of forty,[*] dressed in the orange robe of an itinerant nun, her hair flowing loose like a goddess', appearing one day from nowhere on the temple grounds. Since she was all her life extremely self-conscious of her low-caste birth, she exerted herself constantly in not only a life of virtue but in the appearance of it: to prove herself as conventionally pious as any brahmin. Sanctioning Ramakrishna's relationship with the mysterious brahmin-lady, Yogeswari by name, who was to come to Dakshineswar daily, spending hours in his company, would have been difficult for her.

Rani Rasmani's final days were not peaceful as her mind wrestled with problems of her last will and testament and the noncooperative attitude of one of her daughters. Certain probate matters remained tangled, unresolved, to the end, and she suffered as a consequence. All her good works, her public generosity, her well-meaning nature, her eagerness to be virtuous, could not bring her the peace she wished. We recall her dwelling on a litigation the day she went to Dakshineswar on a special religious occasion, when Ramakrishna had sternly scolded her, recalling Christ in the temple ("Make not my Father's house a den of merchandise"): she was the same woman on her deathbed. What we are in life we will be at the end.

Anxious that the proper brahmin priest should be found, and only the most acceptable food practices followed, for her Ganges temple, ever scrupulous that the most orthodox reports could be conveyed about her, in her last hours she was a slave of shadows, unable even then to immerse her mind in the thought of God, the Substance, since her life had not demonstrated such a capacity. And she was among the most sincere of the doers of good works, of the accumulators of merit.

How many like her in India, like Rani, Mathur, Haladhari, Ramkumar, Chandramani, how many millions of Hindu Pharisees, against whose outlook Christ and Buddha labored, seemingly in vain, each thinking he is leading a God-centered life, each a pillar of virtue in their parochial world, each faithful to their creed, their tradition, and each a world away from salvation, from God-realization—from

---

[*] In order to make the relationship seem more respectable, Swami Nikhilananda on his own authority asserts she was "slightly over fifty" (*Gospel*, 18), while Saradananda (*Great Master*, 185), said that he had heard directly from Ramakrishna himself that she was just under forty.

God-notice: God seeth the heart only. The heart of each twisted by crazes, fears, fetishes, worldly phantoms, egoism, pride of lineage, or whatever, and none with *understanding.* "May that Light illumine our understanding"—the old Vedantic prayer seems to have passed over the lives of all the millions like them. God seeth the heart—and the understanding. Both. The pure heart. The understanding heart. Both are necessary. If both are not achieved, we have failed. Then in our own age, on our deathbeds, we will be senile like Chandra or worried about the law like Rani. The serenity will be missing. The truth. The peace.

Rani, then, almost certainly would have troubled herself over Ramakrishna's strange immediate friendship—his special love-relationship—with the mysterious Brahmani, the itinerant, ochre-clad renunciate, carrying a few precious books, still at forty a beautiful woman, and as learned and devotional as she was attractive. Mathur, though more liberal and able to abide the startling development taking place before his eyes, was suspicious of her on the grounds that she *was* attractive. Full of lust himself, as all worldly men are, as all *men* are until the infinite stirs in them, he projected onto objects of impossible desire the scope of his own cravings, and attributed to them his own tendencies. He did not interfere, however; by now his faith in Ramakrishna's spirituality was enough to reassure him. He simply restrained himself, enjoying his private male skepticism of the wandering brahmin-lady.

Rani, however, would have been prey to the same suspicions which Mathur was able to deflect. That she was removed so suddenly from the scene, and such a short time before the Brahmani's appearance, makes it clear that the new friendship was to be of crucial importance for Ramakrishna.

7
The Brahmani

HE WAS PICKING FLOWERS on the Ganges embankment at the western boundary of the temple grounds when he first saw her and felt the instant attraction of Fate incarnating. Within minutes they were conversing as people do who have known and loved each other for a long time. Perhaps his earth mother some lifetimes back, and now his spiritual mother, she was given the immense role of guiding him in certain inward directions which, following pure instinct alone, he had not yet traversed. Where her learning derived from, or where she had taken her sadhana, bringing her to the high spiritual state she occupied, she did not divulge, nor did anyone ever find out. He himself never questioned her about such things. The direct intuition, the emotional certainty, the personality rapport, deepening moment by moment, was all he needed.

Hriday and Mathur, his physical supports, realized he had never acted this way before with anyone else, male or female. One more fountain of awe opened for them in contemplating the marriage of minds that had taken place before their eyes.

She told him she had received a summons to come to him, and not only did he not question this, he seemed to anticipate it. The source of the summons, she said, was God. The reason was not completely clear, but shortly became so.

He poured out to her the story of his persistent ailments and of particular spiritual experiences that puzzled him. In the absence of any guru-guidance, without any way of confirming his mysticism with the vast tradition that stretched out behind him, and surrounded for several years by people who avowedly expressed doubts of his sanity, he had been unsure himself at times of his own mental balance, and of the meaning of what was happening to him. Unhesitatingly this extraordinary woman reassured him without stint. He was not mad, he was in a rare, high state of spiritual consciousness which only a few saints in the past reached (she named two: Radha and Chaitanya), with the same attendant symptoms he too was experiencing. She vowed to prove her assertion by citing chapter and verse from Bengal India's devotional scriptures (as distinct from the *Upanishads* and the *Gita*), where, she said, everything was recorded. He was, moreover, living testimony to the truth of those scriptures.

All of this, even in the first meeting, there in the flower garden on the bank of the Ganges.

When they had finished talking and, in the manner of mother and son, taking food together, he left her alone for a time in the Panchavati,[*] where Yogeswari offered food to Rama, her chosen Ideal (who was also, we may recall, Ramakrishna's family deity), a stone symbol of whom hung from her neck. She then meditated on Rama and quickly entered into a profound superconscious state, bringing tears without and vision within. We are told that at that moment Ramakrishna, magnetically drawn back to the Panchavati, found Yogeswari still in contemplation, saw the offered food, and, as though hypnotized, began to eat it, meanwhile passing into a deep devotional samadhi himself. She then shortly returned to normal consciousness, saw him in front of her, and the half eaten food, saw that this precisely accorded with her own vision, she said later, whereupon hair on her body stood on end. When Ramakrishna regained the normal state, she expressed anew her conviction regarding the Power that was causing him to do what he did, then and at all times. She felt that in the young man before her she was seeing the living image of Rama and hence, she said, had no more need of conventional ceremonial worship. The stone symbol of the avatar, hung round her neck for most of her life, was superfluous: her worship had been answered forever. In a profoundly emotional mood she walked to

---

[*] Literally a "place of five trees," in this instance five different traditionally sacred trees, including the fig and the banyan, which Ramakrishna himself planted and hedged, making a dark, secluded grove where, almost invisible to sight, he performed many spiritual practices and austerities. The Panchavati tended to replace the jungle burial ground, his chosen site for meditation in the first years.

the Ganges and committed her stone amulet to the sacred river.

Days of intimate spiritual conversation followed in the shadow of the Panchavati, with the Brahmani often reading from the devotional scriptures or from books on Tantra, her other specialty. After a week of continuous intercourse in this manner Ramakrishna suggested that for appearances' sake, and to preserve her reputation intact, they should think of having her at least sleep elsewhere and to visit him by day, to which she agreed. A suitable family, honored to have her stay with them, was found close to the temple in the village of Dakshineswar.

As their exchanges continued and the rapport strengthened, it was the preeminent early sixteenth-century saint of Bengal, Chaitanya, who seemed on numerous points of comparison to be a precursor of Ramakrishna. Their conduct and types of experience, and the painful bodily symptoms, showed much in common. What had cured Chaitanya of his physical suffering, said Yogeswari—a mysterious combination of garlands and sandalpaste smeared over the body—was recommended for Ramakrishna, evoking indulgent laughter in Mathur and others, who had tried many remedies in vain. This prescription, nevertheless, actually worked: the burning sensation in Ramakrishna's chest, from which he had suffered for so long, left him almost at once.

The Brahmani declared that Chaitanya, considered a prophet in the Indian devotional tradition, was manifesting for the present age in Ramakrishna's body. She went further: the signs uniquely found in the bodies, experiences, and behavior of divine incarnations—the avatars— were there in Ramakrishna as well. Which, when he heard of it, pro- voked friendly ridicule in Mathur: avatars belong to history, they are never our contemporaries. But Yogeswari held her ground and tried to convert him to her views. Let some renowned scholar be found, she suggested; let *him* hear what she had to say. Ramakrishna with guileless enthusiasm urged Mathur to do what she asked: only then would all be satisfied—"What she says must be tested."

Soon everyone in the temple compound, and many outside of it, had heard of her remarkable opinions of the one-time priest, and great was the sensation. Mathur felt that the two pundits he planned to invite, Vaishnavacharan and Gauri, both illustrious in that part of India, would soon enough make short work of the Brahmani's extravagant thesis and Ramakrishna would benefit directly by freeing himself of the egotism which must inevitably be creeping into him by virtue of these excessive tributes from someone about whom no one knew anything whatever—and who was a beautiful, unattended woman as well. Mixed motives, then, greeted the arrival of the two esteemed scholars at this unprecedented conclave. Ramakrishna's seem to have been a combination of eager childlike interest in the proceedings, as though personally not involved in what was going on, and calm, resigned faith in the wisdom of the Brahmani, his spiritual mother.

Both of the celebrated scholars, who had come with separate retinues, listened with an amazed intentness as the impassioned nun, so quickly domesticated in Ramakrishna's world, likened her protégé to the most renowned figures in India's devotional history, explained that his many physical ills were but externalizations of inner states brought on by excruciating sadhana, as had been the case, she said, citing the sources, of his foremost predecessors in devotion, Chaitanya, and Radha, the latter the consort of Krishna, the former worshipped among devotees as Krishna *redivivus*. She argued that even a saint could not endure for long the burden of more than a few of the highest divine graces but would forthwith give up the body, whereas Ramakrishna had shown signs of nineteen such marks of divine favor, making it clear that his body was under special protection and that he had been born for the good of mankind, such as had been promised periodically to the world in the *Bhagavad-Gita*. She was questioned closely, with little dispute being raised. Astonishingly, both Vaishnavacharan and Gauri agreed with her, in a tentative way at first, and after some days without reservation, each attempting, in fact, to outdo the other in their celebration of Ramakrishna's spiritual state.

What had made the difference in their response, as compared to Mathur or Haladhari, for example, was that they were long practicing devotees as well as scholars. Vaishnavacharan was the leader of a band of Tantric worshippers, and Gauri, who venerated his wife as divine, was on the verge of total renunciation of the world when he met Ramakrishna, though unaware himself of his own condition. Despite their scholarly repute, both considered spiritual *life*, not learning, as the pearl of great price and both reverenced anyone who had genuinely achieved it. In Ramakrishna they were amazed to find a veritable personification of it—having, indeed, no life left over in him, we might say, that was not spiritual life. Gauri, after contact with Ramakrishna for some time, abruptly abandoned society, disappeared into the Himalayas, it was thought, there to spend the end of his days in all-renouncing contemplation. Many searches were launched for him but he was never heard of again.

The Lord is a consuming fire. So are his God-men. Lives are burned up after a few days' contact. We worship them at our own risk. If we do not wish to become fire, too, we should keep our distance— and settle for a creed.

As did those who judged the Galilean master, finding him wanting, their touchstone being not the degree of spirituality, the living presence, he had attained to, but a book. The Torah. The Law. The letter killeth, Jesus reminded them. He was judged by death, he being life. Death slaying life. The problem every true soul faces in his combat with family, church, and society.

The Hebrew fixation on the past sealed his doom. The divine, they were sure, had intervened in human affairs—Jewish affairs, that is—but it had happened long ago: it was a closed volume. The Hindus, on the other hand, regarded divinity as immanent, perennially returning, periodically incarnating, eternally united with human endeavor in the most intimate manner. The Jerusalem scribes looked for a messiah but not in one who failed to announce plans for an earthly kingdom that would make the Jews once again a world power; not in one who disavowed violence, preached gentleness. The Hindu pundits believed it undeniable that the divine light might take a human form at any time. Lo, it might be him before them now, assuming a humbler guise than ever before.

Why need he always come to found a new religion, or speak in apocalyptic accents? "This time," Ramakrishna said much later, to his circle of disciples, "it has happened in secret."

Who can say whether these eminences were right in their assessment? But that they should both agree, and with little difficulty, with the overzealous Brahmani; that the strength of their conviction should make both descend from their height in society and become humble devotees of Ramakrishna ever afterwards, one seeing him often, returning constantly to his company, the other faithful in Himalayan seclusion, gives us pause.

Mathur and all the doubters at Dakshineswar were overwhelmed by the outcome of the conclaves.[*] Henceforth Mathur was totally at

---

* Some say that it was now, in the moment of his complete conversion, that Mathur denominated the illiterate Gadai after the two most celebrated names in early Hindu (cont.)

Ramakrishna's disposal and he gave appropriate orders to his temple underlings to conduct themselves in the same way.

The Brahmani, her position strengthened and inviolable, was revered as a special representative of the Lord sent to enlighten the world about their rare inhabitant. Her relationship with him proceeded in sweet, harmonious, and triumphant progress, Mathur admiring it, in awed wonder, from a distance.

8
Tantra

THAT RELATIONSHIP NOW LOCKED itself into the labyrinths of Tantra—mystic, esoteric Tantra, always suspect among the orthodox (if one estimates Vedanta, Yoga, and the devotional *Puranas* as Hinduism's traditional paths), while exercising over everyone its almost illicit fascination. One can scarcely credit this chapter in Ramakrishna's spiritual career: the chaste young saint introduced into the mysteries and practices of India's most exotic tradition, involving sexual encounters as its central portion, and guided for nearly two years in these intimate mazes by a beautiful nun who remains a witness (though not a participant) to his accomplishments.

Which may be the best way for a man to achieve not only a heroic but a fulfilling continence: through the grace of a woman-guide steering him through the Scylla and Charybdis of fear and desire that must imperil any male attempting to draw out of the tangled meshes, the shoals and quicksands, of this yoga, this *terra incognita*, the fruits of divine realization.*

The Tantric disciplines have always been shrouded in secrecy but

---

history. The outer-oriented Mathur's fealty to conventional values of society, including the leading religious scholars of that society, would likely have provided the final element needed in his full conversion.

* In Book III of Spenser's *Faerie Queene*, the Elizabethan allegory pitting vice against virtue, the hero acknowledges his dependence on the guru-heroine Britomart for his self-conquest of passion and ultimate embrace of continence.

their essential features are not: the conquest of sexual passion by a controlled, ritualized exchange aimed at perceiving in the partner the image of the divine feminine (and masculine); gaining a mystical insight into the nature of the relations between the sexes as a spiritual transaction; and eventually experiencing the divine itself by awakening the coiled-up serpent power of the *Kundalini* in the sexual region but then carefully, ritualistically, deflecting it from its instinctual into the spiritual channel and so elevating it to higher levels of consciousness and the alchemy of transformation.

Tantra is a path for those who wish to solve the problem of sexual craving not by withdrawing from the lion altogether but by plucking victory from his very jaws. If one proceeds with enlightened caution, accompanied by a sympathetic companion, one may find that the lion's aggressiveness has been largely due to not having been properly appreciated. With a mind worshipful of the divine presence in the woman's body and spirit alike (symbolized in Tantric ideograms by the *Kundalini* flame, of triangular form, depicted in the sexual area), the man discovers he has nothing to fear from the woman. As both go forward, on mounting waves of elation, with a united will of loving vigilance and prayerful wonder, they are cheerfully to hold at bay the enemy that threatens to manacle both and destroy the work of grace: lust.

It is a path for those who cannot give up the company of women but who feel, equally, the desire for self-transcendence—that is, God-realization. At this ambivalent stage in the soul's evolution it is not sexual desire chiefly that draws them to Woman but, rather, erotic love of her—an *esthetic sensuality* in which the lust-element is muted, or easily made so, in the glow of their ardor. They crave not so much fleshly satisfaction as sensual comfort from her presence, the unveiling of her mysteries, her graces, her nobler eroticism. In the West the version of Tantra that is coming steadily, if still somewhat tentatively, into awareness, is known as *Karezza:* love as caressing, an intimate blending of the sexes into a higher harmony through the creation and cultivation of ritualized love-making which has as its end not physical gratification but emotional ecstasy and *spiritual experience.*

Tantra sees the whole universe, and the mind-body unity as well, as pervaded by a single energy, which modern physics, in its completely different approach to the same challenge, has gradually come to confirm. In the sexual confrontation what had begun as a powerful thrust of emotion, pure energy, becomes, during the swiftly rising arc of excitement, sexualized, and man, though a soul at the outset, becomes a body en route to orgasm, depletion, and *tristesse*—soul sensualized, spirit conquered.

Tantra and its Western modification, *Karezza,* offer a medicine for this disheartening condition. By the meditative discipline of its ritual it aims at denying the original surge of love-energy its sexual channel but gently trains the organism to elevate the flow of energy to a spiritual channel, after first allowing it, through the middle stages of the encounter, to become tenderly, amatively, erotic: the poetic, half-way phase between sexual and spiritual. The ecstasy which Tantra claims to be able to bring about is equal in intensity to the orgasmic abandon but is a controlled rapture *and does not end*—rather, can be maintained indefinitely, with heightening intensity, at that level, ecstasy breeding more of itself, in ever-finer degree, as long as the nerves of the two lovers can sustain it. Genuine spiritual realization is possible—is, indeed, the true objective of this rite—if the participants proceed with due awareness and mutual reverence from beginning to end, have initiated the encounter only after solemn prayer, and concluded it the same way.

Ramakrishna entered into this delicate and arduous sadhana with a motivation unique among practitioners for the nearly two thousand years of its history: to discover if Tantra was spiritually genuine or a series of lascivious exercises masquerading as a religious system. It was, he found, all that its defensive adherents, badgered into theological corners by more prestigious Vedantists and yogis, had for centuries claimed for it: a legitimate entry to the hidden truths of the universe and to a realization of their Source, the Godhead itself. When his monastic disciples, imbibing their skepticism from orthodox elders, later questioned him about it, he forbade them—young monks following the traditional path of renunciation—to partake of those disciplines, but he counseled them never to disparage Tantra. It was not the main door leading to the sanctuary, but nevertheless a door. The chief objective, he said, was somehow to get into the house. Tantra, a path hedged with fire, got one into the house too, if breathlessly.[*]

Ramakrishna, raised in the strictest of orthodox backgrounds, all

---

[*] When the monks were not present he would explicitly urge his householder disciples to follow the path of Tantra, which he said was more appropriate for this age than traditional Vedic observances. See e.g., *Gospel,* 311.

his life a defender of traditional pieties, becomes, by his two years of Tantric practice and his acceptance of its philosophy, not only the inaugurator of a new and radical religious path but the embodiment of it. As she steered him through the dangerous waters of Tantra, Yogeswari constantly praised his self-control, astonished as he not only underwent all sixty-four of the disciplines (the first man, she said, ever to do so) but achieved mastery and realization in each in a short time. She brought him naked virgin girls whom he worshipped as forms of the divine Shakti, and she brought him beautiful, trained young women who performed ritual ceremonies of love-making to arouse him to desire—though with him the desire was for divine grace. Actual intercourse, however, prescribed in the Tantric rites,* was never achieved, and was in fact not possible: his genital organ at the slightest hint of temptation, turned inward, not outward—like the limbs of a tortoise being pulled inside the shell, he said, and nothing being able to get them out again. Once more his bodily responses had precisely reflected the state of his mind.

One of the beautiful females was a nun of the same religious order as the Brahmani, brought to him this time not for ritual intercourse but to serve as the embodiment of the feminine principle itself, which Ramakrishna worshipped in her, Yogeswari attending, a muse presiding over the mystical birth taking place in her pupil's soul. Every part of the woman was adored, especially the breasts, identified with the nourishing will of love, human love, and hence the love of God nourishing humanity from the breasts of its infinite compassion; and the organs of generation, known in the Tantric tradition as the *yoni*, symbol of the great *Brahmayoni*—the creative womb, the universal matrix—of the divine principle of the universe.

Any caressive or loving attention to woman's body in its intimate aspects becomes adoration, and thus elevating to the worshipper, so long as sexual pleasure—the animal climax of orgasm—is not sought and, indeed, is studiously avoided. A secret of the sexes—familiar to everyday experience, awesome in its implications—is available to us in the discovery, dreamlike in its immediacy, that if man approaches the female as an object of desire and carnal gratification he misses entirely

---

* A *continent* intercourse. Seminal emission, by disciplined control of thought, breath, and body, was carefully avoided: the climax being the mark of defeat, the loss of power, the return to bodily—that is, ignorant—consciousness.

what she is meant to convey to him, namely, her role as goddess to his role as questor, as votary, as hierophant of her mysteries—which she, without his nurturing devotion, is powerless to discover.

The full view of a pair of lovers enjoying the height of coital union was part of the Tantric sadhana, and Ramakrishna passed this test successfully as he had all the others. He described it as affecting him as a sport of the divine, not as an exercise in carnality. In the language of Tantra, the male represents the power of Shiva, the female that of Shakti, the two in union forming the divine fusion of eternal opposites into a triumphant harmony experienced by both ... except that, Tantra warns, the surrender to the sexual abolishes the spiritual illumination and renders even a god and goddess no more than earthlings.

Despite the endless descents into matter and their sad disillusionments, man returns as endlessly to the same delusive embrace. What is it he *must* be seeking, beyond the ever-diminishing glandular pleasure, in this mesmerizing act? What *is* it that does in fact mesmerize him about it? Some hope of heaven realizable, some glimpse of reality shining through the veil, some sense of immortality to light upon him suddenly? His yearning for something beyond himself, beyond his mortality, to be quenched at last—all too briefly, yet enough to give him conviction of himself as real, of life as real?

The Tantric tradition candidly recognizes this phenomenon and by a ritualized, totally transformed approach to the act attempts to draw from it the divine essence—which Ramakrishna declared *was* there if the body remained under the control of the will throughout.

We have emphasized in Ramakrishna's achievement its application as much as the achievement itself, because it is evident he had little to gain in living for himself—even in being born. "I have done it all," he told his disciples; "now you do one-sixteenth"—and gain an equivalent result. Which means, apparently, that we do not have to attain the same perfection to know essentially the same experience: of God, and of his masterpiece—Woman. Hence the relevance, applicability, the implications of his life—particularly his unique relationship, still to come, with Saradamani—are at least as important as the life itself.

Vivekananda said he could have converted half the world if he had preached Ramakrishna instead of Vedanta—the philosophy of the indwelling God, the doctrine that the soul is all, is omnipresent, is divine and eternal, and is every man's true nature: the doctrine that has penetrated everywhere in the West. Now the time has come to add the doctrine of Tantra, the chief application of Vedanta: namely, that within this woman is the soul, is the Godhead, is the whole divine being, and that is the truth of what she is. By desiring congress with her flesh, thinking in terms of that only, a man debases her soul and his own, and the resident Godhead itself, intensifies the bondage in which life has entrapped them both. Instead, by certain practices and attitudes he must seek her inwardness, her soul—by first remembering he too is a soul. By control of his mind, by prayerful recollection of our common spiritual nature, he can have more than her body—he may experience the presence of her soul, and in the doing will know his own: each of them then experiencing the reality of the One Soul, divided—apparently divided— for the sake of just this discovery.

Vedanta is the great truth for mankind as a whole—as spiritual seekers of this age have increasingly discovered. Tantra is the great truth for men and women as, seeking to sustain their love intact, they struggle to cope with sexuality. Ramakrishna, the personification of Vedanta as no one before in India, was also the perfection of Tantra— the first God-man known to have not only married and achieved spiritual union with his wife but to have spent so long encompassing the whole of Tantric discipline to expressly ascertain the degree of its truth, so that when his wife arrived he would be able to implement with her its profound teachings. *

During the thousands of years when men and women—by custom, fear, religious precept, and mutual ignorance—remained apart, the monastery and nunnery were natural expressions of that cultural condition. In a future which is upon us—*c'est déjà demain*—they will be, for most, unnatural expressions. Everywhere the clerical demand in larger numbers all the time is for optional marriage. Not lust but liberation dictates this demand—the *desire* for liberation, which an enforced chastity has been unable to bring about.

Noble are the disciplines of the renunciate; no less so, those of

---

* The gradual Western discovery of Tantra has been largely confined to the decades following his immersion in Tantric practice, although the ecstatic mingling of the sexes in the love-feasts of early Christians and the erotic symbology of courtly love, whose essential Tantric mystique so disturbed the ecclesiastical mind of its day, manifestly reveal an awareness of the same sublimating tendencies.

Tantra, the spiritual dynamic for the future—thanks to Ramakrishna and those two years he devoted to it, and to a marriage which glorified it. Tantra is *another* way to summon and experience the divine, *another* route to self-knowledge. It has been awaiting the advent of the modern age, for which—unlike the monk's way—it is uniquely suited, if man will pause in his passions long enough to give it the chance to prove itself.

Its time has come, Ramakrishna its annunciator. It will liberate man like nothing he has known for many centuries—and woman also. *Spiritual* man, that is. Not the mass man. Not *l'homme moyen sensuel.*

There is an absolutely new current of thought abroad today, respecting the sexes. All feel it. Few have found its meaning. Tantra is its meaning.

Sex is opposed to spirit; male and female must not cohabit if they seek God—these are superannuated ideas. The traditional religious view of man and woman, and of their love-relation, has gone forever. Tantra has appeared, crystallized in Ramakrishna's life, to supply what is needed. It and Vedanta will constitute the religion of the future for untold centuries.

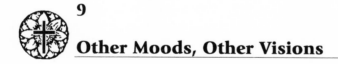

9
Other Moods, Other Visions

FROM THE INTENSE SUBLIMATIONS of Tantra, wherein he had come to love all forms of life as the divine itself manifesting in them and discovered in woman the infinite mystery he had from his childhood sensed in her, the next stage in his instruction was inevitable. Yogeswari initiated him into the disciplines of *bhakti*, or spiritual love—the Tantra of the unseen.

Since his own innate tendency was in that direction, the path was very natural for him. But she gave him tested methods and secret mantrams for concentrating his fervor, of which he had known nothing. Most of all she gave him modes of devotion beyond the basic servant-and-master or child-and-mother modes: the "serene" mood, of friend-to-friend; and that of parent-to-child, where the deity is regarded as the child, the devotee as the parent—a strange aberration to a Western mind, though in Magdalena da Jodi and certain other Catholic women saints we have some approximation of it, notably in St. Thérèse of Lisieux's adoration of the Child Jesus. In this devotional *genre* the goal is to eliminate every trace of awe towards a helpless infant or winsome child. Once distance is removed a dramatic closeness with the object of one's devotion becomes possible.

In the midst of these disciplines Ramakrishna was given a metal image of the child Rama, became devoted to it, and in a short time seemed to experience the real nature of the ancient God-man embodied in the metal form he fondled. The vision of Rama soon followed—the divine nature appearing to him as a boy: a mode of spiritual communion largely unknown beyond India.

In the West we have not wanted to get *that* close to the divine, lest our thralldom break. By a transcendental distancing we observe proper reverence, fill the sky with apostrophes to supernal majesty, and nourish our human difference from *that*. But it is a suspect reverence, since we follow it, during our secular obsessions, with characteristic forgetting of the divine splendor and with throwing upon one Man the burden of our insufficiencies.

Eros sublimate—the amorous mood—was still another powerful way to find access to the celestial bosom, drawing its inspiration from the phenomenon of intense passion between a woman and her paramour. Love, thriving (like Life) on obstacles, delights in illicit connections: secrecy is catnip to its craving, fuel to its fire. The greatest lovers have never married, except in propitiatory death-rites. Marriage is what society needs, but love flourishes outside the marital fold. The best of married lovers do not dream of the absoluteness and self-annihilating ardor of the best of unmarried contenders for the prize of Love's votary, which illicit passion always captures. The hidden lore of Hindu devotion, as the Brahmani unveiled it to her precocious pupil (his instant responsiveness astonishing her at every step), reveal an honored place for this other kind of love, whereby one desires the Lord clandestinely, with total, soul-sacrificing fervor, single-minded intensity, the way a woman engulfed by love adores her paramour.

It is doubtless a shocking way of addressing the Eternal One, though if we ponder the *Song of Songs* it will appear less shocking:

Let him kiss me with the kisses of his mouth: for thy love is better than wine.... A bundle of myrrh is my well-beloved unto me;
he shall lie all night betwixt my breasts.... Behold, thou art fair,
my love; behold, thou art fair; thou hast doves' eyes.... I sat
down under his shadow with great delight, and his fruit was
sweet to my taste.... His left hand is under my head, and his
right hand doth embrace me.... Thy lips, O my spouse, drop as
the honeycomb: honey and milk are under thy tongue; and the
smell of thy garments is like the smell of Lebanon.... Thou are
beautiful, O my love, as Tirzah, comely as Jerusalem, terrible as
an army with banners. Turn away thine eyes from me, for they
have overcome me.... I am my beloved's, and his desire is
toward me.

To many, alienated from subliminal energies, such rhapsody has
seemed unsuitable for a "holy" book, but if the power of human emotion at its most intense be our touchstone the passion of lovers cannot
be disregarded. This is the kind of insight that occurs, becoming inte-
grated into devotional practice, when Indian mystics down the ages
occupy their minds with all the ways the deity can be experienced and
described.[*] Occupied as the West has been with other themes, we naturally find the contribution distasteful and grotesque.

Ramakrishna mastered each of the five major modes of Hindu
devotion. In the erotic vein he turned himself into a woman to love
the masculine god, Krishna, the vision of whom was granted after an
appropriate delay: neither in divine nor human love affairs does the
beloved too quickly unveil the innermost Form to the suitor's hungry
gaze. Historically the love of Radha, ultimately to be the god's chosen
consort, became a synonym for total, all-consuming passion, supreme
bhakti, such as only Ramakrishna, according to Yogeswari, had
equalled—with one exception[**]—in the more than thirty centuries
intervening. She explained that the polarity of sexual attraction, when

---

[*] There have always been individual Western mystics, of course, who have
shared the same psychology but they have been the exceptions invariably.
Madame Guyon: "The soul ... expires at last in the arms of Love." *Mechtild of
Magdeburg* prayed that if she could "put my arms around you lovingly (cont.)

[**] Chaitanya, whom we will recall from the preceding chapter: the celebrated
saint and yogi of Bengal in the sixteenth century.

sublimated and purified by the grace of sadhana, gave an enormously greater power to one's devotion. Accepting the subtle rationale of this, he promptly began to identify himself with the feminine elements in his constitution. He dressed like a woman for six months—moved, spoke, thought as a woman exclusively: *became* a woman, became the paramour of Krishna, the Universal Bridegroom.

From boyhood these elements were always evident. We recall his ability to impersonate women so well that women themselves were deceived. All his life his intuition of the feminine nature was strangely prescient, intimate. The most revealing photograph of him, taken

---

the rapture of your holy love will flood my soul with ecstasy." *Jacopone Da Todi*: "O Love, take me in a sigh!/ Glad and spent I lie./ O love, my Bliss!/ O Love's Kiss!/ O quench my soul in love!" *St. Bonaventure*: "O Sweet Lord Jesus Christ, pierce the marrow of my soul with the suave and beneficent blade of your love!" *St. John of the Cross*: "He lay upon the breast/ I kept for Him immaculate and fair./ He closed His eyes in rest,/ and I caressed Him there.../ His gentle fingers clung/ About my neck—O tide/ Of ecstasy in which my senses died!" *St. Francis de Sales*: "Our Lord desires that our will should be satisfied with sucking the milk which He pours into our mouth..." *Blessed Margaret Mary Alacoque*: "Hold back, O my God, these torrents which overwhelm me." Her biographer reports that she "felt loved by God to distraction.... One day, at chapel ... the Son of God leaned towards her like a sweet lover, giving to her soul the softest kiss ... and the following Sunday, while she was thanking God for this favor, behold the Son of God ... took her in His arms as if He were proud of her..." *St. Teresa of Avila*: "I saw in the angel's (cont.) long spear of gold, and at the iron's point there seemed to be a little fire. He appeared to me to be thrusting it time and again into my heart, and to pierce my very entrails .... to leave me all on fire with a great love of God." *Richard Rolle*: "O love everlasting, inflame my soul to know God, that nothing may burn in me but His embraces. O good Jesus ... shed Thyself into the entrails of my soul!... Inebriate my mind with the hot wine of thy sweet love.... O holy Ghost, come into me and ravish me to Thyself.... Come, my love, with mellifluous heat into a soul longing for Thee ... enlightening with Thy light my inmost parts...." *St. Maria Maddalena De' Pazzi*: On one occasion she stripped its adornments from an image of Jesus, saying: "For me you shall be naked, O my Jesus, for I cannot endure your boundless virtues and perfections. I want your naked, naked humanhood.... I saw how Jesus united with His bride in closest embrace. He laid His head over the head of His bride, His eyes upon her eyes, His mouth upon her mouth, His feet upon her feet, all His members upon hers so that His bride became one with Him and wanted all her Bridegroom wanted ... savored all that her Bridegroom savored."

The transparently erotic nature of the imagery here only confirms the basic premise of Tantra: that sexual desire and spiritual longing are integrally, divinely related.

some years later, shows his breasts developed like a woman's, despite the beard and the body otherwise masculine in contour, as well as the characteristic expression: his cultivation of the feminine (though not sustained beyond the six months' period) had obviously become manifest in his body, like so many of his other mental and emotional states.

The modern Westerner may find such practices bizarre and repellent, passing well into psychopathology—such as when Rufus Jones the Quaker too hastily judged thus the stigmata of St. Francis, later to suffer on the slopes of Mount Alverna, where the saint had been deified, a repentant humiliation. They are difficult to assimilate into our more decorous religious passion, but very likely they are what we will have to undergo also when *our* time comes, when being content with a few years of civilized meditation will far from satisfy the juggernaut appetite of the Supreme for utter extirpation of egoism in his *Homo sapiens.*

At this juncture Ramakrishna found it natural to adore the Lord Krishna as though he was a new Radha—nay, as though Radha herself. As Kali had not been able to resist him earlier, neither could Krishna. And when this pinnacle was scaled he returned, with equal ardor, to his previous role of male lover of the feminine principle, taking different forms: Durga, Parvati, and others, but most of all his Kali, who, answering to his psychological needs, became a seductive mistress, a guileless girl, a magisterial queen, a forbidding scourge.

In many subtle encounters between them the Brahmani must have been the beneficiary of his complex achievement in the highest reaches of *bhakti*, as earlier during the travail of Tantra; their relationship must at times have mirrored, in part, the shifting splendors and occult mysteries of his communion with the Ineffable shining behind the forms of Krishna, Rama, Kali, and the others. But surmise is all that is left us. Lips were never unsealed, by her or her prodigious pupil, in so provocative an area.

The intricacies of Jesus' devotional sadhana—unless, as some have claimed, he reincarnated in Kamarpukur—remain likewise a sealed volume, though all true *aficionados* of his mystery have attempted, through wonder and inference, to pierce the veil. We can never be certain if he, also, penetrated the inner recesses of the paramour's cave of love, but the fact that one of the hermetic traditions (which Edgar Cayce has revived in the modern age) has placed him under the tutelage, for a time, of a female adept, leads us to speculate. His special fondness for a woman once enslaved by sensual impulses adds fuel to the speculative flame.

We know for sure of three other modes he practiced, those of child-son, servant, and friend. The latter is evident on those occasions when he thinks of himself as a peer of the Lord, when his consciousness is filled with a sense of conquests won, of heights attained, of truths known for all time—occasions when his mind burns at the center of the universe in the self-realized splendor of "I am the Way, the Truth, the Life," and "He who has seen me has seen the Father." It is the *soul* that is the way, the truth, and the life, the soul that is the resurrection and the speaker only a consciousness identifying with that soul, thinking of itself *as* the soul, and with no effort of will in so doing.

If one feels one *is* the soul, feels simultaneously a total disregard and indifference toward the body and all its works, then obviously it is not difficult to think that one is the truth also, and the way to the truth, and the life that truth manifests; it is not difficult, also, to say that "before Abraham was, I am"—the soul being an eternal presence—an eternal *present-ness:* it being the soul quite literally that is speaking all these famous phrases, not the man, not the Galilean, not the creature. It is, in a word, a *consciousness* that speaks—ours, his.

This is the serene, magisterial mood of friend speaking to Friend, the divine Comrade. It was Buddha's characteristic state. But even great devotees, like Jesus and Ramakrishna, have often known it. All of the seventeenth chapter of John is a reflection of this mood:

> Father, the hour is come; glorify thy Son, that thy Son also may glorify thee....
>
> That they all may be one; as thou, Father, art in me, and I in thee, that they also may be one in us: that the world may believe that thou hast sent me.
>
> And the glory which thou gavest me I have given them; that they may be one, even as we are one.
>
> I in them, and thou in me, that they may be made perfect in one; and that the world may know that thou has sent me, and hast loved them, as thou has loved me....
>
> O righteous Father, the world hath not known thee: but I have known thee....

Because of their temperaments, however, devotional prophets more often revert to the familiar modes of child-parent and servant-master. Normally Jesus is the loving, obedient son, the typical state in which we encounter him throughout the gospels. During the long night in the garden of olives he dramatically exhibits the servant-master mood, doing the will of the Supreme with an effort that ordinarily he did not have to exert, resisting it for a time because of the weight of nature casting its baleful shadow over the edge of his resolution; the weight, also, of the burden of all humanity condensed into a draining cancer at the core of his strength from innermost chambers of his will. Here he is not the son, not the friend. He is the tormented servant doing what he must do but not understanding it completely, though in the final surrender in the garden there came great peace, always the by-product of renouncing any course of action contrary to that of the divine: the eternal secret of all peace.

On the cross the serene friend and child-parent moods alternate: "Woman, behold thy son.... Son, behold thy mother," "This day thou shalt be with me in paradise," "Father, forgive them, for they know not what they do"—are utterances of the immortal friend speaking to his bosom Companion just on the other side of the veil. But "My God, my God, why hast thou forsaken me?" is the cry of the child-son temporarily lost in the thickets of the body's assertive impulse to retrieve its departed empire, not of the majestic personality who declared he was the Way, the Truth, and the Life.

In brief, he was the Way, the Truth, the Life—sometimes; at other times the child, the loving son, ever aware of him who *was* the Way, the Truth, and the Life; and at times the servant struggling to do the will imposed upon him by the mysterious Presence that was his being.

Christ's nature regarded in this light enables us to comprehend, to a degree, Ramakrishna's effort to be all things to the divine and to discover in the Godhead all possible relations to himself.

10

Jesus and Magdalene

JESUS' HAUNTING RELATIONSHIP WITH Mary of Magdala, the prostitute he converted into penitent saintliness, has never found a satisfactory explanation, at least none of record, and doubtless, in the absence of certain knowledge, and fuller documentation, none is actually possible. An attempt must be made nevertheless.

All the gospel narratives place her at the center of the women at Calvary and during the dramatic hours following the crucifixion. Her continuing gratitude and devotion to the extraordinary man who had rescued her from sensuality and from much else would account for this. But how can we explain the fact that after his death he first appeared to her *alone*—as Mark and John specifically state? For such a unique honor why was Peter, the delegated leader, not chosen, or John, who understood him best, or Mary of Bethany, she who had sat at his feet enraptured by his presence? Why the Magdalene?

Let us for a moment recast the gospel story as an oriental epic in which the hero, possessed of occult power and mysterious antecedents, is put to death by enemies but because of his thaumaturgic gifts is able, as he had prophesied, to rise from the tomb—and to appear first to a woman, one not long before caught in the snares of fleshly lust, greeting her by name in a soft voice at dawn in the garden of his resurrection. We would conclude that he loved her in a special way, that they had either been lovers in that life or in some other. We would *assume* this.

We should make the same assumption about Mary and the Galilean.

The only other time we find them together is the scene in Simon the pharisee's house (Luke 7: 36-50), coming shortly after her conversion from the "seven devils" that had plagued her in her life of sin. Uninvited, she makes her way into a gathering where Jesus and his disciples are seated and where her long-standing promiscuous reputation is well-known. Acting not as a devotee nor as a woman understandably grateful for her liberation from misery but as someone possessed by a trance-like compulsion, she cannot remain apart from Christ but falls at his feet, washing them over and over with her tears and then with the expensive ointment she has brought. In her love and adoration and, seemingly, in the grip of some other, more obscure emotion, she cannot do otherwise—her craving to be near him, to touch him, to wash his feet, to weep over him, completely overmastering her. This impassioned, compulsive behavior is—there cannot be any doubt—that of a woman at the feet of her lover. Whatever else it might be, it is that, first of all. If asked to interpret the actions of any other woman in such a situation, that would be our response; it should not be different because the woman was Mary Magdalene and the man Jesus.

Thus, in the only two scenes where they appear together, something most extraordinary happens and in both cases we are led, though by very different evidence, to an identical conclusion about them. Both incidents exude a strange kind of intimacy and both reinforce the same insight, which, had it not been for the habitual state of reverential numbness in which we gloss over our scripture-reading, would have been self-evident.

Since the fragmentary records in the text regarding this relationship (and so much in Jesus' life) are unsatisfactory and—perhaps deliberately —incomplete, we are forced to speculate, guided by intuition and by the light of normal human experience. This is where we might be led:

To render her so sublime an honor as their secret appearance together that morn he must be acknowledging some personal tie, some private debt which for long has been left unpaid. She must have served him well—somehow, somewhere—but not in a merely personal sense. The service would have been, necessarily, to his higher self—more likely, to his *evolving* higher self as it was at the time of their association (a perfected self obviously needing no such service); and further, if she had been able, and permitted, to serve someone who in time was to become the Christ of the Western world, and so significantly that in recompense he chose her to whom to appear at one of the portentous hours of his life, the association had to have been not only deep and intimate, but *of long duration*.

Many lives they must of have known each other, becoming ever more closely linked—like Gautama and Yasodhara—probing the depths of the other's soul through every possible psychological mode. They would have been parents to one another, children, siblings, friends, husband and wife, lovers, teacher and student. At some point he would have begun to move steadily in a purely spiritual direction, with each lifetime mounting rapidly toward ultimate illumination—which finally came in Palestine, on a cross. That would have been reached several, perhaps a dozen or more, lives prior to the Jesus of Nazareth embodiment. It would have come during or immediately after the last time they had been emotionally united: as lovers, as husband and wife. That would have been the time when their love, in power and depth, had been at its apogee.

What had begun to separate them would have been his growing commitment to the spiritual path *per se*, the path both of them had been treading for a long time: the undergirding principle in their relationship. For her to have been the feminine presence in the life of someone destined to become a world savior means that she, too, would have possessed, by that stage, or by the time they had met—fifty or a hundred lives previously—a spirituality proportionately rich, at least potentially so. But along with it, growing simultaneously, was a nature capable of enormous ranges of creaturely emotion, which, because insufficiently purified, inadequately *grounded* in mystical insight, fell prey to some negativism by virtue of its very intensity, locked her into a dominantly human attachment—with accompaniments of anger and jealousy that universally appear at that stage—clouded her spirituality, and began seriously to block his own movement toward higher and higher perception of truth.

Thus her love, by its very passion and the totality of her commitment to him as a *man*—which prevented her from making an equal commitment to him as a spiritual being, as an emerging saint—became, with tragic irony, fatal inexorability, an obstacle on his path: on the world's path, too.

She would be falling into despair, or disease, or dissipation, possibly suicide at this point, though the agony (*mutual* agony) would have been protracted through *hundreds* of scenes over *many* lifetimes, the tie between them so powerful, the soul rapport so profound, the fabric of their shared karma so densely woven. Only slowly, resistingly, would she have drifted into the control of inauspicious emotions that would have sought escape in one addiction, passion, illness or another, each one like a devil—that is, each with the power, demon-like, to blot out the divine light that *had* been potent in her, the power to dominate her emotional life increasingly, and all of her life, for her heart had ruled her life, *was* her life, was her soul too. (By the time she is born in Palestine some lifetimes later the "devils" have accumulated and left her deranged as well.)

Slowly he, the polestar of her existence, her other half, would have felt an urge, a divine implantation, to move away from her, but might indeed have resisted it, might have chosen instead to die with her than live without her, as the poet Emily Dickinson sang:

> And were you lost, I would be—
> Though my name
> Rang loudest
> On the heavenly fame.[*]

Or as Milton, in Book IX of his great allegory of human fate, shows us Adam speaking to his Eve after her fall:

> Certain with thee my resolution is to die.

Unable to solve the knotted tangle of their psyches, unable—because of his own attachment to her—to guide her into freedom and clear understanding of what was taking place, unable, in short, to help her, he might have chosen to follow to the end the long course they had by then traveled together.

Their separation, brought about at last, would have required divine intervention, taking one form or another, bringing her to death perhaps, while he was still in the midst of strength, coercing him to proceed without her—the divine unwilling that a spiritual potential already so formidable should serve only creaturely drives, only *human*

---

[*] From her poem "I cannot live with you."

life—and in the next lifetime, apart from her, his mind is absorbed in other themes, and for the lifetime following, dedicated to work, to sacrifice, to austerity, to contemplation, to ego-conquest, heart-conquest, too, the light advancing in him rapidly, as five, ten, or more lifetimes pass, and she is forgotten as, following another course, she continues to slip away from the height she had known when they had been last together, slipping away ... down, down.

But she has given him much, more than can be uttered. Only God could give him more, and we might say she had been an instrument of the Lord in giving him what she had over such a time span, so that he is in her debt forever. Indeed, appearing to her that momentous dawn outside the sepulcher could not match the magnitude of her gift, the treasure she had bestowed on him.

What *was* the treasure?

The total knowledge of Woman. Through their all-absorbing union, perfected over many incarnations, he had come to know, each time, a new phase of womanhood in her evolving love for him. She would have told him: *you can experience all of Woman through me.* With each facet of the feminine unveiled to him through the symbiosis of their love, he had discovered corresponding facets of himself. Between them the universe of manifestation had become known. Insofar as human relations can provide the incentive, he had come to know what could be known about himself, and about Her, his soul's companion through the ages. For this gift, there was nothing to truly compensate. He did what was possible. When they met again, in Galilee, he saved her from depravity, and on the morning of his appearance in the astral state, called the Resurrection by Christians, it was to her that he chose first to come, whispering her name, as only he could, and as only she could hear it: *Mary.* But she had borne many names, and he had. She had known him once, perhaps, as—Adam.

When all she could give him was received, and she could give no more, but only the Source of life, including womanhood, could instruct him, he had to turn, or be made to turn, to it instead—with what anguish we may imagine.

In Luke 8: 2 (immediately after the scene in Simon the pharisee's house) she is identified as formerly afflicted with "seven devils"—with the lust, fear, rage, addiction, and self-hate which had replaced, with equivalent intensity, the love she had nurtured over so long. Jesus, who would have received her precognitive image in meditation before they met again, recognized her early in his public ministry—feeling a sorrow and heartache beyond our comprehension. Some unrecorded meetings would then have passed between them, during which he would have transferred to her, through his yoga power, the knowledge of who she was, who and what they were to each other, the knowledge of all their past. She would have been stricken, traumatized by wonder, delirious with relief, gratitude, incredulity, adoration beyond measure inundating her.

Again we see her trailing into the pharisee's house after Jesus had entered, standing behind him, weeping, with her tears washing his feet, kissing them, wiping them with her hair, anointing them with the oil she had brought in the alabaster box, and had been doing so from the time he entered the house, for when Simon objected silently to his tolerating the presence of a known sinner, Jesus, perceiving his thought, remarked: "This woman, since the time I came in, hath not ceased to kiss my feet." Then adding, perhaps addressing himself to an audience unknown: "Her sins, which are many, are forgiven: *for she loved much.*"

How much, and whom, he alone there knew—and she herself.

The protracted weeping, and washing, kissing, and anointing of his feet—among people who scorned her because of her reputation as a sinner and her known "possessed" character—is difficult to comprehend, but in terms of the background traced above, her conduct becomes perfectly understandable. In one stroke she has been liberated from her diseases and lusts and simultaneously reunited with her soul's love over so many ages! Her behavior seems wholly natural, innocent, touching, beautiful beyond words. Again she is a being possessed—but by love now. A woman's love—and the humble love of a penitent: both at the same time.

Is he penitent too? With his yogic vision he could recapture their past, and might have wondered if he could not have acted more wisely during that crucial lifetime when their paths had diverged for the first time, could not have managed her agony better, could not have known himself more accurately, could not have prevented the tragic disjunction from taking place—while still pursuing his path to glory. Could not the will that was driving him to immortality have been matched with sufficient wisdom to cope with the problems destroying their love, to find some alternative to abandoning her to a baleful destiny, which ten lives could not bring to an end?

We cannot but feel the intimacy of her gestures in Simon's house, going beyond that of the penitent only. There seems a trace, at so long a remove, of the old passion mixed with the penitence in her prostrate weeping and caressing of his feet, mingling with her tears the sighs of a lover's heart reborn. In John 12: 3 Mary of Bethany is seen also anointing his feet with oil but the manner of her doing so is purely devotional, worshipful of the *messiah*, not the man. The outward similarity of the two women's ritual of adoration has led some to think of them as the same person but the difference in mood and attitude obviously springs out of two quite different feminine hearts. And when we see Mary with her sister Martha in the famous domestic interlude (Luke 10: 39-42), her serene absorption in the Master's words contrasts fundamentally with Magdalene's devastated unbelief on finding herself free while clinging to the feet of her Adam.

Then there is the scene where Mary of Bethany informs Jesus of the death of her brother Lazarus (John 11: 32), in the manner of a devotee— not as the tragedy-laden Magdalene would have acted. The death of a loved brother, coming soon after the time of the sinner's illumination, could not, in all candor, have been regarded as a momentous incident— as it manifestly seemed to Mary and Martha, for whom the spiritual path was not a recent revelation and for whom, therefore, their brother's sudden death would have had the decisive impact it, in fact, did have.

An avatar's actions always have a double meaning. Beyond the crucial personal aspect of the Resurrection there is the powerful symbolic factor. Christ's appearance to a woman is deeply appropriate on that ground alone, for woman symbolizes the soul, represents the soul in human life, and to her, man—the perfected man, especially he—must render homage. Even the adulteress, the harlot embodies the divinity of the Universal Woman, the eternal feminine, and so Christ in one stroke reaffirms woman's divine nature, worthy of special reverence and tribute.

At the same time the masculine and feminine principles are fused into a living unity. Mary is the divine woman, the Christ *without*, the feminine half of pure being. Although Jesus, become the Christ, has achieved this union of opposite principles within himself, his appearance first to her outwardly symbolizes the fusion of the two eternal polarities.

Not least of all it is an act of sheer gratitude. Three of the four accounts show him abandoned by everyone on Calvary—except for the few women who stayed to the end. At the center of whom, as the reports make clear, was the Magdalene, ministering with her heart's tears to the world's newest savior, but herself a savior also—*his*, so long ago, remembered by them both now, and by the gods who keep watch over mankind's laborious ascent into the light from out of the prehensile darkness.

11

On Charisma and Powers

WITH ONE EXCEPTION, RAMAKRISHNA tended to discourage the embracing of his feet by female devotees. The close physical contact he had experienced with women during the unique Tantric practices had been part of a *discipline* not meant to be perpetuated. Hypersensitive to influences around him, he felt that a woman holding his feet was not in his best spiritual interests—or in hers. The single exception was his wife, Sarada, who massaged his limbs, often at his own request, every day of their years together—her character pure, her mind flawlessly reverent toward him, all potentially inauspicious vibrations rendered inactive.

Upon reflection, this was essentially true of Mary of Bethany and, in a special sense, of Magdalene also, whose earlier sins had been washed away by the grace of her immortal lover and by the power of her sacrificial urge to immolate herself in the flame of his glory: a consecrated craving which brought her to purity and perfection.

Jesus' extraordinary psychophysical sensitivity was strikingly demonstrated in the scene (Luke 8: 46) where, pressed by various people in a dense crowd gathered about him, he asks, "Who touched me?"—and then explains to his puzzled disciples: "For I felt virtue go out of me." The touch of what turned out to be a diseased woman—

steeped in negativity of mind as well—had burned him, causing actual physical pain and a sense of power lost, an experience Ramakrishna had on a number of occasions, even when a rupee coin (symbol of Caesar's realm) was covertly placed against his skin, which he compared to being bitten by a scorpion.

The avatar's body, including his transformed nervous system, becomes delicately susceptible to others' influence—spiritual and sensual, healthy and diseased, acutely vulnerable to the nature of everyone who touches him, to a degree utterly beyond ordinary conception. During times of emotional distress, such as often afflicted Ramakrishna when the omnivorous flame of his spiritual hungers threatened to consume him, and as afflicted Jesus, for example, in Gethsemane, their bodies, passive to the imprint of every current of thought carried through the nerves, will sweat blood, the flesh at these times having become a transparent outer covering of the mind.

In the light of such wondrous sensitivity, it is notable that Jesus was able to absorb the stately salutations of Mary of Bethany, not to speak of the more prolonged caresses of Mary Magdalene, whose hands would have conveyed to him all her soul's ardor as few women can ever have conveyed it. He would have had to place himself, during their embraces, in a yogic state of Tantric sublimation, whereby their ministrations became—as Ramakrishna had discovered them actually to be—the chaste and loving touch of a mother, and he the child of each. Given the pronounced likeness of their temperaments, Ramakrishna's self-conquest would have been won by Jesus following similar psychological methods. [*]

Had either possessed the more austere nature of a Buddha the challenge would have been mastered by refusing to see the woman as a female at all, as in fact anything different from oneself; by denying any significant difference—nay, any difference whatever—between her touch and his own body.

---

[*] In the devotional saint, strongly oriented to states of feeling as he is, there remains, in an esthetic and emotional sense, an awareness of the opposite sex-principle. So with Jesus and the women who worshipped him by prostrations as well as by prayer. So with Ramakrishna (as we shall see) and his adoration of Sarada, his fascination with the female saint Gangamata. By virtue of their devotional natures they had not extirpated the root of sex-awareness, nor tried to: though of course this awareness was radically free from purely carnal elements. Buddha, on the other hand, after an excruciating struggle, succeeded in transcending all differences of sex. Hence (cont.)

• • •

About this time, perhaps a little earlier, as a result of the intense and prolonged Tantric sadhana, there emanated from Ramakrishna an unearthly beauty that hypnotized those who saw him—spirit radiating through the thin envelope of flesh, which, mortified by the severe temptations of the Tantric regimen, superadded to the years of ascetic devastation prior to it, yielded up all resistance to the divine presence within. The gospel evangelists allude to a similar charismatic power in Jesus, who, by a mere glance, could draw to him those who, with his preternatural insight, he saw were fated to be his disciples.*

The eight supernatural powers, by-products of his all-consuming disciplines, began to appear about the same time. Patanjali in his *Yoga Sutras* describes these but warns they are to be shunned by anyone committed to the ideal of divine realization: indulging or exploiting them will inexorably block further progress and will indeed regress the individual who succumbs. Ramakrishna, now and in years following, made scant use of these powers, such as reading the minds and comprehending the past lives of his disciples, foreseeing those destined to come to him, and the like. In answer to a prayer as to what they signified he had received a vision of falling excrement, and for the rest of his life acted as though the powers were not his.

Not every Hindu has acted thus but the greatest—like Gautama Buddha—have. Their self-restraint reflects a view of man profoundly at variance with that maintained in the West, where body-consciousness dominates religious as well as social life. In the metaphysics of the Western world the self to be saved includes, as signs of the divine favor, a body to be healed and a physical life to palpably thrive. Hence our blazoning of miracles, powers, psychic phenomena, and material prosperity: the latter an obsession with the Christian Science, Unity, and

---

his characteristic mood of serenity and detachment. Yet he had had great ardor at the beginning—transmuting it into great peace. By dint of his ardor, indeed, he had slain its root—for his *feeling* was grounded to some degree, inevitably, in a sense of separateness. By uprooting *this* he also killed its branches and limbs of personal emotion. It was then that his compassion became like a waveless sea.

* When Ramakrishna's own disciples actually came to him, however, years later, it was not because of his hypnotic beauty, which by then had largely faded. Distressed that increasing numbers were attracted to him only by his appearance, he prayed constantly that his beauty be removed. "Make it go in," he is reported to have entreated the ever-attentive Kali, who in time answered his singular request.

New Thought schools.

The view in the East is that man's powers are really the Supreme's, which, at a certain point, he finds himself in possession of; therefore he must have little or nothing to do with them. *Thine* is the Power....

Christ, a master yogi, evinces yoga prowess, it is true. Had he not, no one would have noticed him except even fewer disciples than he gained, and doubtless the anchorites with whom he studied during the unknown years. Throughout the Bible the Jews manifest traits immediately recognizable as Western: the outer-directedness, the materialism (Job equating a life of virtue with an abundance of the world's goods), the egotism, the contentiousness. Consequently a pure gospel of nonviolence, humility, and the love of God would fall on psychological soil almost as barren as it would have been in Muhammad's Arabia. Some feats of healing, raisings from the dead, thaumaturgic bedazzlement generally, was essential, for to the Western mentality already crystallized in the Jewish environment these things were identified with spiritual greatness—especially with someone reputed to have a mandate from God. In short, all the people around him, including his simpleminded followers, believed that if you came from God you had to perform miracles to prove it. A pure life, a lofty teaching, a radiant character, a mission utterly selfless— these were not enough, as they have been in the East. Wonder-working had to be part of it.

Yet he is often reluctant to gratify those who keep asking him for a "sign" and in the total context of his activities the miracles play but a modest role. In key moments—at the Last Supper, Gethsemane, Calvary—they are absent. In the historic utterances the psychic is ignored. In the Sermon on the Mount there is no promise that one will heal the sick or raise the dead if one follows the path prescribed: only regeneration and the new life is offered.

In essentials he resembles the supreme figures of India. All his miracles—though Christians are blissfully ignorant of this—are reproducible among advanced yogis in the ancient land and have never made a deep impression on the Hindu soul; they have been gently laid aside, allowance being made for the people with whom he had to deal, the age, and the culture. In his profoundest characteristic he has been adopted as one of India's own, one of the reigning stars in a pantheon of gods that includes, among the greatest, the other subject of our study.

12

Conquest of the Ultimate

AFTER HIS VISION OF Krishna, his proud maternal guru had placed
Ramakrishna in the choice company of Radha, Krishna's actual consort,
and of the St. Francis-like master saint, Chaitanya. It was toward the end
of 1864. Yogeswari, who had performed inestimable service for the
three previous years, had good reason to rest content with her labors.
Never had a teacher such a phenomenal pupil. Still only twenty-eight,
he had already completed the entire circuit of devotional spiritual practice, with only the forbidding realm of the Nameless unexplored.
Henceforth his renown must spread across India, and her own name be
forever linked with his: not only in that century, but for centuries to
come.

In fact, his sadhana was far from complete. Despite the unscaled
heights where, by power of longing and force of will, he had attained
his goal, with visions of Krishna and Radha alike, not once but daily,
almost *continuously*, equalling the *poverello's* identification with Christ,
and not so much experiencing the divine presence as being experienced
by it—despite all this, more disciplines, more transformations, all of
them unprecedented, and greater heights, lay before him, beginning
immediately. The sweet taste of triumph for Yogeswari was to be
short-lived.

Tota Puri—Nangta, the naked monk, as Ramakrishna was fond of
calling him—brought it to an end and overnight made Yogeswari feel
an outsider to his new practice: that of the Impersonal path, whose end

was the conquest of Brahman, the Absolute, the Immutable, the Nameless, the One without a Second, the Pure Light of the Void, the Womb and Tomb of the Universe, beyond the gods and incarnations, beyond Rama, Krishna, Kali, Vishnu, Shiva, and all the other suprasensual forms Gadai had known, so inconceivable, so awesome, that even God the Creator—Allah, Father in Heaven, Jehovah—was only *his* creation, formed to do *his* bidding, and silenced eventually when *his* design was completed—more properly, *its* bidding, *its* design—and all returned to the primal calm of Brahman Alone, the Ground of God—the vast universe of previous manifestation resting a cosmic memory in his bosom, wherein he communed with perfected parts of himself: Buddha, Krishna, Christ, Lao-Tzu....

Few had known that experience, glimpsed that white, remote bosom, few had entered into it: Buddha under the Bodhi Tree that famous night; the Christ who announced "I and my Father are One"; St. Francis, whose cosmic love for all life came not from the stigmata but from the knowledge of *That*, which shone back to him afterwards in everything; Eckhart, who had had the boldness to *conceive* there being planes beyond Christ, beyond the Father in Heaven, and then the rare fortune to attain them. (Other mystical eminences like John of the Cross, Teresa, Jan de Ruysbroeck, had not been able to imagine any spiritual reality beyond the Creator-God, the God of Love, the Personal Lord, the Father of Jesus, and so had not *realized* what lay beyond it.) There was also Dionysius the Areopagite, for whom the divine Darkness was an experience transcending that of the Personal God; Plotinus, whose life-hunger was for the One beyond forms, the Unity beyond multiplicity, and who on at least three occasions had his hunger sated. And others, no doubt; but indeed few.[*]

In the West we are fixated in the unconscious assumption of the body's *reality*, the essential existence of the personality we have, and the concomitant role—also implicit, rarely examined—of the creaturely ego as the dominant center of consciousness. Even our religious philosophies are geared to that ego-center, flow out of it, and tend to justify its naturalistic promptings. How far this is from the viewpoint requisite for realizing the One without a second: namely that there *is*

---

[*] The engrossing *phenomena* of the psychic and spiritual worlds prevented Jacob Boehme, greatest of the Protestant mystics, from joining this select company.

no ego, no mind, no consciousness, no life, no reality at all—only that One, that Immutable, that Eternal Being. Thou alone art, declares the Upanishads. *Thou alone art.*

There is no indication that woman—symbol of the creative power and its manifestation alike, the *personal* dimension of life incarnate—has ever known him. The Creator God—Brahman's projection, Brahman activating—is the limit of her transcendental experience. Radha and many others—St. Teresa, St. Catherine of Siena, Rabi'a, Mira Bai—had known that reality; transcending it was unthinkable. Their natures— grounded in love, feeling, response—were also grounded in *separateness;* they could not conceive going beyond what they were in their quintessential core. Woman, including the women saints, is rooted in forms, things, appearances. She accepts the world as real *and makes it real for men.* She is an *element*, capable of being purified, not of being changed. She is Brahman's foil *par excellence.* Small wonder that Yogeswari was anxious, Cassandra-like, when she divined that her spiritual son was embarked on the perilous journey which the naked monk with matted hair held out to him. She felt dread, as any woman would have.

She warned him that his devotional nature would dry up. But he could not turn back. The Niagara of religious yearning that had stormed through his being for so long, after a due respite following his struggle to exhaust all aspects of devotion, was raging again, its insatiable power drawing to him with irresistible magnetism, a man—one of the few in India—who had actually realized Brahman, or who was said to have done so: one who, at any rate, had experienced the Reality sufficiently to teach him.

Ramakrishna's biographers suggest that the Divine Mother pressed her will on him and "made" him adopt a role, follow a path— that of the Impersonal, which now beckoned—not truly suited to his devotional nature. But long before the hand of Kali was evident in his life he had emotionally identified with Shiva, the great male deity, the god of ashes and renunciation—to such an extent that on that "night of Shiva" in his early teens he had passed into an hours-long state of samadhi. On the basis of this experience we might argue that his first love was the impersonal, and the personal path a later development. And now at last he was returning to his heart's desire, the path truly most suited to him, having in the meantime navigated the deeps and shoals of all the currents of devotion known to religious practice.

Further, the mind that was able to consecrate itself exclusively—but separately—to Rama and Krishna and Kali, for months at a time in each case, was clearly able, sooner or later, to detach itself from all forms, gods and goddesses whatever, and immerse itself in its own element—the Impersonal.

Which Tota Puri, the famous monk, had intuited when he first laid eyes on him at Dakshineswar, stopping there on a tour of Bengal, where, as everywhere on his travels, he planned to stay no more than three days. One glance at Ramakrishna revealed to his yogic perception a rare prospect for the impersonal path—the Vedantic disciplines leading to the direct knowledge of the God of Vedanta: *Brahman*, the Universal Self. With some annoyance he intuited the unique development of devotional tendencies also, but beyond them he saw a new Buddha in potential, a *knower* of Truth, not merely a lover of its forms.

We can agree with some of this. We may add that Ramakrishna, already supreme in devotion, would probably become supreme in knowledge too, and thus in one life incarnate the highest development of both tendencies hardly ever found to an advanced degree in the same soul—one more facet of his life for which the mind finds no precedent, one more instance of the incredible.

Tota Puri, powerfully built, aged about sixty, wandering free like a lion, the master, it was said, of seven hundred monks in a monastery of western India, after forty years of iron-willed struggle had realized his goal: the direct knowledge of Brahman. His name was circulating through India, and wherever he went his reputation preceded him. His nakedness was an emblem of his refusal to acknowledge sensory or societal realities anywhere, for which he was widely admired by victims of those same realities.

In fact he was not yet truly free. He had fetishes, which he believed strengthened him in his monastic rigor—itself, for a man of enlightenment, a bondage. One of these was his refusal to linger anywhere more than three days for fear of attachment, the monk's cardinal sin: an attitude more appropriate for one undergoing disciplines *toward* illumination than for an illumined soul itself. If people or places had potential power to coerce or fetter him, he was not yet free, and his Brahman-experience not yet definitive. At most, he had probably touched the outer edges of the Brahman world, and emerged calling it conclusive. His intimidating, leonine independence of society then seemed certain confirmation of his claim, and Hindus—a gentle folk— would have been docile to accept his self-evaluation.

This is not to suggest he had no greatness. For the momentous task facing him with Ramakrishna no ordinary sadhu would do. It is only to remind ourselves that even the knowledge of Brahman will not, at first, free us of ourselves totally. The Nature we have worked with, conspired with, identified with, for so many lifetimes, is not to be removed by a blaze of illumination or forty years of yoga. In a sense, we may think of it as past karma to be worked out, still operative, on the level of personality habits and tendencies in fringe areas of the mind where the core experience of illuminative intuition has not reached. Perhaps, in areas closer to the center than we would like to admit.

In short, while the central part of our personality becomes changed, much of the rest of us remains either unchanged or only sub- dued by awe as it stands in relation to a transformed master. We have been led to believe, inadvertently by mystics themselves and by our own desires, that superconscious experience will change us utterly in, essentially, a single stroke of overwhelming insight. This wished-for consummation might, in reality, come only after several lifetimes spent as Tota Puri was spending his, after the *first* enlightenment had dawned, to be followed by others more significant, more penetrating, more cleansing, until *all* the areas of the mind, at last, are transformed, and the *true* perfection we have heard about appears in its Buddha-like splendor.

Ray upon ray from the divine sun deep within the mind must, over lifetimes, penetrate the vast labyrinths of darkness we have woven through thousands of incarnations. By darkness we mean ignorance and egoism cemented together by endless accumulations of the karma of bondage, the product, as well, of that same ignorance and egoism (delusion, as Buddhists term it). Asceticism, disciplines, "living the life" prior to spiritual experience, it is true, remove some of the obstacles, but so many remain untouched by our mortifications that it is shallow and childish to believe that a partial mystical experience (and all are par- tial until the whole interior world of darkness has been purified) will, as in dreams, when revelations take place at the wave of a hand, accom- plish everything else for us—*exploding* us into perfection.

Hindus are as naive as any other people about these matters, more naive, because terms like liberation, enlightenment, and samadhi, representing extremely rare states, have become common counters of exchange—of folk *banter*—for centuries in India; in the process the reality of these states is increasingly colored by ego-desire and trivialized by casualness. Pretending to know much about divine matters, they know nothing; other people admittedly know nothing either—but do not pretend to.

There is another aspect of this—the inevitability of experiencing, in the mystical crisis, what is already in the mind. No Christian mystic has experienced Buddha. No Buddhist has experienced Christ. No Sufi has experienced Krishna. The Supreme gives the mind whatever it wishes and, in the forms he grants, he appears to the individual soul. Those who, like Tota Puri, erase the effect and memory of all forms, seeking the Formless Reality, experience, at least in its lower reaches, the nameless Godhead, the Pure Light of the Void.

Tota Puri from his adolescence, under the tutelage of his guru, himself a famous yogi of the time, was taught the Vedantic philosophy only: Brahman alone is real, the world is unreal. All sense objects, forms, images, all manifestations of Nature, all modifications of mind, everything pertaining to phenomenal existence whatsoever—unreal: because they change, are creations, perceived by what is itself a creation, a sense organ. Only Brahman is real because it changes not and cannot be perceived by anything created. Even the mind, properly speaking, cannot perceive Brahman: it perceives itself *through* the mind—the mind being only a reflector of the light within.

This is the path of *jnana yoga*, its practitioners known as jnanis. It is the path of Knowledge, of Discrimination, of the Rational Will. The jnanis tend to feel they alone are responsible for their spiritual achievements. They reject the alleged power of *Maya* to deceive and resist aspirants in their freedom-seeking endeavors and disdain the weaknesses of men that prevent them from fulfilling their spiritual possibilities. They stand, as Tota Puri preeminently did, on the strength of their own wills, their individual powers, confronting the challenges of the universe from that indomitable stance. More, they tend to scorn other paths, especially those of devotion, as being of a much inferior grade leading to inconclusive realizations—if they are not (as Tota Puri felt them to be) fantastic self-indulgences.

This contempt, like all contempt, is a vice, and Tota Puri inherited it because of the path he had grown up in. His realization of Brahman—that is, of a portion of Brahman, with a mind *partly* able to do so (not yet purged of its weaknesses)—was of a reality of which he had been hearing for forty years, and *that* reality he came to know. A reality vindicating his indifference to or scorn of all other paths except his own, his persuasion that the world and its forms of sense life were unreal and were simply to be disregarded. Missing on his path was the compassion of Buddhism and the gentleness of devotional Hinduism—serious lacks, indeed.

Although he had had an experience that convinced him of the immortality of his spirit and his oneness with the distinctionless Brahman, he still saw distinctions everywhere. Clouded areas of his mind created previously by a more ignorant viewpoint remained so, largely untouched by the light of his experience; indeed, they were vindicated in their unregenerate tendencies since his ego-sense, not by any means expunged by what had happened, was justified in any of its impulses because it had been persuaded by the experience that it was divine and anything that opposed or annoyed or inconvenienced it was unreal. Anger, therefore, accompanied him on his travels and was frequently resorted to like a weapon to keep unwanted individuals away from his ever-burning fire: they being unreal, the fire being Brahman itself.

This was one of his fetishes: the conviction that fire was especially sacred. It is an ancient idea in India among certain orthodox sects, to one of which he belonged. Wherever he went the first thing he did was to light a fire, in all seasons, and kept it burning day and night, sleeping or meditating by it—as though the fire *itself* contained the secret of truth and was not simply an excellent symbol of it.

His nakedness was another fetish. Its symbolic power one understands—in rejecting clothes one rejected society and all worldly values, and one's nakedness then became a constant reminder of one's true orientation, one's dedication to immutable values, spiritual realities. But other great souls, like-minded, have not felt the necessity of such a defiance of those who surround us on the planet. Neither Shankara (the idol of the Vedantic monks in India) nor Patanjali (the compiler of the yoga system which Tota Puri practiced) nor Krishna (the hero of Hinduism itself) nor Buddha nor Jesus nor Moses nor St. Francis nor

Zarathustra nor St. Paul nor Lao-Tzu nor Milarepa has advocated such a course, nor any scripture of India or of any other religion even intimated it, from which we may conclude that it was a fetish of the mind, an aberration of the ego organized into a sectarian principle in the monkish order to which he belonged. It resembled that practice of certain Jains who, slavishly adhering to the doctrine of nonviolence, never bathe their bodies for fear of killing germs and in the process become an offense to all.

Clearly he had much to learn, as the Brahmani did, in coming to Ramakrishna—engrossed as both were in the certainty that their own paths were the only true ones. At some point the monk had chiefly to discover—by some experience to be gained, perhaps, with the help of Ramakrishna—that the world that is denied is a product of Brahman, who is *responsible* for it, who has conceived, projected, and sustained it from the beginning. More, it is Vedanta itself, in one of its greatest metaphysical flights, that insists that Brahman *pervades* the world, has *become* it, gives life to every part and parcel of it—including, most particularly, the human beings where he resides as the soul of each. Lip service only is given to this crucial idea by the jnani, who prefers the more ego-consoling attitude of *contemptus mundi*, world-unreality.

The mystic discovers that everything that happens to a holy man comes to him directly from the divine intelligence, as part of the continuing drama being played out between soul and Deity; and, above all, any human encounters are weighted with divine significance. This is what Tota Puri did not seem to realize sufficiently: another reminder of the limitations of his spirituality—a reminder, also, that one may be able to realize God and retain much of one's egoism.

Despite our reservations about the degree of the monk's enlightenment, that he was brought to Ramakrishna specifically by the same universal intelligence that had sent Yogeswari, it is difficult to doubt. There was the sudden psychic recognition of Ramakrishna by a total stranger, the immediate conference about spiritual practice, the almost instant offer to guide him in an untrodden path—as with the Brahmani. And the timing was uncanny. When there was nothing left for him to attain in the fields of devotion, there came a messenger from an entirely different realm.

According to legend, he responded to Nangta's bid to scale the impersonal heights by first withdrawing to the Kali temple where, in devotional samadhi, he sought the permission of the goddess to proceed. Which was readily granted, and, as well, the knowledge that the monk had come explicitly to teach him Vedanta—had, indeed, been sent by her for that purpose: to indoctrinate him in the philosophy and practice of the impersonal path to Brahman, the Godhead. Thus reassured, he returned to Nangta but with a new demurral when he was told he would have to be initiated by the monk into the impersonal discipline in traditional fashion, renouncing ties to home and society and all that the world held dear. He insisted that the ritual be carried out in secret—lest his mother hear of it and be grieved.*

Shortly before, his aging mother had left Kamarpukur to live at Dakshineswar, where she remained for the rest of her life. She had arrived, in fact, about the time he had completed the Tantric experiment: that is, when he had come not only to believe in but to *realize* the divinity of woman, the mother of his flesh—reconciled to him in his changed consciousness—was allowed to join him in his place of struggle, near to his spiritual mother Yogeswari. When, in other words, the last vestige in him of male *reaction* to the female in all her vagaries had been burned up in the fires of knowledge, of Truth itself, then his earth-mother, embodiment of material consciousness, of mere Nature, was freed to share in his emancipation.

At length Tota Puri, observing the conventional rites, initiated him into *sannyasa*, the vow of total renunciation. Then he instructed him in the lofty monism of Vedanta: only the Self is real, all else is *Maya*, illusion, name and form imposed like a mirage over the immutable reality which is the Self, Atman-Brahman, the Absolute. In the type of meditation proposed, he was to detach his mind from all sensory objects, all mental reactions to these, and courageously elevate his being to the realm beyond the body, beyond the mind itself—to the purely spiritual level, where the Self existed in its own glory, in the body of its own bliss, free, infinite, eternal, the Truth of all truths. Abandon every other concept, however inspiring, plunge the mind into the bosom of the Self alone, and be free forever.

---

* Untold numbers of monks without benefit of special mandate had renounced the world, blessed by their parents, but she who was said to have received dreams and visions attesting the birth of a divine son found the notion of *his* renunciation insupportable.

Without delay Ramakrishna followed his instructions, finding it not difficult to do everything enjoined upon him until he reached that level of his mind—deep in samadhi—where there appeared the blissful form of God he had come to adore, that which he termed the Divine Mother: "the effulgence of pure consciousness" as he told of it. To the jnani this is one more modification of the mind that has to be transcended, however bliss-producing it may be, however much above other modifications with an earthly origin. To Ramakrishna it was the essence of essences with which—with *whom*, rather—he had communed in his most cherished moments of samadhi; his soul's core, his heart's joy. Several times he attempted the ultimate ascent, following Tota Puri's instructions, and each time his mind, bathed in the *ananda*—pure bliss—of the vision of the Personal God, transported with ecstasy, forgot its specific goal: the unconditioned Absolute, the transcendental One—the Self, the *Urgrund*. He confessed his failures to the monk, who importuned him to take the sword of Knowledge and cut his way through firmly and decisively to the domain *beyond*, which is what he was able finally to do, on the third day of trying. When the Personal Vision appeared once more, this time, using his discrimination as a sword he clove her in two. "There remained then no function in the mind, which transcended quickly the realm of names and forms"—plunging into the sea of Absolute Unconditioned Consciousness. This was the state of *nirvikalpa samadhi*.

The will that could "cleave her in two" had proved as unthinkable as his devotion had been.

Despite his impatience Tota Puri was astonished to see what had happened. Had Ramakrishna accomplished so quickly, almost in a day, what it had taken him forty years of the most intense struggle to achieve? The two were in a small hut which the monk had chosen for the momentous matters going on between them. Still stunned at Ramakrishna's state, he left him alone—his body rigid, all functions suspended, eyes closed, seated in the traditional cross-legged posture—locked the door behind him, and waited in the Panchavati for his pupil's call. Three days passed; all was silence. Returning to the hut, he found Ramakrishna seated in the same posture, his bodily functions completely stopped, his face, however, radiating a serene, divine light like a magnet in the center of the small enclosure, his mind immersed in the Self, in the absolute being of Brahman. Half-unbelieving, Tota

Puri studied him closely, examining key areas of his body—the heart, the breathing—but there was no pulse, no breath, no vital functioning. It was true. His eyes did not deceive him. The ultimate had been conquered.

With a great effort, repeating certain mantrams over the motionless form, he slowly brought his pupil's mind back to the normal state. The three days that was the maximum he spent anywhere had expired, but he made no move to leave.

The ultimate had been conquered—by Love. Pure Knowledge—direct experience of the Real, the Absolute—had been made accessible, been made *possible*, by pure Devotion. The discovery: the two paths, the two realities, were not different, as everyone had assumed, as both Yogeswari with her anxious warnings and Tota Puri with his monkish condescensions had, they were the same, two sides of the same coin, two facets—Bliss and Consciousness—of the same Godhead, separated by man's intellect, by his empirical compulsions, by his limited spirituality—but in reality inseparable, as Ramakrishna's life had demonstrated irrefutably.

A revolution in mystical philosophy, in the knowledge of the divine, and of man's nature, was now available to moderns.

Far from having sought the Impersonal, he had tended to avoid it. And yet five minutes before the supreme Experience—which, after the monk's departure, he would know still more radically, on the scale of the Buddha Enlightenment—while yet enveloped in the fragrances of devotion, he had been fully capable of it, was even then, just prior to the ascent, already a knower of Truth, without having had mystical corroboration in that supernal ecstasy.

Beyond his sadhana of devotion he had needed no further discipline to take him to the depths of the Brahman world, had needed no training in the yoga of the *jnani*, the path of Discriminative Knowledge. Love—carried to its limit, to be sure—had been enough. Love at any earlier stage might have persuaded him of the apparent differences between Loving and Knowing. Taken to its extreme, Love revealed its true nature, as only extremes reveal the truth of things. Thereby he had discovered, and from his example we have discovered also,[*] that love in its innermost depths is equivalent to Knowledge.

[*] In Jesus, St. Francis, and a few others the same example was evident, had we (cont.)

Buddha, also, treading the path of the Impersonal, found that the depths of Knowledge led to infinite Love for all creatures. Starting from opposite ends of the spiritual spectrum, they had met in the center, had had the same mystical experience, emerged with the same teaching, the same transformation of personality.

In the later years Ramakrishna would urge monks—on *their* path— not to have anything to do with women, while urging householders, on *theirs*, to practice devotion and Tantra. *Many* paths, he knew—and almost alone knew—would lead to God-realization. The Impersonal was true, because he had had the experience of it. The Personal was true, for a like reason. Renunciation was a true path—but a continent, enlightened sexuality was true also. He knew these things, as well, from his own experience. Devotees know one thing—Love. Tantrics, one— the mystique of sex. Monks, one—renunciation. Yogis, one—the mind. Partialists know only their own thing. Ramakrishna, beginning now, would come to know that all are possible, that all may lead to the One. It is what we are to try to do also, and to attempt to become. As Christ in an earlier time was "the first fruits of them that slept" (1 Cor. 15: 20), so Ramakrishna in ours may be the first fruits of modern men, groping in their sleep state, struggling to awaken. As Christ's was the core life for past ages, so Ramakrishna's may be the paradigm for us, and our successors.

The austere monk, trained in nonsusceptibility to sensory influ- ence, found Ramakrishna's presence irresistible. Weeks, months passed. He spent long hours every day in meditation but often the two were steeped in conversation on the science of Yoga, and on Vedanta and its uncompromising metaphysic. Nangta conveyed to him the fruit of his forty-years' study about every aspect of nondualism, and from time to time, though still for brief intervals (strangely brief), Ramakrishna brought his mind again to the state of Brahmic bliss. To some extent he tried to relate his earlier, pre-Vedantic experiences to the monk but with little success, Tota Puri's impatience being all too apparent when- ever anything pertaining to devotional practices was brought up.

He was struck by his teacher's continued practice of meditation despite the realization of Brahman: despite, that is, having achieved the purpose of meditation. The monk pointed to his glistening water-pot,

---

been able to study them to the degree that we can study Ramakrishna.

noting that it would lose its luster if not polished every day. So with the mind, he said, which would accumulate dirt if not polished every day by meditation.

"What if the water-pot be gold?" His own mind was such that he would tend to *avoid* meditation and instead seek ways of fastening his mind to *this* world. With him it was precisely the opposite of other men, including yogis like Tota Puri. He was so much possessed by the divine that his problem was how to keep his mind interested enough in worldly things—some, at least—to continue to remain in the body.

Once, while they were immersed in the high philosophy of Vedanta, Tota Puri, in a semi-meditative state at the time, did not notice one of the temple garden servants approach his fire and draw out of it a burning coal with which to light his pipe. When the monk saw this act of impiety committed against the sacred flame, he was enraged, leaped up, seized a pair of tongs, shook them at the offending servant, and threatened to beat him.

Ramakrishna, convulsed with laughter, pointed out that he had been preaching the whole world was nothing but Brahman and that all names and forms were only manifestations of *That*—and here he was, caught himself in the delusive net of Maya, *angrily* denouncing one of those manifestations and on the verge of beating it. The *Maya* whose existence he denied, Ramakrishna went on, was once again demonstrating its inscrutable sway over everyone, including men of "realization."

Here, in a flash of revelation, we see that the depth of Nangta's experience, though genuine, was limited. Shallow in comparison to what it might be one day—when he departed from Ramakrishna, perhaps.

The monk, touched by the incident, vowed to give up anger henceforth. But he would not be able to do so unless he also renounced the center of his personality whence the anger had arisen: a much more difficult task. And that could not be accomplished save through a humbling of his ego before the divinity of the world, the divine spirit behind the world itself—not only the transcendental spirit which, eternally nonattached, brooded above it.

Some ten months after his arrival at the temple compound the final act of the drama commenced with an attack of dysentery, which slowly grew more serious, causing him intense pain and discomfort. He attributed the cause to the poor water of Bengal and to the heavy humidity with which, as a native of northwestern India, he was unfamiliar.

The real Cause, of course, lay deeper. What had happened was the beginning of a particularly powerful onslaught of *Maya* intended to transform him from the hard-minded ascetic he was into the true man of Knowledge he might be.

Although the pain brought him much bodily suffering, his mind, made strong as adamant through years of mortification, was at first, during meditation periods, free and invulnerable to pain. Often, during this stage, he went to Ramakrishna meaning to bid farewell but unable to take the step. Gradually the increasing severity of the disease spread through his entire system, affecting his mind, making it difficult to do what had always been a matter of pride: achieve profound states of withdrawal and concentration on Brahman. He decided to put an end to his earthly life and cease to undergo his humiliation any longer. Clearly and overwhelmingly he had understood, by direct experience, that he was not the body—a cage of bones and flesh—and therefore had no need of putting up with its interference and morbid illnesses. That very night he resolved to drown the troublesome vessel, which Vedanta claimed to be the very seat of illusion, and take his mind to another orbit where unbroken contemplation on the Self could be enjoyed for as long as he wished.

When all was still, about midnight, he waded resolutely into the Ganges nearby, determined to leave his disease-emaciated body a watery corpse to be discovered in the morning, but to his amazement found there was not enough water to drown himself—it seemed to recede the more he plunged into it, struggling all the way to the opposite bank. He turned around. Suddenly, caught up in vision, he saw that life pulsed through every object before him—houses, temples, stairs, grass, flowers, the river itself—eternal, infinite life manifesting in every form that met his dazzled eyes, a creative power of unlimited potency and mystery pulsating through all, pervading all, making all things divine, appearing as river, as men, as flowers, as buildings, and simultaneously as the power that bound them together and transcended them too; in short, he was seeing the hidden face of the creator God—immanent, omnipresent, the support and reality and life of all things, as Nature and as the power behind Nature, as Life and as Energy supportive of that Life, as Human Nature and as the Divine Nature manifesting, palpitating through that Human; a shoreless infinite ocean of consciousness trembling dynamically in every atom of existence, making it all significant by its own immortal presence, full of mystery, profundity, beauty beyond description, the One in manifestation, in creative palpable form, only another face of the same unmanifested One he had worshipped all his life, the other, manifesting principle wedded to the unmanifested forever, as Shakti to Shiva, as Night to Day, as Yin to Yang, as outer to inner, as world to world-creator, all of it an equal undifferentiated Unity he had never before glimpsed, or guessed, but which now poured its reality into the portals of his startled brain and became a part of his knowledge, his transformed being, forever.

He spent the night in meditation, untroubled by the body's pain; in the morning he told what had happened to Ramakrishna, who seemed to have anticipated it. The disease, it was evident, had been divinely sent to bring him to this new knowledge. He was very humble, full of devotion, prayers, cries of worship. Together they went to the temple of Kali and prostrated themselves there: Kali, for Tota Puri too, at last, a symbol of that divine, creative Life whose presence in the world of men made it as sacred and as meaningful as the world of the unmanifested Self of Brahman.

A few days later the monk, now truly a man of realization, took his leave. He had arrived as the teacher, had left as the student. He never came back. They never met again.

Eleven months before, Ramakrishna had plunged his mind into the kingdom of the Absolute, where all sense of personal identity and all distinctions vanish, an immense and infinite Oneness of perfect Bliss, Knowledge, and Being, but had only returned to that colossal experience intermittently in the ensuing period. He had to wait until the monk's knowledge was complete. Tota Puri's mind had to be softened by hundreds of hours of conversation with him before it would be ready to receive the revelation that was coming. And the steady psychic exposure to the vibrations of his personality further conditioned the monk for the grand awakening that night on the Ganges bank.

Now he felt free again to seek out the stupendous aloneness of the Brahman world, with the most sensational of all his mystical achievements: *remaining in the state of nirvikalpa samadhi for six unbroken months.* The recorded history of mysticism, among its greatest practitioners, shows no experience comparable to this in magnitude and fullness. The nearest seems to be the seven weeks of total ecstasy that Buddha knew after his enlightenment. Even his own devotional experiences, though they had prepared the way to it, and made it possible, vastly recede before the enormity of this, and here more than ever the idea of the incredible presses upon the mind of the investigator. His earlier mystical triumphs had established him as India's chief devotional saint since Chaitanya but this achievement left him *sui generis*, bringing him to the unsurpassed height in the sphere of pure Knowledge that he had attained already in pure Devotion: matching the greatnesses, let us say, in one commingling, of St. Francis and Gautama Buddha.

Further, the *nirvikalpa samadhi* led directly, in a few years, to his mastery of faiths outside the fold of Hinduism and to the discovery, which has set him apart from earlier prophets, that every faith is only a path, that all are inspired, that the same divine is manifesting in each. This truth, now a permanent part of world mystical teaching, was inaccessible to him by devotion alone, for in the path of love and worship the aspirant can see nothing except the object of his fervor: whether Krishna, Kali, Rama, or Allah, Buddha, Jesus, or the Father in Heaven. Unsupported by knowledge, unleavened by reason, love enslaves us to one idea exclusively. Without the ballast and catalytic influence of Knowledge it remains an expression, however spiritual, of that egoism which pervades every level of our being, from animal to spiritual. Emotion differentiates, judges, excludes, clouds. In the name of the love of God what crimes have been committed! On the other hand, Knowledge without Devotion gives us at best a Tota Puri, more often the ignorant, overbearing ascetic.

The combination of Love *and* Knowledge is necessary, which the major saints possessed, needless to say: the Love of God and Knowledge of the Ground of that God in the experience of the Self, as the Vedanta would describe it—the devastating discovery that not only is there a God we can love and adore but that that God is not outside us, after all, is *within*, in his—or its—pristine glory, essence, reality, and divine ground, in Eckhart's memorable phrase, and is one with the individual self once the nature of that self is analyzed and unfolded—and experienced.

It is "the pure unitary consciousness," as the Mandukya *Upanishad* calls it, "wherein awareness of the world and of multiplicity is completely obliterated. It is ineffable peace. It is the supreme good. It is One without a second. It is the Self. Know it alone!"

It is the Eternity within, beyond time, the Immortality within, beyond mortality, the Infinity within, beyond limitation, the Peace within, beyond understanding. Kali is not enough, nor Krishna, Shiva, Jesus, Buddha, nor Allah. They are only expressions, or conduits, or names, or forms, of *That*, which alone exists, say the *Upanishads*, which alone is the real, say our hearts, which alone is the Truth, say our minds. It is Existence-Knowledge-Bliss Absolute, it is the Real Existence, the eternal Consciousness, the infinite Life, beyond good and evil, beyond male and female, beyond all modifications whatsoever, beyond time, space and causation, beyond thought and mind, and all distinctions, an immense and absolute Oneness of which we have heard so often but which, according to those who have known it, can actually be experienced in the depths of our own beings.

That is where, amazingly, it is to be found. Within. But *deep* within, *far* within, like a diamond in a mountain. It is our own souls that we find. It is the heart that has been beating in us, so near, so intimately, so faithfully. Our own hearts. It is the silent, soft bosom on which we have been riding like infants throughout our life.

There the ego disappears and, at sufficient depth, is dissolved forever. Fears vanish, never to return. Death is vanquished like a dream forgotten. The Real Man grounded in the Real Existence stands immersed in his own glory, of which all love, all earthly joy, is but a foretaste.

Six months in that state became Ramakrishna's habitat. Somehow a wandering monk, a nameless successor to Tota Puri, drifted into the Dakshineswar temple garden (one more strange happening) and came to understand that he should take charge of the rigid form suspended like an upright corpse—as its possessor's mind was lost in other worlds—and make sure that for the good of humanity some physical life be maintained in it. By continuous attentions, sometimes by vigorous and violent actions, he occasionally brought the contemplative's mind back to earth for a few moments, pouring needed liquids and a few morsels of precious food into his mouth. So life was preserved. After the six months ended the obscure monk disappeared.

In the days following, Ramakrishna, as he told of it later, discovered that he was to hold his mind thenceforth in a balanced poise between the Absolute and the Relative, the Impersonal and the Personal, what Hindus call the state of *Bhavamukha*, where he could maintain contact with the Brahman state and its ineffable bliss and at the same time the world of Creation (the sphere of Kali, of the Personal God, of Allah, of the Father) which, because of the transformed nature of his consciousness, he would perceive as a universal expression of the Supreme One. *Bhavamukha:* The One and the Many, the Many being the One manifested—the One appearing *as* the Many. Nirvana and Samsara of Buddhism: Nirvana the Undifferentiated Experience, Samsara the manifestation of Nirvana in the world of becoming. Being and Becoming. Brahman and Kali. The Infinite and the endless power of Creativity among the Finite, transforming it into the essence of the Infinite. ("To see a world in a grain of sand...") All of this the play of the One, the Omnipresent unity, and Ramakrishna like a man standing at the threshold, able to see one world, the phenomenal, in front of him, and simultaneously aware of another, the world of the Absolute, behind him.

This was the state he was to occupy for the rest of his life.

Could he rest at last, since there could be nothing beyond what he had already experienced? He had conquered the ultimate. But his sadhana was not ended. New challenges awaited him.

13

The Mysticism of Christ

RAMAKRISHNA'S SUPERCONSCIOUS EXPERIENCES ARE corroborated by many and by his own descriptions; the unfolding process of his mystical development can be clearly traced. We cannot do the same with Christ, whose mysticism is to be *inferred* by actions and teachings that could only have issued from a supermystic.

But do not the miracles demonstrate his mystical power, establish him as a great mystic? They, least of all. That kind of mystic is common in the East, where they have been fascinated by the internal world, including its powers, for thousands of years. Apollonius of Tyana, a wizard of the miraculous and a contemporary of Christ, performed scores of miracles that equal or surpass those of the Galilean, as many have long noted. Tibetan Buddhism, Zen, Sufism, and Yoga, between them, have produced hundreds of thaumaturgic adepts, like Milarepa who rose from his bier because a late-arriving disciple wanted one last look at him alive, including many who can heal any disease known to man, others who have remained in well-posted graves in a living death only to emerge at an appointed time; a number who eat no food of any kind, yet remain healthy; some who altogether dispense with sleep. (Christ took food, and slept—are they not therefore superior: the counter-argument for those who argue Christ's uniqueness because of *his* powers.)

Unfortunately, from this standpoint, he appeared among a people who demanded "signs" before they could believe anything about a messiah, who required material proofs of spiritual greatness because they lacked the spirituality to discern that greatness as it was in itself; appeared, as well, in a part of the world that would persevere in the same interpretation of spiritual truth, and require healing and miraculous powers—inconsequent gifts though these are in lands where the inner realities have been tirelessly explored by thousands since the Vedic age—as heralds of messiahship or mystic authority.

Emphasis on healing, stress on the miraculous, is a psychic display, not a spiritual manifestation. Many heal who are charged with egotism; many have access to the miraculous who are full of themselves, not of spirit. Miracles and healing are attempts to make us at home in the body, to revive our faith that the body healed means *we* are healed, and because our bodies are so dear to us (as Ramakrishna often said) that any major healing of their ills becomes proof, *ipso facto*, of God's existence!

Christ, we have noted, would have died unsung, unwept, had he presented himself to the Jews as only a holy man with a lofty message of spirituality. His pearls of discourse would have dropped silently like dew in the hot desert of Judaic legalism and, except for a few attracted to him, would have been forgotten in a generation. The message *and* the miracles was the combination that drew attention to *him*, then to his teachings, then to his mission. Likewise with Moses, who had to deal in the prodigious before the Israelites accepted him. Muhammad, while lacking the miraculous power and the deeper mysticism alike, became the prophet militant, put himself at the head of conquering armies and in his own time vanquished Arabia for the new creed of Islam—in Arab eyes attesting to its truth.

But Confucius and Lao-Tzu conquered in China without a single miracle. Buddha's victories were all spiritual. As were Shankara's, India's peerless philosopher. In the life of Ramakrishna, though he possessed all the powers, we search for miracles almost in vain: the three or four minor ones, secretively performed, for some special occasion, are not worth one's trouble to examine. Patanjali's warning against the use of the miraculous as a serious obstacle to further spiritual development included the reminder that psychic powers were a natural part of the human constitution when it reached a certain state of evolution and had nothing directly to do with spirituality. In fact, the exercise of spirituality and of psychic powers are diametrically opposed; one cannot have both for long. The choice must be made. In the West it has generally been made in favor of the psychic—healing, clairvoyance, communion with other planes, prophecy, and so on—because of inadequate knowledge of man's nature and insufficient development of that nature towards its total fulfillment.

A little metaphysical insight, the excitement of early spiritual seed-time, combined with a large unexamined store of egoism, results in the cultivation of psychic phenomena and healing activities. This kind of behavior, in turn, reinforces the existing egoism in a subtle, insidious way, debarring the individual, as Patanjali warned, from further inner unfoldment.

Christ, it is true, performed miracles, healed many, for the reasons we have noted. But he was an avatar who, with full knowledge of what was taking place and the necessity for it, could exhibit such powers with no harm—or little harm—to his spiritual nature. Others cannot claim such control.

It is often overlooked that his pristine teachings find no place in them for encouragement of the miraculous. The profound statements in John's Gospel avoid any mention of psychic powers as, chapter after chapter, they develop the theme of the mystical Christ, the divine principle in man. As we have observed, his most notable utterance, the incomparable Sermon, makes no reference to supernatural powers. He does not promise that if you follow his teachings you will perform occult prodigies. Perfection he does promise (Matthew 5: 48).

His mysticism and true grandeur shine forth for reasons entirely different than the wielding of powers accessible to yogis and wonder-workers of many lands, who are not studied for their wisdom nor followed for their love: evoked, rather, by radiance of personality, weight of deed, and the hierophantic profundity of his teaching.

His devotional nature is evident through the gospels. The struggle in the Garden: "Let this cup pass from me.... Nevertheless.... Thy will be done"; the cry on the cross: "My God, My God, why hast thou forsaken me?"; the prayer he gave to his disciples as a summary of his beliefs: "Our Father Who art in Heaven—"; his exhortation to Nicodemus to "love the Lord thy God with all thy heart and all thy soul and all thy mind and all thy strength"; his solitary prayer after the Last Supper: "Father, the hour is come—"; the innumerable references to his Father, to his own Sonship, to the relation of love and trust between them ... all demonstrate his powerful devotional nature. But he had known more than the Personal Father, the God of Love, analogous to Ramakrishna's Mother Kali. He had known the Godhead itself, the source of his being and the ground of his incarnation as a divine embodiment. That he had known it to a substantial degree does not admit of doubt.

I and my Father are One is one of the strongest statements of this experience. The Father here is not the Personal Father of his many devotional allusions, for no devotee would have either wanted such a realization—actual oneness and identity with the object of his adoration—or attained it; recalling our principle that the mystic experiences in transcendental consciousness the fulfillment of contents already in his mind. The content in the mind of the devotee is that of a divine, loving separation between Lord and worshipper. Ramprasad, the medieval Hindu poet-mystic, put it succinctly: "I don't want to *be* sugar, I want to taste sugar." I don't want Unity, I want to be able to taste the Divine Otherness of my Beloved. I don't want to become God, I want to adore Him. *I and my Father are One* transcends this fundamental approach of all devotees of the Lord, and means that just as Ramakrishna had gone beyond the sway of Kali in that scene with Tota Puri in the hut, so Christ at some unrecorded moment transcended the world of his Father as Creator and attained his Father as Divine Ground—the slight confusion resulting from his use of the same word to denote two different dimensions of cosmic reality: though of course essentially the two are aspects of the same Oneness, the one abiding ever-changeless *Tao*, as Ramakrishna's celestial ascent to *nirvikalpa* made unmistakable.

So established is he in the devotional strain, however, that even after this transcendental experience he returns to his characteristic role of son to his Father, searching out His will, mindful of His Love, as Ramakrishna, after *his* immersion in the ultimate, returns to being son to Mother Kali. Astonishingly, he now thinks of the Absolute as his Father, as Ramakrishna thought of Brahman as the inactive ground of Kali's active, all-creative being. The result is a devotional nondualism rarely seen.*

God as Love gave Jesus his gentleness, emotionality (weeping when he heard that Lazarus was dead), his sacrificial hunger—his feminine desire to immolate himself for the salvation of the world. But God as Knowledge gave him his majesty, serenity, profundity, and indomitable masculine will.

Under questioning from Pilate (John 18: 37), he replies: "For this cause I came into the world, that I should bear witness unto the truth." The *truth* is the experience of the Impersonal, love the experience of the Personal. On the cross the devotional passion possesses him, but before Pilate the Buddha-like mode is dominant, issuing from his transcendental knowledge of the Godhead, the "truth."

You shall know the truth, he says elsewhere (John 8: 32), *and the truth shall make you free.* Love is the dynamic mode of our communion with the created world and with its creator but Truth is its foundation. Love, says St. Paul, is the fulfilling of the Law—by which he means the Truth, the Truth of Being. Love is the fulfillment of the Truth. But it is truth that it fulfills, not itself alone. Christ, the preacher of love, says that *truth* alone will free us (significantly, not that *he* will). We are presently in a state of nonfreedom, due to some ignorance of which we are unaware—wheels upon wheels of delusion. It is like a dream of nightmarish proportions that fully possesses us, utterly convinces us of its reality, even though in actuality it is not real, as we discover when we awaken. So our ignorance and bondage are not real either, and never were**—precisely what the knowledge of truth reveals to us. That experience—a *mystical epiphany*—simply makes us know the truth, namely, that we are now

---

* Shankara (fl. 800) is another instance. Renowned for his Vedantic monism and uncompromising adherence to the impersonal path, he was the author of hundreds of fervent hymns in worship of the God of Love. More recently Swami Vivekananda is an example of the same rare, complex development.

** A cardinal theme in Vedanta philosophy, most subtly expounded by Shankara in his *Upanishads* commentaries, most eloquently by Vivekananda in modern times.

free, and always have been, that the bondage that was so seeming-real was an illusion: a killing one, an illusion nevertheless.

Love will not entirely free us from the nightmare, only Knowledge. When one *knows* what the truth of one's situation actually is, then and then alone one is free of what was binding and terrifying us. The spell breaks, the dream vanishes, the ignorance that constituted our *lack* of freedom—rather, our *nonawareness* of freedom—dissolves. But only Knowledge—the truth—can bring it about—and the realization that we always possessed it.

Further, he says, it must be *known*—but in some way unfamiliar to us. We may "know" the truth in many conventional ways: hearing it, reading it, uttering, memorizing it, being instructed in it, through analysis, comparison, philosophy, and so on; but whatever the truth was that Christ had in mind none of these ways of "knowing" is going to "free" us. For we have gone through all of them—like the philosopher, the theologian—and still are not free. What *will* free us is the way the mystic knows—through mystical intuition we directly perceive the truth of something at the core of our being: we know with the organ of truth within us, the divinely indwelling intuitive power that represents the soul in its active principle. That is, an authentic experience, *only,* will dispel the dream that makes us feel we are in bondage; it alone will furnish the kind of knowledge that will enable us "in the twinkling of an eye," as St. Paul says, to realize what our real nature is: divine, one with the Father, as Christ discovered his to be.

Love will not entirely free us, despite Paul's hymn to its power (1 Cor. 13). Its bliss is so overpowering that, bondage or not, we remain content with any condition only so long as we can go on loving. It is the sun of Knowledge alone that drives away the mists and fogs of our ignorance, freeing us. In Hinduism the path of Knowledge—jnana yoga—leads to the ideal of Liberation—from bondage, ignorance, our present condition. Precisely what Christ meant in: *you shall know the truth and the truth shall make you free.*

The command to love thy neighbor *as thyself* (Matthew 22: 39) is not the utterance of love but of Knowledge—that is, emanates from the experience of the Impersonal rather than the Personal Being. The purely devotional saint is always aware of differences, though he apprehends them through veils of love. They are, to him, images of Love's infinite variety in its power to relate ever more richly to unending aspects of the Loving Father's (or Mother's) infinite bounty. He is, in a word, a dualist, though a purified one, whereby the harmful ego, the self-centered ego, which he once knew, and which all other men still know, has been refined away and only a mild ego-consciousness remains; harmless, but there. He sees his neighbor as his brother (in the Lord), but *not as himself. His* version of the command would be: "Love thy neighbor, for he too is a child of God" or "he too is an image of God" or "he is your brother and the Lord is the Father of both of you."

To see another man as yourself is possible only if the power of perceiving differences—the ego, a universal impediment in the human constitution—were removed, and that is possible only in an experience of the undifferentiated being, the One without a second, *without any other thing than itself in existence.* A unitive experience of That will make us resemble it sufficiently so that when we emerge from the light into the dimmer world of ordinary life again every face we see will be our face, the center of our consciousness will no longer be, as now, in our body, but everywhere, in every other life as well as our own, recalling St. Augustine's "God is a circle whose center is everywhere and circumference nowhere." Every life becomes our own, because there is, we discover, truly only one Life after all, *the Life of That,* but since we are united with it we share in that and if our experience is sufficiently profound and perfect, as it ultimately was with Buddha and Christ, and with Ramakrishna (but had not been so with Tota Puri), then we too become that life, become protective toward all because the All beats in us now as its newly-realized center.

> In me the caresser of life wherever moving ... not a person or
>   object missing....
> Absorbing all to myself and for this song....
> And these tend inward to me, and I tend outward to them,
> And such as it is to be, of these more or less I am,
> And of these one and all I weave the song of myself.[*]

Our power to perceive differences and to act on that perception has

---

[*] Walt Whitman, "Song of Myself" (Secs. 13, 15).

been melted out of existence by the heat and light of the Godhead known by our souls in the divine darkness of mystical illumination.

My neighbor, therefore, becomes myself—no longer my neighbor or my brother alone. *My self.* Such a declaration, coming from Jesus, could only be accounted for in terms of the unitive knowledge of Brahman.

The kingdom of heaven ... the kingdom of God ... is within you—is another mystic precept that seems too bold for the self-effacing devotee, who, though he might sense this truth, tends to place the onus of all glory on the Lord, drawing *his* significance from the Power felt to be different than the nature of his creations. The nondualist, however, is known for *not* shrinking from bold conclusions. The Kingdom is the awakened, realized spiritual consciousness. It is the soul glimpsed, discovered at last. Heaven, he finds, is *within.* The Kingdom is the Truth. Experiencing the Kingdom in mystical ecstasy, we come into the truth and are made free. Perfection or its potential must be within us if heaven and God and Truth are. There must be no limits to what we can spiritually attain. The devotee, perhaps nearly perfect already, hesitates to attribute so grand a state to a creature, as he still tends to think of man (unlike the nondualist who, after *his* experience, thinks of man as the soul and does not conceive of the soul as having been "born"—rather, thinks of it as having existed always, coequal with the Supreme Presence that is its ground). But in the midst of the Sermon on the Mount (Matthew 5: 48) we read: "Be ye therefore perfect, even as your Father in Heaven is perfect"—be perfect as God is. How is this possible? *Because our nature is the same as that of the Lord*, because we are truly made—as the nondualist, the impersonalist alone has discovered, verifying the Genesis *principium*— "in the image and likeness of God."

The realization of the Pure Light, the Blissful Center, convinces the mystic that he has not had an experience unique to himself, but one that is the potential birthright of every man. He is convinced of nothing more than this. Hence Buddha's refusal to accept praise, his constant turning the tribute back upon the disciple with the reminder that he could reach the same heights if he would tread the same path. Every soul, the nondualist finds, has the potential to experience, directly, in immediate intuition, the transforming truth into which he himself has arrived. The discovery makes him perfect—rather, draws out of him the perfection that was there. Then he invites others to have revealed unto them the sublime truth of what their nature truly is. The line from Christ's favorite Old Testament mystic, which he dramatically cites (John 10: 34; Psalms 82: 6)— "Know ye not that ye are gods"— restates this idea in other terms. It is well known that even the greatest devotional saints never address their hearers on the premise of their being gods and of attaining a perfection equal to that of God himself. Their realization being incomplete, so also is their understanding of the full scope of human nature.

Likewise, as we have noted, a pure devotee would not have said: *"I am the Way, the Truth, and the Life."* Christ has told us that the Truth will make us free—the *knowledge* of the truth: obviously a state to be known in the most organic way possible to human knowing—which then liberates us from some previous state of ignorance and frees us. Therefore when he says that "I" am the Truth, he means, necessarily, not a man but that condition, that spiritual state, which he has known and *become.* Hence it is that spiritual reality which is speaking here and on every other occasion like it, in John's gospel especially, where indeed the central theme is that very state, that Christ-mind which is the completely awakened consciousness available to everyone. It is the soul that speaks—ablaze with knowledge of its own being, in the full consciousness of its own reality. The *soul* is the Way, the soul is the Truth, the soul is the Life.

The soul is the Kingdom, the Kingdom is the Truth. We sell everything when we have glimpsed the Truth. It is the Truth that frees us, saves us, gives us Life, is the Door, is the Way, changes us into Sons and Daughters of God. When once we touch it we are changed forever. We become what we have experienced—unlike worldly experiences, which leave us as we were. We pass into the likeness of what we come to know. "I am the Truth," declared Al Hallaj, for which in 922 he was executed in Baghdad, charged with blasphemy. (Jesus would die for the same charge: placing himself on a level with God.) Some know the truth a little, some more, some a great deal, some almost totally, a few totally. All move in the same direction. Worship of God, love of God, the whole path of devotion, is a step towards that goal, the chief step. Christ is one of the pathfinders, having discovered by experience the Truth of immortality that is the Soul's nature. He becomes That. He *is* That. The "I" that speaks ... the "I AM" that speaks—has become *that* ... *is* that.

Jesus the Nazarene has been transcended. Soon he will die and will never come back. His soul is immortal. The Christ—*Christos*—is immortal. Truth is immortal. Christ is a name for Truth, as Buddha is another name for the same Truth. Jesus once, Gautama another time, entered into that state, became that, became the soul. The soul is Truth. No *man* is the Truth, no man is the Way, no man is the Life.

No man cometh unto the Father but by me, he adds, in that same celebrated remark. No man can achieve the knowledge of Truth, of divine reality, except through the realization of his own soul, as I have done. The soul speaks here, the Christ speaks, not Jesus the son of the carpenter. "Without me," says Eckhart, another knower of the Absolute by direct, immediate experience, "God would not know that he exists." By which he does not mean the fourteenth-century German Dominican monk. Rather, the consciousness he has become, has completely identified with, is the identity that speaks—the soul speaks—the "divine ground" within Eckhart speaks, and it is that which mirrors back to the Creator its own being.

I am the Resurrection and the Life—that is, in complete self-identification with soul-consciousness he has been resurrected out of the tomb of body-consciousness, and the life he now embodies is Life itself—the life of God. Not the dim, cave-like existence that passes in the world for life. Hence his "resurrection" after the crucifixion (his appearance in a shining astral body to men and women who would have misinterpreted such a resurrection as from the dead, being unschooled—like ourselves—in realities beyond the material form) only externalizes in symbolic form what has been essentially accomplished.

"The glad tidings of great joy" that Mary Magdalene reported were, in fact, that the soul is immortal, that the soul is risen out of the death of the body and death-feeding body-consciousness. "He is risen!" she cries. But the He she refers to is the pure consciousness that Jesus the Nazarene, now the Christ, has become. The glad tidings are, truly, that everyone's soul is immortal, that the fetters of mortality are broken, and are to *be* broken—once and for all: that Christ's ascent, his conquest of death, verifies this supreme fact.

He who hath seen me hath seen the Father—is one of the more dramatic enunciations of the mystical Christos principle and one of the clearest repudiations of the traditional rendering of "me" as "Jesus of Nazareth," since the pure Spirit—the Father—cannot be a man, or a form, or even an incarnation, but it can be the Christ-principle, the soul within, the consciousness elevated to the highest, transcendental level by the blasting light of *nirvikalpa samadhi*. "I have attained the state of infinite knowledge," said Buddha. That is: I am the infinite, I am that which is. If you see me you do not see a man (as he often declared), you see the Awakened, you see the Enlightened, you see the Truth. I am the Truth, he said. He who hath seen me hath seen the Truth.

In Matthew 11: 27 we read a corollary sentence: "No man knoweth the Son, save the Father; neither doth any know the Father, save the Son"—a passage on which Eckhart the seer makes the pertinent commentary: "In truth, to know the Father we must *be* the Son." *Father* is Jesus' highest word for the ultimate knowledge he has gained of the divine. He has asked us to "know" the Truth—in *mystical* knowing—since spirit cannot be known except by spirit. But how can we unless we are of the same nature, related to it as intimately as Jesus? How can we know the Father if we are not also the Son?

Christ's devotional temperament compelled him to continue to refer to the oceanic consciousness as the Father, for personally he preferred to remain in a loving and devoted relationship with the Power he also knew was within him and *was* him. As did Ramakrishna.

In John 8: 58 Jesus, trading repartee with the Jews on the subject of Abraham, remarks that he has lived before Abraham, at which his auditors take great offense. He concludes with the cryptic utterance: *Before Abraham was, I am*—another dramatic reminder that his experience of the divine included dimensions transcending that of the Personal Deity. He is saying—to those who have ears to hear—that he is no longer a person but a being, no longer a man but a consciousness. For no man could have lived before Abraham, though a consciousness could have.[*]

---

[*] I AM recalls Moses' request of God to tell his name (and, by implication, his nature, for in mystical tradition the name of something evokes its nature as well), and the memorable reply: Tell them I AM hath sent you (Ex. 3: 14).

It also recalls that moment in the *Bhagavad-Gita* when Arjuna questions Krishna's statement that he personally communicated the truth of yoga to ancient sages, and Krishna's response:

You and I, Arjuna, have lived many lives.
I remember them all: you do not remember.
I am the birthless, the deathless....
I seem to be born: it is only seeming....(cont.)

The Christ—eclipsing the Jesus born in Palestine—lives eternally. The Buddha-Man, according to Buddha, is infinite and unborn. In the Vedantic tradition the Atman (Brahman conceived in an individualized mode) is considered the true man: the Soul itself. Each term refers to the same state. In the Old Testament the version is I AM.

The state emerges out of the Impersonal alone. However lofty the experience of the Personal Deity may be, by the very nature of it *two* are presupposed. But the Christ, the Buddha, the Atman, the I AM, are *one* with the essence, with the Truth, with the Godhead, and cannot know itself without that experience. The Religion of Love, of worship of the Personal God, is offered to mankind as the best way to progress upward on the ladder of spiritual development, but direct intuition, unitive knowledge, of the Supreme awaits us at the end of that ladder.

Along the way our spiritual practice will be free of fanaticism, exclusivism, patronizing toward other (and therefore lesser) devotions, if we immerse the mind during contemplative hours in the atmosphere of impersonal reality, gradually accustoming it to what must be, sooner or later, in this or some other life, its cumulative, apocalyptic encounter.

The three recorded mystical experiences of Jesus—his baptism, the temptation by Satan, and the Transfiguration—do not represent mysticism at its deepest or most significant. The supreme moments of truth by their very nature must exclude not only any witnesses (such as we find in the Baptism and Transfiguration scenes) but the possibility of any relevant or authentic description by the mystic himself. (Moses' dialogues with Jehovah, often a complaining and quixotic Creator, as so many have noted, are patently allegorical, as are all the Old Testament versions of prophet vis-a-vis deity.) He can only hint and suggest; even then the reality of what he has undergone is scarcely credible or comprehensible to those who lack personal acquaintance of what he is painting in metaphorical language.

The scene at the Jordan after John's rite of baptism, at the very outset of Jesus' ministry, is more of a symbolic *manifestation* than a genuine superconscious occurrence, and may have taken place for the benefit of the faithful John who, for so long, had been awaiting the

(IV: 5-6) trans. Swami Prabhavananda
and Christopher Isherwood
(1944, 1951).

messiah and now had the great fortune to baptize him; for the benefit, also, of anyone else of potential spiritual nature standing near—some nameless disciple who, but for the voice seemingly from above and the glorified expression on the stranger's face, might never have awakened to the new life. The incident really marks an *overture* to the career about to begin rather than a profound moment of spiritual growth.

Directly following, the temptations offered by Satan indicate that Jesus, unknown at the time of this experience, has not evolved to the personality of the immortal utterances. For Satan's presence means that the satanic element in him—as in everyone—was still somewhat active. The *ego*, that is. He clearly rejects the advances of the temptation principle, but because the encounter takes place at all—in his consciousness—means that he is not yet totally united with himself, utterly free from any *thought* of exerting power in the pursuit of his mission, not yet illumined by the Pure Light of the Void within, not yet the Christ, not yet in full possession of I AM.

He exerts his will, and emerges innocent, triumphant. But the fully realized soul transcends will, enters into the realm of being itself—*becomes being*, beyond contraries, modifications, temptations, becomes Bliss itself, Knowledge. Satan is a lost dream. He smiles at the thought of Satan, and all such contrary principles. He is the One, incarnate. But to those not yet the One, such as Jesus in this scene, Satan—or the enemy within—is no memory, is a matter for intense concern: being the last, still tenacious obstacle to enlightenment.

The Transfiguration, while a genuine illumination for Jesus, is, by his yoga power, converted into a psychic experience for the benefit of the three disciples with him, none of whom at that moment is prepared for spiritual insight but rather, baffled and awed, for psychic excitement, which the "vision" provides. (We may remind ourselves that all his actions and teachings were carried out chiefly for their benefit, since upon their shoulders would rest the success or failure of his mission after death. Therefore everything would depend upon the degree of their conviction of his divinity. Because of their Jewish belief that the wielding of miraculous power was a sure sign that the possessor was likely to be the messiah, the miracles were one of the major ways to accomplish this. The Transfiguration was a late attempt, while he still lived in the body, to impress upon their fairly simple minds the extraordinary nature of their *guru*.)

In a spiritual experience of the personal or devotional type forms may appear—forms of saints or divine personalities, such as appeared to Jesus in the so-called Transfiguration; otherwise, it is a psychic experience. The latter issues from the mind and the senses, the spiritual from the spirit—from beyond—from the divine world, which has the prerogative of generating in the in-gathered consciousness forms, sounds, or emanations from itself to strengthen or enlighten the worshipper. Other sense manifestations are either without much significance or are delusive phenomena produced not by the divine but by the mind in its unfamiliar areas—subconscious, fringe regions of itself—from which it is capable of producing endless sounds, lights, colors, forms, to intrigue the meditator into the fancy that enlightenment be nigh. Even when the forms of divine beings appear, the higher planes of devotional contemplation transcend them (except the form of one's ideal, such as Buddha, Krishna, Christ), not to speak of authentic knowledge of the impersonal reality in *nirvikalpa samadhi* when all sense of egoism, individuality, apartness, separateness is dissolved, even the memory of the chosen ideal, in the melting unity of the fire of pure spirit.

The Transfiguration, then, is an important spiritual *darshan* in which the forms of prophets appeared to Jesus, but it was far below the higher levels of devotional ecstasy when his soul would have communed in rapt love with the heart of the Divine Father, not to mention his experience of the divine Ground, beyond not only all forms but beyond their creator, the Peaceful Essence that Buddha declared was at the central core of the universe.

That the mount theophany had witnesses makes it, spiritually, of a lower type. A one-to-one relationship is the norm in the divine world where the *ecstasis*, in Plotinus' phrase, is a "flight of the alone to the Alone." The Transfiguration, something considerably less, was, to repeat, brought about for the benefit of the three bystanders, who would play vital roles in the virgin period of the new creed and, if necessary, had to be overwhelmed (as Saul on the Damascus Road would be) into faith and conviction.

But despite this unique infusion of grace, giving them a vision of ancient prophets, and despite the miracles, and two or three years in the presence of a God-man, the conviction was something less than invincible.

In the great crisis of Jesus' last days, enveloping them in a dire sense of Fate and Necessity, there were few heroes. Peter, a natural-leader type, was given the honor of being named group spokesman, but we note with shock his weak-mindedness when stead-fastness was called for, and his blustering lack of self-knowledge in pro-claiming (John 13: 37) that he would be true to the end, would lay down his life for the Master—and then his repeated denial, as the trial was under way, that he had ever met him.

His weakness is an object lesson for us. The power of the lower nature is not only strong—all will concede as much. It is also vast, treacherously subtle, with uncanny reaches of perversity to command when the life of the seeker is on the threshold of spiritual break-through. An infinite number of reasons for suggesting withdrawal—nonacceptance, refusal of the challenge, a return to what used to be—are available at instant readiness, and responding to its provocations are the extensive sleeping areas of the mind that have not yet been touched by any light, any awareness of the divine—regions of which, in the early years of our conversion, we remain blissfully innocent. Simple, conscious-level, outer-directed personalities like Simon Peter are partic-ularly unaware of this phenomenon and hence the tears he compul-sively shed after his conscience had reawakened must have been bitter indeed. He may have been tempted at that juncture to choose the fate that overtook the hapless Judas.

In Jesus by then the lower nature's manifestations in the submind—seen outwardly, for example, in his constant wrangling with the Jews, and in his scourging the money-changers out of the temple—had been purged; but he was not free from the shadowing nemesis of Nature her-self in the final dark days. Even someone who has known the ultimate experience—the direct knowledge of the Absolute—may not be immune to this shadow—as we see, with awed wonder, in the Garden and on Calvary. There is a body-consciousness which lingers on well after illu-mination, just as the bodily functions remain and the natural processes leading to bodily death. It appears to assert itself especially at those moments when the individual being is about to plunge deeper into the abyss of God and become, by degrees, more of the deity than it has been. This *hubris* of the enlightened will awakens the latent forces of its eter-nal antipode, Nemesis, and the individual self, during the moments of the clash of opposites, seems to forget—for such is the nature of the mind, even of saviors—the splendor of its past accomplishments, and the height of its realizations. For yesterday's realizations, while they provide momentum, will not serve for today, which demands its own victories, at penalty of annulling altogether the glory of the past and, indeed, converting it into opprobrium.

This is the price we pay for reaching for the stars and the price, still to be paid, after we have touched them.

This is the moral of the drama, reminding us that on the threshold of *our* crucifixion we will undergo a similar pattern and can only hope—such is the paradox of spiritual life, reversing all worldly estimates of themes like sacrifice—that in that hour we will be able to undergo the death of our ego-self. Resurrection is the reward—ascension of consciousness—to be repeated as often as necessary until the Godhead is ours and we are its.

Meanwhile our perfection, like Christ's, will be wholly inward; the outer man will at times show forth passing, visible weaknesses, to be attributed, finally, to a force surrounding the man rather than to the man himself, that is, to the body—to the bodily environment under the mastership of Nature: able to sway and shake and confuse him occasionally—at the peak moments—but not able to keep him from persevering in his committed task, bearing onward into the diminishing darkness of himself the torch of his burnished will, honed through so many vigils, fueled through uncounted meditations, offered as a saving gift to his fellow men laboring still in a profounder darkness.

14

 The Family Reassessed: The Two Compared

HAVING EXPERIENCED THE GODHEAD supporting the gods of all faiths, the truth toward which the thrust of all the scriptures pointed, Ramakrishna came to understand that each religion was genuine in that each endeavored to articulate its version of common, underlying principles. As many faiths, so many paths, he declared. All led those who devoutly practiced them to the transcendental goal: knowledge of the universal reality. And the greater prophets were either messengers or incarnations of the Creative Power behind the universe. Those in the Hindu tradition— Rama, Krishna, Chaitanya—he was intimately familiar with. From the outset, he regarded Buddha as of the same rank and all his life remained susceptible to his incomparable character.

But what of Jesus Christ and Muhammad, and their religions? Although he had already exhausted the full spectrum of Hinduism's vast scope of mystical possibility he hungered for still more types of experience. No one was yet available to teach him the religion of the Nazarene properly, but a Hindu convert to Islam—to its Sufi mystic sect—was on hand: Govinda Ray by name. For some days, under his guidance, Ramakrishna entered with total absorption into his study and practice of the new faith, dressing like a Muslim, eating Muslim food, repeating the name of Allah, avoiding the Hindu shrines, living outside the temple compound. At the end of a few days he had a vision of a long-bearded sage of radiant, impressive mien, who seems to have been Muhammad. This was followed by the mystical knowledge of the Islamic personal God, Allah (that is, Brahman with attributes), and finally an experience of Brahman itself, *al Haqq*, "the Real": revealed as the source behind Allah, as Allah was the power behind Muhammad, and the prophet the inspiration of the Koran.

Despite the immense misunderstanding Hinduism and Islam had of each other, cohabitants as they were of one country, they were similar after all: each led to the same truth, each inspired by the same divine mandate.

He began to convey to others—wandering monks, sadhus, ascetics, drawn to the Kali Temple because of its reputation for generosity to itinerant holy men—the essentials of his discovery, citing an ancient Vedic aphorism but never understood in that era as it was now understood by him: *Truth is one: sages call it by various names.* He found, however, that the sages he encountered embraced the names more easily than the oneness that underlay them, and saw how long it would take to persuade conflicting religious men of the truth of the harmony of religions. But a start had been made. One man, at least, believed in that truth.

Both his nervous system and intellect alike were radically altered because of his Vedantic experiences whose psychological issue was that all indeed *were* one, bound at the depths of their separate beings by the One Undivided Being he called Brahman, the common single life animating each; and all had the divine *potential* he had discovered in himself, each was latently a god, a saint, a magazine of all Truth. Even animals and plants were pervaded by the blissful impersonal spirit that constituted their very existence, as St. Francis, likewise a knower of the nondual reality transcending his devotional passion for Christ, had demonstrated. Ramakrishna, once the devotee only, had loved others because they were children of the Divine Mother. Now, the knower of pure Truth, he *identified* with them, and with the whole world, as before him the master of Assisi and Buddha had done unforgettably.

In the Upanishads we are told that "he who knows Brahman becomes Brahman"—which, after our examination of Tota Puri (held to be a "knower" of Brahman), we may take with some reservations. In Ramakrishna's case none need be lodged. We might vary the statement to read: "He who knows that Life becomes that Life." This quite literally seems to have happened. One day as he was resting near the Panchavati, where a plot of virgin grass was growing, a man walked across a protected area of the fresh green blades and as he did Ramakrishna felt simultaneously a lash of pain across his body, which quickly became unbearable and lasted for hours. Another day he was standing close to the Ganges where two boatmen at the nearby landing-ghat were quarrelling bitterly, when suddenly the stronger of the two beat the other fiercely on his back. At which Ramakrishna felt instant pain and cried out, bringing Hriday to the scene, who noted the red welts on his master's back and heard with incredulity what had happened.

This kind of incident, as much as anything else, supports the claim of his followers that he was an incarnation of the divine.* Tota Puri, for example, although a master yogi, was very far from such empathy with all life. As were the saints. Who (to our knowledge) besides St. Francis and Buddha possessed this super-sensitivity, this infinite tenderness toward everything as well as everyone that breathes? On that count alone may we not include the Italian saint with Buddha as one of the avatars?

After the prolonged transcendental experience of Brahmic bliss it was clear that continued raptures of this kind would mean the end of his

---

* Earlier, such anecdotes would have seemed the myth-making of credulous devotees; at this stage of our study little about him is likely to surprise us.

bodily existence and the preclusion of any message of experiential wisdom he might have offered to his countrymen or to the world. That was why the command had come—and henceforth it became his habitual condition—to remain in *Bhavamukha*, the state of spiritual consciousness just between the impersonal and personal levels, where he would have instant access to the former—the Immeasurable—at all times, but simultaneously the world of creation and of *Maya*, the world of the Personal God, would constantly be before his vision, enabling him to interest his mind in what was happening around him sufficiently to "remain in the body"—and thus minimize, or prevent, the risk of plunging too deeply once again into the dissolving, annihilating ecstasy of the Absolute.

Meanwhile the prodigious sadhana of the Impersonal path had taken its toll on his health, which again was poor. Various diseases, including dysentery, assaulted him. The laws of Nature are one of the ways by which the deity has both limited and manifested itself and normally cannot be evaded any more than any of its other laws. He was urged from various quarters to visit his home country to recuperate, and without delay he agreed. Leaving his mother behind at Dakshineswar, and accompanied by Hriday and Yogeswari, he left for Kamarpukur and its environs in 1867, his first visit in nearly eight years.

The green paddy fields, the village lanes, the unchanging thatched houses, the little river, the tired peasants chanting hymns at sundown, the old, familiar faces—all heartened and refreshed him after the long, monumental struggle he had passed through, made him feel a surge of gratitude and love for the plot of earth that had given him life, given him a body, made it possible to become what he was. He drank in the sights, sounds, and smells of home as he had never done on the earlier visit, before the storm had been weathered, before the peace of realization had arrived. The relatives and villagers, delighted to have him back, noted his calm, outgoing response to them, dispelling their fears that the rumors of his madness, which continued to circulate year after year for the past decade, might be true. Their beloved Gadai was with them once more—so strange in many ways, so radiant, inspiring them with awe and shyness, a transformed Gadai; and yet the same boyish, amiable, high-spirited traits they remembered were not entirely vanished. They could not get enough of him—nor he of them. It was a mutual love feast.

And the fresh air, the purer water, the fragrant countryside, added to these more personal vibrations, quickly restored his health. Month after month the idyllic period went on, a serene, sequestered lake of content after the years of stormy sadhana.

The mutual rejoicing at his return shows him in a light of surpassing charm: the saint or prophet returning to his hearth to receive the embraces of faithful relatives and village friends, awed by his greatness but unable to restrain their delight in his presence once again. His other brother, Rameswar, having died, as well as Ramkumar, and his mother having remained at Dakshineswar in the care of Mathur, it was mostly relatives outside his immediate family that represented kith and kin now, it was to them and to the friends and neighbors of his youth that he paid tribute, as though discharging a debt not only to family but to his birthplace itself, and to those who had lived there with him.

This is a higher note than we have received in the teachings of other mystics, Christ notably.

We recall, inescapably, the Galilean's *A man's foes shall be those of his own household* (Matthew 10: 36) and something considerably less than sympathy that flourished between him and his brothers and sisters. In John 7: 4-5 his brothers are seen belittling his mission, suggesting he is afraid to "show himself to the world," and the evangelist openly declares that they "did not believe in him." To their insinuations Jesus replied: "My time is not yet come: but your time is always ready. The world cannot hate you; but me it hateth, because I testify of it, that its works are evil." The world cannot hate them, as pawns of nature, because they, the family, are the "world"—its spirit, its flesh, its devil—in every sense. In encountering the spirit of the world he finds embodied in the family reality, the spiritual seeker gains his first, and most painful, taste of what is in store for him during the early years of his struggle. The world "hateth" the Christ-principle, which exposes its darkness and evil works. Inevitably, then, his brothers, like the brothers of any saint or mystic, cannot "believe" in a reality of which they can have no conception: the Christ-consciousness.

Pressing upon us also is the far from abundant relationship between Jesus and his mother, first noted in the temple in his twelfth year, and then at the marriage at Cana when, in response to her remark that the hosts had no more wine, he declares, speaking to her symbolically for the benefit of his disciples (at least one of whom was present to transcribe the exchange): *Woman, what have I to do with thee? My hour is not yet come.* What do I—the enlightened consciousness, the higher principle in man—have to do with you, who represent merely creature-consciousness, materiality as opposed to spirituality, nature as opposed to spirit? Do not importune me with worldly matters, *your* concern: they are not mine.... Compounding this emphasis is the scene recorded by Matthew (12: 46-50):

> While he yet talked to the people, behold, his mother and his brethren stood without, desiring to speak with him.
>
> Then one said unto him, Behold, thy mother and thy brethren stand without, desiring to speak with thee.
>
> But he answered and said unto him, Who is my mother? and who are my brethren? And he stretched forth his hand toward his disciples, and said, Behold my mother and my brethren!
>
> For whosoever shall do the will of my Father in heaven, he is my brother, and sister, and mother.

Again there is the dichotomy in his mind, and in the instruction he is at pains to convey to the disciples, between what his mother -and-brothers represent (namely, the doing of some other will than his Father's) and what his followers symbolize: his true family, the brethren of his spirit.

The most innocent suggestion that the life of nature, of the family, including his own, is divinely favored, encountered his immediate resistance:

> And it came to pass, as he spake these things, a certain woman of the company lifted up her voice, and said unto him, Blessed is the womb that bare thee, and the paps which thou has sucked.
>
> But he said, Yea, rather, blessed are they that hear the word of God, and keep it.
>
> (Luke 11: 27-8)

All he will concede is the reluctant *Yea,* followed at once by "rather—"

with the implication that all under the influence of nature cannot keep the word of God because, deafened by materiality and the complacent egoism that is the mark of nature's presence in us, they cannot hear it.

I have come, he says elsewhere (Matthew 10: 35), to set son against father, daughter against mother. And: "If any man come to me, and hate not his father and mother and wife and children and brethren and sisters, yea, and his own life also, he cannot be my disciple" (Luke 14: 26). Fanatic cults, taking their cue from fundamentalist Christianity, have—in wanton mischief or tragic ignorance—interpreted the "me" and "I" of such passages as referring to Jesus the man, when of course, as in the passages preceding, the reference is to the principle incarnated in him, that of spiritual consciousness as opposed to the earth-consciousness represented by family. Flesh and blood cannot give birth to spirit, cannot understand spirit, and is—as we saw when studying Gadai's family life—compulsively opposed to spirit, particularly when it appears in their own midst.

The phrase, *and hate not his own [creaturely] life also,* illuminates his symbolic meaning precisely. Family members embody outwardly the same principle of creaturely egoism which is all too active in even the potential disciple, and it is *that*, clearly, which is to be "hated" (that is, "totally opposed"), in oneself or in the family, not the person, not the soul, not the divine latency.

We understand what he is saying. Nevertheless there is, too, an overriding sense of his unchangeable disillusionment toward families as such: his thinking in these passages comes through unmistakably, in spite of the manifestly symbolic emphasis.

Nor was there much more affection for the neighbors and townsmen who had known him from childhood, and who, when they discovered his powers and genius, were far from pleased:

> And when he had come into his own country, he taught them in their synagogue, and they were astonished, and said, Whence hath this man this wisdom, and these mighty works?
>
> Is not this the carpenter's son? Is not his mother called Mary? And his brothers James, and Joses, and Simon, and Judas? And his sisters, are they not all with us? Whence then hath this man all these things?
>
> And they were offended in him. But Jesus said unto them,

A prophet is not without honor, except in his own country, and in his own house.

And he did not many mighty works there because of their unbelief.

(Matthew 13: 54-58)

Mark (6: 4) has a similar passage, adding "and among his own kin."

It is not that Ramakrishna had not experienced how difficult families are for spiritual seekers. Recalling the early years of his struggle, he remarked: "I could not then bear the very atmosphere of worldly people, and felt when in the company of relatives, as if my breath would stop and the soul leave the body.... Relatives appeared to me to be enemies trying to push me down into deep pits; ... I could have peace only when I fled from them."* This is certainly as strong as, or stronger than, Jesus' sentiments on the theme, like the advice to his disciples much later: "When a man feels utter dispassion, he looks on the world as a deep well and his relatives as venomous cobras."** But the psychic devastations of *nirvikalpa*, after the complete dissolution of his separate ego, had made it impossible any longer to harbor such views. From which we conclude that Jesus' abrasive viewpoint toward family and villagers of Galilee reflects, at the time he gave voice to it, a more limited knowledge of the impersonal realm, suggesting that those sentiments were expressed at the outset of his career or else that he may never have fully ascended to the heights scaled by Ramakrishna.

The nondual enlightenment of Brahman, the divine Ground of the world, made Ramakrishna perceive every individual as a walking divinity, every religion as a sanctioned path to truth. Jesus, it is true, tells us "to love your neighbor as yourself"—counsel, as we deduced, derived from the highest illumination revealing very clearly to the mystic the *actual* oneness of life, and hence the truth of the idea that your neighbor, in his essence, *is* yourself.

But he cannot always follow his own instruction. With his family he obviously did not, nor with the Nazarenes, nor with the scribes and Pharisees whose gibes and mocks he returned in kind, no doubt retaining an inner control but occasionally giving vent to impatient, perhaps scornful ridicule of their willfulness and stiff-necked ignorance—an atti-

---

* *Great Master* 362, 366.
** *Gospel* 896.

tude we never encounter, for example, in Buddha, the epitome of gentle restraint, and, at worst, ironic ambiguity when challenged by obtuse intellects.

The traditional gentleness of Hindus—though more an ethnic than a true spiritual quality, to be sure[*]—doubtlessly facilitated Ramakrishna's loving embrace of the Kamarpukur villagers where the harsher tendencies of the Jews would have obstructed Jesus' attempts—as such undoubtedly were made—at similar *rapprochement* with relatives and townsfolk. We should also remember that some element in his karma had brought him into incarnation as a Jew himself, inheriting to a degree the same ethnic proclivities. This would explain what so often surprises us in the gospels—the animus, the strain of scornful impatience in his repartee with skeptics and adversaries. Admittedly their aggressive provocations would not conduce to peace of mind in any but the rarest. But he *was* the rarest. Or one of the rarest. His lack of perfect equanimity with them—unlike the poise, for example, he was able to exhibit with Pilate and throughout the last scenes, reminiscent of Socrates' similar conduct with *his* judges—may have been the product, in part, of that element in his constitution, in his karmic potential, namely, his Jewishness, which responded emotionally to aggressions in personal exchange according to the ancient mandate of the Hebrews: an eye for an eye.

Here, again, is an instance of that inexorable influence of nonspiritual factors—in this case hereditary traits—on one's spiritual character, even one of lofty development; a reminder that inner perfection may cohabit—nay, must—with an outer or personality pattern of tendencies that seems inconsistent with it, but which in fact proceeds, on the whole, largely independent of it.

In this area we have undeniably glimpsed considerable disparity between the two souls under study, and seem to perceive in Ramakrishna a more profound spirituality than that of the Galilean master—a spirituality that would have been too ethereal, too strange, *too* unprecedented for the earthliness that has always been a strong admixture in the Jewish character, even when it has attained spiritual dimensions. Consider how inconceivable in Buddha's emancipated personality are

---

[*] That is, what is ethnic is *from nature*: what is spiritual is *from will*. A merely *natural* gentleness could coexist, for example, with cheating or deceiving tendencies but a *spiritual* gentleness would be the result of the overcoming of such.

Moses' proneness to indignation, David's headstrong ways, or the vitu-
perative gift of the Hebrew Prophets generally, their native power to
denounce: all recognizable human traits, needing no divine guidance for
their implementation.

Necessary for the Jews—for Europe also, looming as a historical
shadow in the background—was a spirituality that would accommodate
itself to the ways of Westerners, among which were a love of debate, a
capacity for anger (witness the rout of the temple money-changers), and
a continuing concern over the ills of the body—hence the role of bodily
healing in Jesus' mission, something we do not find in Ramakrishna's
career nor in Buddha's, both possessing the Galilean's powers but declin-
ing to exercise them.

And, of course, a dramatic, commanding personality was what the
Jews would expect in a messiah, since the Hebrew tradition identified
leadership of any kind with capacity for *power*, for dominating the center stage of his time, such as they found in the long line of prophets and
patriarchs. In the West, too, the preacher-pastor becomes archetypally an
activist, somewhat thundering figure and inevitably much of his concep-
tualized *imago* conditions our expectations of the Christ-personality—
just as many Christians have *needed* a close, classic love-relationship
between the divine mother and the divine son, despite the clear evidence
to the contrary, and the result is the image immortalized in the *Pièta*.
What we need acutely enough we get. Except that with Jesus of Nazareth
we get something created not out of imaginations but out of considerable
evidence, much of it not too comfortable for the searcher in mystic
waters.

Some egotism in their savior, in other words, is what the Hebrews
and the West generally have required, to correspond to the characteristic,
ruling egotism of the Hebrew and sequentially the Western character. It
is not fundamentally different in the Muslim world. Imagine a St. Francis
attempting to generate in the Arabians of the sixth century a renewed religious spirit and preaching, to that wild, nomadic race of horsemen given
to blood-feuding, his message of nonviolence and universal tenderness
toward all creatures. He would have been fortunate to escape with his life.
But see the compelling Muhummad, with his message of conquest (not
unmixed, to be sure, with ethical incentives) and his readiness to take the
sword when necessary, and how swift his rise, how impressive his ascendancy, among a people for whom "resist not evil" and "turn the other

cheek" would have been received as the height of folly. So each people receives the prophet it can assimilate.

Jesus was right for the Jews for the reasons we have noted. They rejected him only in part because of his spirituality and his gospel. The more significant motive was that they felt he would be a menace to the state if his movement was allowed to flourish and they took the deepest offense in his equating himself with God—conceiving man divine, as well. (They killed him because his suggestion that they were immortal souls was unendurable.) But though the Jews rejected him (with what results history has witnessed), the West has not, for his personality meshes well with the Western concept of what a messiah must do: present a lofty message and at the same time a savior-image that would be comforting and not too unfamiliar to enable ordinary men to attach themselves to *him* in lieu of accepting his call to higher realizations, an image that would not be without certain minimal signs of ordinary self-centered humanity to make identification with him possible for the millions who would, before long, populate Europe.

The miracles are an example of this self-centeredness. No one can perform the wonders Jesus did without calling attention to himself as a man. His message obviously meant more to him than the prodigies but throughout his ministry the dramatic, almost the theatric aspect is inescapable. This is what was required, what the West expected in a savior.*

His frequent reminders that "my time is not yet," "my hour is not yet come" is another illustration of the same self-dramatizing trait. Undeniably what he said was true: his hour *had* not yet come, but *would* come when the Higher Will ordained it. A divine script *had* been written, with certain scenes fated to unfold, to which he held the master key. But both Ramakrishna and Buddha became aware, early in their careers, that they were pursuing more than their own particular destinies, that the happiness of millions of others would hang on the success or failure of their struggles, that they were but instruments in

---

* The expectation has continued to the present, evident in the widespread anticipation among fundamentalist sections of Christendom of an Armageddon to be fought at the end of time, with Christ, his early evangelical, wonder-working image now perfected into a triumphant, militaristic genius overpowering hordes of atheists and Antichrists: the adherents of this messianic hope forgetting that his message is one of nonviolence, sacrifice, and loving one's enemies!

the hands of powers that be. Yet no self-dramatization emerges from either. They shrink from any attention being called to themselves in any way whatever. With Jesus the drama is highlighted, externalized. The script is public in Palestine, private in Asia, because the Jews, and their descendents in the West, needed vicarious participation in a divine melodrama to be impressed—either negatively or positively—with the messiah's teachings. Since the secret to the inner world was open to only a few, others had to experience that world in vivid outer symbols before their minds would pause to wonder at their significance. Jesus marches to his fate in perfect rhythm with the hidden chords sounding in his soul from supernal regions, but all eyes, fascinated and mystified, are always on him while he lived, and in the intervening centuries the phenomenon has continued. The man has overshadowed the teachings for everyone except those few mystics who have seen in the teachings the universal gospel of mysticism. The man, not the message, is felt to save—yet surely only the message is the saving power. "You shall know the truth," he said, "and the truth shall make you free"—but he acted, perhaps in spite of himself at times, as though he himself could free. But no *man* can free us, no *man* is worthy of adoration. Only the divine may be adored, only the truth—universal, impersonal, beyond time and personalities—will save us.

What, then, of our earlier conclusion that Jesus had experienced the same nondual transcendental Reality that Ramakrishna, though more powerfully, had known, and as a result had truly become the Christ? Qualified by these reflections, the conclusion may stand. He had, we cannot doubt, become united with the Absolute Existence— "I and my Father are One"—but not to such a degree, and not for so long a period, that his ego was completely effaced. During the transformative experience itself it would have been totally *neutralized*—immobilized, rendered latent—but the seeds of its reality would not have been destroyed, would have stirred into life after his return to the normal plane—stirred sufficiently for him to act in the manner we have sketched.

A man in whom the ego had been extirpated could not have driven anyone, using a whip, out of the temple, whatever the provocation. We do not say what his response would have been. But it would have been different.

This is not to suggest the anger was involuntary. For certain, it was largely voluntary, assumed for a purpose, *put on*, as it were, the way a mother puts on anger to sweep her naughty children out of the pantry where her pies are stored and the moment they are out she puts the anger off. So with Jesus and the money-changers that day. He, master-yogi that he was, could easily have pretended an anger he did not feel but the impression conveyed, because of the effect of his yoga power, would have been anger indeed—striking fear into the hearts of the profaners of the temple.

The action served, again, to draw attention to himself not as a messiah or as a prophet but as a man: a dominant personality when he wished to be. Every European reading his Bible, for centuries to come, could identify with him and with the incident, and see himself doing the same thing, for the same reasons (though *compulsively*): for such a man it is not enough to be godly; one has to act like a dramatic hero, too.

Christ's moment of destiny on Golgotha is *visibly* great—publicly so, one may say. Buddha's comparable hour, equally celebrated in Buddhist lands, is all internal: the struggle for enlightenment. The lesson Jesus wishes to impart by his crucifixion is the immutable necessity of sacrifice as the way to our own awakening and resurrection. But for us in Western lands, outer-oriented as we are, this universal message, endlessly preached in Hinduism and Buddhism for thousands of years and pervasively assumed by their sages, does not come through clearly unless we see it demonstrated in an outer, iconic fashion. Only a divine incarnation of a certain type can serve that purpose and carry out the action with powerful effect and charismatic beauty, as Jesus so flawlessly does—one in whom exists, along with the divine properties, an admixture of sufficient egoism to enable him to act in such a way as to strike significant chords of empathy in us who still have so much egoism. One who, while close to his divine Source, is capable of the grand gesture, the mesmerizing act, the magisterial utterance: "This day thou shalt be with me in paradise." We have the incarnation we needed.

In India they would have accepted and glorified his message (as historically they have) of the indwelling divinity and the way this divinity is to be realized—*Blessed are the pure of heart, for they shall see God*—but they would have felt (as indeed they do) that the miracles were unnecessary, that too many yogis possess the same powers, that they were but a distraction from the purity of his teachings, a kind of *panem et circenses* provided for the masses not enough awakened to practice meditation and seek the inward flame. They would have preferred a combination of his deathless teachings with a character more resembling that of St. Francis, who, in point of fact, is regarded in India among the spiritually discriminating as an avatar.*

Indeed, the Umbrian saint seems in some respects an advance beyond Jesus, although climbing on his master's shoulders to surpass him, toward the dizzying heights of character-transformation achieved by Ramakrishna. The more of the human there remains in the man the more attractive on one level he may be to us but thereby we are assured of the limits of his unfolded divinity. Nor must the self-effacement be practiced only: all of us are practicing it constantly, achieving it seldom. It must be established, *it must be* the *man himself,* after he has passed through the fires of the ego-life, of which there seems less in Francis than in Jesus—and therefore there will be more cosmic sense, greater universality, more of the divinity realized, just as Jesus goes so far beyond Moses and the Hebrew prophets, who, though mystics genuine enough, were more rooted in the Jewish ethnic passion than he and far from the universal seer the mystic aims toward, and whom in our dreams we still prefigure.

In the same way Ramakrishna appears to represent a similar evolution of the Indian religious personality, but since his predecessors, except for the sublime Tathagata, are so little known in the West, a comparison would bear little fruit. Beyond him, casting a contemplative glance into the future, we cannot conjecture the lineaments of *his* superior, would have no real way of visualizing him, since he himself is beyond our power to comprehend. As Jesus the Christ surely is. All the God-men surpass our understanding and in attempting to assess them we grope forward through the passages of minds rarely touched with the brilliance that guided *them* at every step.

Returning to the idyll at Kamarpukur, we find Ramakrishna tender toward everyone, seeing the divine light shimmering through every face—that light, resurrected permanently in his soul, enabling him to perceive everything in its luminous fire. The Vedantic truth of "love

---

* Hundreds of Hindus every year can be found making a reverent pilgrimage to Assisi and the legendary mountain.

your neighbor as yourself" became actualized, a fixed reality in his mystic gaze, full of effulgent love. Gone were the "vipers" and "cobras" and "enemies" of the early years. He saw them as perhaps the Personal God would see humanity if he could incarnate. It is doubtful that Jesus' interpretation of the world of relatives and family represented the highest the Supreme itself could achieve in an embodied state. Higher is Francis' identification not only with human but with all life (again, like Buddha in this respect), including that of the animal kingdom. Birds were said to hearken to the language he spoke to them and the understanding he brought to theirs, and wild beasts, in the same legend, were said to be tamed, dissuaded from their destructive courses by his appeal to reason. Nor did he exclude plants and trees from his embracing pity. Even the elements stirred in him a motion of affinity: water and fire, in the well-known canticle, inspiring surges of animistic response.

Although Ramakrishna's injunctions to caution when dealing with relatives, treating them at times as wild animals conditioned to swallow up our virgin spirituality, were communicated long after his Kamarpukur apocalypse of love, it does not mean that he regressed. The mind that perceived his village neighbors and kin with such burning empathy was not subject to further deviations, to a sliding back to previous levels: to where, for example, he had truly *felt* the reality of those objurgations, when the sting of the emotional experience that had given rise to them was indeed real, felt on his nerves. An actual *transmutation* had taken place. A mind formerly of brass or bronze was now of gold (to recall one of his exchanges with Tota Puri), that alters not, whatever the conditions to which it is exposed.

Those injunctions obviously were intended to apply to spiritual life in its early stages. They were designed to kindle vigilance and determination in the aspirant as he struggled to fledge his way through the morass of bondages, attachment, discouragement, and emotional blackmail to which family and relatives resort to forestall the launching of the new consciousness, the commencement of our eternal life, they representing, as we have seen heretofore, the force of matter in human relations, the self-perpetuation of blind habit. Ultimately the light of God may be seen radiating through their eyes if sufficient visionary power is brought to bear upon the perception (such as the pure Divine itself would do), but the fire of pure egoism is more immediately apparent, a dark force of intimidation and conformity that must, like the lions of legend, be faced down and overcome before the gates of the sacred temple will open to the questing soul.

During that period Ramakrishna's early warnings and Christ's similar pronouncements are realistic, clear summaries of the actual psychological condition we face. To the spiritual man his enemies shall indeed "be those of his own household"—for the household, as we have seen unmistakably in the passage where Christ retorted to the insinuations of his brothers, represents everything the soul does not, and must fear and avoid if it is eventually to discover itself, know its own powers in direct mystical experience, and then turn back to those same enemies and "cobras" and, if the advancing experiences are deep enough and—lest we forget—*impersonal* (that is, universal) enough—see them as Ramakrishna saw them, or at least some approximation of that, and as Buddha, who had forgotten his father during the years of his titanic struggles, later saw him, eager then to return to visit him: "No opportunity should be lost," he said, "to do reverence to those who have given us life." We are, in short, to the degree they can receive it and to the degree we can impart it, to transmit to them the gathered grace of our transformed consciousness.

To parents first of all, then to family and relatives, must be paid the immense and unpayable debt of life, of rearing, education, and numberless other hidden obligations, as well as providing the resistance to our spiritual awakening that enabled us—through sheer necessity—to assert, out of the dark inner depths of the subconscious world, the power of our wills, the force of our resolution, and to do this not once but many times, until the forging of a strength undreamed-of is completed: in the process having gained self-knowledge, insights untellable into the nature of things. By then we are apart from them, lost in the solitude of the city, or in a hermitage, or desert, but with the ripening of the process, and the deepening of our mystical intuition—that is, our insight into the true nature of life—we return to the nest and attempt, if with uneven success, what Ramakrishna was able to do to such perfection, in that rare tableau at Kamarpukur after the eight years' absence.

So all-pervasive has Christ's influence been in the West, however, that an uncountable number of Christian monastics have been led to adopt toward their families the attitude enjoined upon them by statement, and by implication—such as his distant, symbolic relationship with his mother. In the first years of spiritual striving the ego is at its most inflamed as we take steps to control and atrophy it. The psychic sensitivity that results as it strikes back to reclaim its lost terrain often unbalances our interpretation of difficult or ambiguous scriptural passages and leads us to construe them in ways *dictated by the ego itself* (so rampant and permeating is its power in the first years) though of course we are not conscious, or not entirely conscious, of this serpentine mechanism. How easy to conclude, from Christ's warning about the nature of household life, that the family is actually our enemy in every way, and not merely symbolic adversaries by virtue of material, earth-centered power that has them in thrall. And the passages about setting family members against each other, and "if any man come to me, and hate not his father and mother ... and brethren and sisters ... he cannot be my disciple"—how difficult not to gather from these strictures confidence that the acute resentment one feels toward the family during those anguished first months and, it may be, years, has divine sanction—a resentment generated, in fact, not so much by *their* unreasonableness and egoism but by the retaliatory power of our own as, lacking yet spiritual insight, we attempt to cope with their oppressive ways on the creaturely, egocentric level, with the resulting pain and suffering, to an intolerable degree, that this brings. *Then* the beatitudes do not charm us in the measure that the anathemas fortify.

And in all this no suggestion that it was only a phase we pass through on the way to worship of the parents as gods, and a reverent embrace of other family members as ours in life—perhaps ours in past lives. No suggestion from Christ—but none, either, from other major *gurus* of mankind. Here, too, Ramakrishna was breaking new ground for the spiritual world to take heed, making it clear that a climactic, unitive approach to one's family is to be the way of the future, demonstrated first by him during that epochal 1867 visit, which, appropriately, proved to be only the first in a number he made to his home region in the years ahead.

Although the chief figure in this revolutionary teaching—his mother—did not accompany him to the inland village, his relation with her over the preceding four years not only reflected the sweeping change he was inaugurating in his outlook but anticipated it. It will be recalled that she had come to Dakshineswar (never to return home) soon after the completion of the Tantric disciplines in 1863, the delicate and arduous regimen that had placed at its center, in its innermost core, the figure of a woman, requiring the acolyte to worship her, surrender his powers to her in acknowledgment of her divine character, and in the realization of this unique nature to gain illumination for himself.

The esoteric heights of Tantra mastered, he stood ready to receive his mother, regarding her now in a changed light, and offering not only the reflexive veneration stipulated in brahminical tradition but a liberated reverence derived from his changed consciousness. The significance of her arrival just then is all the more marked by her coming to the very place of his tortured discoveries, the very cave of his struggles, the lair where he had bearded the lion and transformed it into a lamb of gentleness: the sanctuary where the bright new wisdom had descended on him was visited by her who, prior to that, had epitomized the enemies of his life.

Every day since then, and every day in the years to follow (until she passed away at the age of eighty-five in 1876), he spent some time with her; it always pleased him to bring some food to her and stay while she finished it. Everything about his demeanor toward her confirmed the statements he often made, that he thought of her as the veritable manifestation of the Divine Mother whom, in secret contemplation, he worshipped at the Kali Temple ... though every mother, it should be remembered, not Chandra alone, would equally reflect this ideal.

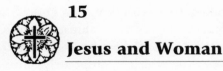

15

Jesus and Woman

ALTHOUGH JESUS AND HIS mother, from the available narratives, did not enjoy this kind of interaction, one intuits that, somewhere in his hidden journey to greatness, along a road that may have taken him to India (as has traditionally been believed in the arcane schools), he had passed through the Tantric fires and emerged the worshipper of the feminine that women have always felt him to be—hence their continu-

ing adoration century after century. Not only the conspicuous tenderness that resonated between him and Mary of Magdala but his graceful
guidance of the devotional Mary of Bethany and her more active sister,
Martha, suggest an easy rapport with woman's nature which only the
sensualist and the realized soul attain: each seeing in her a mirror of his
own character.

There is also the life-like exchange with the Samaritan woman,
where high philosophy is discussed with a female member of a people
despised by orthodox Jews, whom he had encountered by chance at a
drinking well after a long day's march with his disciples through the
country of Samaria. His unhesitating engagement of her in conversation, asking her to pour him a drink, reveals not only his disregard for
current mores—which he has demonstrated often before—but his tacit
assumption that the woman—an ordinary, rather superstitious woman,
we discover—is capable of grasping the subtle, enigmatic philosophy he
is propounding. The scene resounds with a sense of trust on his part,
admiration and awe on hers (she thinks he must be a "prophet" because
he can "read her thoughts"), and a naturalness and ease displayed by
both toward the other.

His magnanimity appears modern, indeed, and offers us a significant
advance over the skeptic views toward woman we find in the Light of
Asia, who, it is said, refused to allow women into his monastic order on
the grounds of their inherent inability to grasp high spiritual truths and
their unstable character. Only with reluctance did he yield to his disciples on the issue. Buddha in this respect—if what was attributed to him
was true—was victimized by the myth of female intellectual incapacity
which had for so many centuries flourished resistlessly in complacent
male psyches. Krishna expresses the same "craze" in the *Gita* (IX, 32),
where, grouped with the lowest castes, women are denied the essential
qualifications for spiritual attainment.[*]

But here is Jesus, tired and thirsty, stopping at a well in the alien
district of Samaria, speaking alone to a strange woman he encounters
there, one whom he also knows, at once, has led a promiscuous life.
That she is a member of a despised group, and is immoral besides, he

---

[*] Another interpretation is that both God-men knowingly reflected the views
held about women in their respective ages. To have shown greater liberality
would have disturbed their audience so much that their credibility would have
been tarnished and the impact of their essential message blunted.

ignores, perceiving something else in her able to absorb his allusive symbolizing and to respond to him personally. And if this woman, it would seem, then *any woman*—any feminine consciousness—was able to recognize the voice of truth whenever she encountered it:

> Whosoever drinketh of this water shall thirst again:
> But whosoever drinketh of the water I shall give him shall never thirst; for what I give shall be in him a well of water springing up into everlasting life.
> The woman saith unto him, Sir, give me this water, that I thirst not....

They discuss ways of worshipping God. There were the ways of the past—

> But the hour cometh, and now is, when the true worshippers shall worship the Father in spirit and in truth: for the Father seeketh such to worship him.
> God is a spirit: and they that worship him must worship him in spirit and in truth.
>
> (John 4: 13-14, 23-24.)

This famous passage we would remember wherever we found it but it is all the more arresting for appearing where it actually occurred: at Jacob's well in Samaria, delivered to a woman never seen before, whose name we never learn, destined for no role in the story. Just a woman....

Nor can we overlook the graphic encounter, etched permanently in the mind of everyone who has read it, involving Jesus and the woman taken in adultery, against whom a mandatory punishment of stoning was to be invoked by the scribes and pharisees who, gloatingly pious, vindictive in their righteousness, had brought him to her to test his adherence to the Law, and his immortal response: "He that is without sin among you, let him cast the first stone" (John 8: 3-11).

Man must not condemn any woman, even the woman who gives herself to men, freely or for hire, since her role would not exist, would not have to exist, if men's natures were different from what the world so well knows they are: dominated by lust, incapable of continence except for rare and palpable divine grace. The immoral woman, sacrificing herself on the altar of male necessity, is an instrument of the Supreme easing the pain of men he has himself caused, and therefore to reject or stone the woman who lives for men, at whatever cost to her own integrity in the end, is to contravene the divine will directly. No man, then, may condemn her.* To the man of truth *realized* the prostitute is like an incarnation of the Lord coming in melancholy guise to make the lives of certain men a little more tolerable—to give them by her comfort a hope to go on living in their almost unendurable folly.**

In the interval between the woman's condemnation and Jesus' reply to her accusers he seemed to write something on the ground, "as though he heard them not," mystifying them, causing an inner shift in their mood of sadistic triumph. During this dramatic important pause the flame of their zeal cooled sufficiently for his pregnant remark to burn its way into their consciences, reminding each of the truth of his condition: that at every moment he was in a state of sin, and in imagination, at very least, had lived more profligately than the accused woman.

---

* Moses' legislating of a harsh fate for the fallen woman seems to reveal the limitation of his vision, as compared with Christ's, but the task confronting him was unique and formidable, and only an iron-willed taskmaster, as well as a man of God, could have accomplished it: the forging of a unified nation, religiously grounded, out of a mass of murmuring, wayward malcontents. This mandate was, moreover, from the Supreme—it *had* to be successfully carried out. Governing by love alone, by pure inspiration, under the circumstances, was out of the question. Governing by love alone, by pure inspiration, under the circumstances, was out of the question. Governing by fear, mira cle, mystery, and intimidation was also necessary—as Muhammad, a latter-day-Moses (so similar their personalities, their peoples, and their missions), also discovered two thousand years later. Unquestionably his stern rule left its ineffaceable mark on the Hebrew character for the rest of time— instilling into it its fixation on the letter of the law, but nevertheless his methods succeeded: the nation *was* forged, the tradition established, and Christ when he came (for whose coming Moses had governed and Jewish history prepared), found accessible to him that nation and tradition, by then long-standing and powerful, which would serve his own messianic dream, and his own mandate—to inspire the founding of a new faith like none ever seen in the West. Without the Judaic tradition there had been no Christ, no Christianity, no Western civilization. Seen in this light, the fiercer elements of the Mosaic code, like their counterparts in that of Muhammad, take on an aspect of historical necessity, despite the individual suffering it produced.

** Ramakrishna, being taken to Calcutta one day some years later, shocked his disciples in attendance by halting the carriage, dismounting and prostrating himself before several prostitutes seated in front of a well-known house of ill fame.

I do not condemn thee, Jesus tells her at the end of the scene. *Go and sin no more.* Neither condoning nor condemnation. The via media of compassion and understanding—of forgiveness. The Buddha's way. The way so rarely followed in many Christian sects, where condemnation of carnal sins has been malignantly widespread for centuries—so much so that "to sin" became, in Christian lands, identified with "sex," though there was no justification for this trend of thought, no sanction for condemnation of sexual misdeeds from Christ himself. No condoning, but no condemnation. Yet here in this scene, as well as in the exchange with the Samaritan woman, he had rare opportunities to declare his mind on the subject, which untold numbers of clergymen would not have overlooked. The sanction for judgment, not issuing from the gospels, must have arisen in their own breasts.

How often Christ seems to be connected with such women, even in the fragments of his life the gospels furnish us. If we had the full record how many more such encounters we might expect. Reincarnationist philosophy reveals that we draw to us those experiences still part of our karma, for good or ill, to be worked out until we are free of them. Christ's mysterious relationship with Magdalene seems to have been of this nature, with some final series of actions on his part necessary before the balance could be restored and both he and she stand free of the complex web of a karmic past. In the same way, to test the depth and authenticity of his compassion toward all such women—each of them aspects of a universal womanhood—various other promiscuous females would be drawn into his orbit to receive the grace of his forgiveness, his courteous tenderness, his inner worship—to be freed, then, of the sins or lifestyle that had bound them theretofore.

Her sins, which are many, are forgiven; for she loved much, he had chided Simon the Pharisee, distressed over Mary Magdalene's protracted adoration. The correspondence between her many sins and her much loving is clear. The way of life such a woman chooses brings happiness to men but to herself degradation, though, as we have just observed, she can be seen to some extent as a sacrificial figure, offering bliss and comfort to men anguished by lust—one of woman's divine functions. On this level the function is abused and the woman sensualized into ruin, but the function itself is not lost, nor her innate feminine capacity (almost unlimited) for loving, and the sexuality we see as an aspect of, indeed an expression of, the vast power of love in the feminine soul. This is an integral theme in Tantric philosophy, which recognizes in even the prostitute and her ways with males a variation, however tragic in the long run, of the power of the eternal feminine to bring joy and encouragement to struggling men. Jesus' behavior with women of this type suggests an exposure not only to the philosophy but the practice of Tantra. That his once-beloved woman, his feminine principle in those by-gone lifetimes, Mary of Magdala, had become one of them would only have intensified his compassion and renewed his awareness of the divine nature of their role, despite its spiritual debasement in the end.

No wonder women—the men fleeing—followed him to the cross and to the tomb, hoping when hope seemed lost, and they have been following him to the same cross through the centuries, feeling his magnetic pull, his charismatic love for them, his graceful ways, his intuitive tact and gentle irony at times, his noble seriousness. For woman—ever tempted and tempting, ever aware of her weakness—he has always been the ideal man.

If, while he lived, his apparent neglect of his mother and other relatives indicates an enlightenment less than perfect, his relation with women generally—Mary and Martha of Bethany come to mind at once—and with sensual, lust-bound women in particular, is beyond praise, due, very possibly, to the profound revelations of *Tantra* being brought to bear upon the operation of karmic ties, and compensates for the other deficiency, redressing the balance.

16

Departure of Yogeswari

TWO MORE WOMEN ARE to be accounted for, both of surpassing importance to Ramakrishna, confronting each other for the first time during that landmark 1867 visit to Kamarpukur: one representing the past, one the future. The confrontation was dramatic and, for all concerned, painful. Throughout, Ramakrishna conducted himself with the same impeccable grace we have observed in Christ with the opposite sex. The two women were Yogeswari and Sarada, the girl from the neighboring village of Jayrambati to whom, eight years before, he had been betrothed.

Eager for a reunion—actually a first meeting, since she could scarcely recall her husband from their brief contacts then—Sarada, almost fourteen, spiritually developed far beyond her years, joyfully visited him in Kamarpukur for some weeks during his sojourn, and he delighted himself in her presence. He began to give her not only simple spiritual instruction but advice on many domestic, social, and worldly matters: she should study the ways of behaving appropriately on all occasions, suiting her words and manner to the time, place, and company. She should learn to judge the character of various kinds of people, men especially. She should know how to handle money. When boarding a carriage or boat she should enter first in order to find a good seat, and when leaving depart last to make sure she hadn't forgotten anything.

Sarada later said that she felt in those weeks as though a pitcher of bliss was constantly pouring in her heart.

What Yogeswari felt however was not bliss but jealousy, masked to others and to herself as maternal concern for a spiritual son, who for so long had been traveling out of her reach and beyond her understanding. Gripped by the unique destiny that had brought them together, that had graced her life with a mantle of mentorship to a God-man, she had been unable to leave Dakshineswar when her work was done, unable to turn from the effulgent flame generated by his ongoing austerities and divine inebriation, and powerless to overcome the promptings of her own possessive love. She felt that his continued close relation with the beautiful girl might jeopardize his continence and did not hesitate to tell him so. We recall her apprehensions, two years earlier, when Tota Puri had arrived at the temple. His love of God would be destroyed by the dry wind of Knowledge, she argued: not suspecting that if the experience of Knowledge is profound enough one's love is intensified beyond measure, for now it springs not only from emotion but from will, from reality itself.

In fact, she was jealous and anxious toward anyone who gained his attention, attributing to herself an importance in his life that surpassed what it had genuinely once been. Spiritual pride, the most pernicious and tenacious of the deadly sins, thoroughly possessed her: if people did not listen to her they would come to harm; by obeying her they would be doing the will of God.

Ramakrishna, while maintaining his respect and devotion to her, had gently but firmly paid no heed to her on past occasions, nor did he now. The daily intimate exchanges with his maiden-wife proceeded and Yogeswari became resentful, her conduct gradually growing more erratic, vain, unchecked. When someone discussing spiritual matters with her indicated that he planned to get Ramakrishna's opinion as well, she was heard to retort: "What can he say? It is I who have opened his eyes!"

She began to bicker over trivial matters with the women of the family, which placed them in a difficult position: they knew, to a degree, the role she had played in the career of their beloved Gadai and also respected her as a high brahmin lady leading the life of a nun. Sarada, instructed by Ramakrishna on how to behave with her, was a model of reverence and service, knowing, of course, that it was her own relation with the master that had precipitated all the discontent which, increasingly, raged around them. But while everyone else struggled to show Yogeswari the respect they felt her due, the nonmeditative Hriday had no such scruples and quarrelled openly with her, particularly when Yogeswari, educated and disciplined among unlettered rural folk, went so far as to disregard their established regulations on the matter of food, the cleaning afterwards, and similar long-standing customs. Within a short time everyone was vexed, the situation rapidly reaching toward a climax, Ramakrishna, noninterfering, alone remaining calm in the tempest his former guru had generated.

Somehow the Brahmani's anger at length cooled sufficiently to enable her to reassess her behavior in circumstances where she was, after all, only a guest, not a mistress, and she was able to realize she had been in the wrong from the outset, including her shocking conduct toward Ramakrishna. Repentance followed, and a meeting with him that reconciled their minds once again. But she had lost face so badly in that setting that she knew she must leave—to renew her monastic vows and re-engage her energies in neglected spiritual disciplines. Making a bouquet of flowers for Ramakrishna, she worshipped him as the God-man she had been the first of all to proclaim, and then quietly went her way—heading for the holy city of Benares, where, according to legend, liberation follows if you depart this life there.

• • •

From the behavior of Yogeswari, following our analysis of Tota Puri, we are confirmed in the melancholy truth that egoism—with its derivatives: attachments, aversions, cravings—is the problem of life. Nothing seems to be able to kill it except the experience of the Supreme at some ultimate psychic level. Short of that, we can at best hope to control or check it, perhaps disguise it, hopefully reduce it, but given enough provocation, or inattention from inferiors, or rejection of our advice, or whatever, it will leap out in all its fiery manic willfulness and pull down everything rather than yield. So formidable is the power of nature and the original nature-given identity, from which this phenomenon of egoism takes its rise, that the tremendous spiritual realizations that gave saints and mystics their power, brilliance, magnetism, and self-control, *overlay* much of the native character, leaving large areas of it intact from grace, secure in its self-assumption that the possessor is not only saved—as Yogeswari assumed—but the instrument of others' salvation. In short, the instrument comes to believe he is the initiator.

Generally we do not like to contemplate such possibilities. The saint is an archetypal figure in our imaginations, and we transfer that mythic character to the perceived man. But the reality has been so nakedly brought home to us that it behooves us to revise our dreams of sainthood, while still aspiring to that estate—still believing the truth of Leon Bloy's *mot:* "There is only one sorrow—not to be a saint." In later years Ramakrishna is reported to have remarked that "The vanities of all others may die out, but the vanity of a saint as regards his sainthood is hard indeed to wear away."* Which seems a precise summation of his experience of Yogeswari—and earlier, of Tota Puri—in the last years of their relationship.

She had misjudged his relationship with Sarada grievously and in her assumption that his experience of the Impersonal reality would destroy his devotional nature she had been totally mistaken. But, in the Kamarpukur crisis, for having seen her error and presumption, her elitist arrogance, for having accepted the difficult fact that it had been she who had been in the wrong, not the others, she deserves credit. And for gracefully withdrawing from the scene of Ramakrishna's life into the obscurity of solitary monastic practice, she deserves praise.

---

* F. Max Müller, *Ramakrishna, His Life and Sayings* (1899), 172, cited in William James, *Varieties of Religious Experience* (New York, 1902), Modern Library ed., 357 fn. Also: Mentor ed., New American Library (1958) 282 fn.

A few months later, while touring sites of pilgrimage with Mathur and Hriday, he met her in Benares. They had several warm and joyful meetings together in the house where she was staying; from there he went on to Vrindavan, associated with the childhood of Krishna, and she accompanied him. Before he left, a few days later, he requested her to remain there permanently, which she did. Shortly after his departure, she passed away.

When the seven months in Kamarpukur ended, Ramakrishna returned to Dakshineswar, Sarada went back to her own village, and they were not to meet again for nearly five more years. But now she knew what her husband was like, and he knew her. When the call would come to go to him there would be no hesitation on her part. A new theophany for modern man awaited their reunion.

 ## 17

Ramakrishna as Pilgrim

AFTER HIS RETURN TO Dakshineswar the stay was short. Within a few weeks he was traveling again, in an extravagant pilgrimage tour planned, organized, and financed by Mathur, who brought with him, besides Ramakrishna and Hriday, one hundred and twenty-five persons, including dozens of servants, all to visit the venerable religious shrines in north-central India along the Ganges and its tributaries. Several railway cars were hired as part of the huge expense involved in the housing and feeding of so many.

En route they passed through a village where the inhabitants had been reduced to starvation. Ramakrishna asked Mathur to feed them and give them some clothing. But since money spent in this way could not serve the purpose of the pilgrimage, a considerable part of which was the exalting of Mathur's image as a benevolent devotee of God, he objected to the added expense, and when he persisted Ramakrishna got

out of his carriage, sat down with the villagers, and refused to go on.
Mathur's money, he declared, was his only in trust. It was actually the
Lord's, he merely its steward. This was an idea to which Mathur paid
contented lip service but being an *outward* man could never actually
believe in. Nevertheless when he saw that Ramakrishna would not
move until he relented, he was forced to yield. There were other occasions when an almost identical scene occurred.

After twelve years of close association with a Ramakrishna,
Mathur, his walrus mustache reinforcing his status, was still at heart a
zemindar—just as Hriday, despite an equal length of time of even closer
association, was similarly unchanged. (Buddha in the *Dhammapada*
remarked that a fool—for whom we may substitute a worldly man, who
is another kind of fool—traveling with a wise man can no more obtain
true knowledge than a spoon can taste the flavor in a bowl of soup.)
The man who objected to feeding the outcaste poor, an act that could
add nothing to his reputation, did not object to feeding large numbers
of brahmin pandits and their families in Benares and giving them money
when he left, a philanthropy which would not go unreported.
Everywhere he went he moved in princely pomp, with servants before
and after, expensive maces borne on either side, a silver umbrella held
over his head. After the fortune spent on this tour, he organized one or
two similar ventures during the next three years, with Ramakrishna
their chief justification. Wherever he went people saw the holy man of
Dakshineswar and with him constantly—the power *behind* him, his
patron, protector, discoverer, the famous devotee: Mathura Mohan
Biswas of Calcutta.

It is curious to observe Ramakrishna making a pilgrimage, since his
religious passion had been focused inward so intensely for a decade past.
Pilgrimages, which have an ancient place in all religions, are mostly for
seekers who have not discovered the reality of inwardness. He went
partly to satisfy a lifelong desire actually to *see* some of the famous
shrines about which for years he had heard so much. And he went to set
an example to others, those present and to come. While he knew that
the universal religion of mysticism—intuitive, direct knowledge of the
divine—was present in all religions for those who wished to find it, he
also knew that few others had as yet this understanding, including few
of his countrymen. For them, pilgrimage was almost as essential as it

was to Muslims for gaining the divine favor; to strengthen them in that assumption—a necessary stage in their evolution to higher insight—he was seen to make the rounds of available shrines, to spend time at each, to manifest sincere devotion to all, experiencing ecstasies constantly.

At Benares, dedicated to Shiva, he had a vision of the god—assisted by Kali, his consort—liberating the souls of the recently deceased, as the legend of the place promised, but his autonomic, vision-fed imagination would have been so prone to such an experience, so inviting of such, that it would have been strange if nothing of the sort had taken place. Krishna appeared to him in Vrindavan—as he had to so many others *looking* for him there where he had sported with the milkmaids in his boyhood.

At Navadvip, the birthplace of Chaitanya, the vision was more impressive. He had gone there to discover if the area suggested anything of divine ambience, since he was not yet fully convinced that Chaitanya was what his devotees claimed he was: Krishna reborn. For some time he wandered about the town, assessing it with mystic measures of the inner world, finding no indication of special divinity until he was ready to leave, when a sudden and overwhelming revelation seized him, producing instant samadhi, as the spiritual form of the saint, of molten gold, entered into him in a fire of ecstasy. After this, Chaitanya was included on his list of unique personalities who had appeared as divine incarnations—*avatars;* those who *descend* from beyond to illumine mankind.

Pilgrimages served another purpose in his life: to excite in his mind desires—spiritual in nature—for visible, earthly objects. A mind of gold, as his had become after six-months' immersion in the Brahman-world, would have difficulty finding reasons to keep returning to the embodied, dross-dominated condition, despite the divine injunction to do so. Desires—which plague other men by their plenitude and insatiability— in him were so few that his mind, more than ever, found its natural habitat in the mystic realm of *samadhi*, the state beyond desire, beyond distinctions, the state of essences. His problem, as we saw, was to keep his mind sufficiently interested each day in the life around him, or in the prospects of things to come, so that he could carry out the divine mandate and not lose himself forever in the undifferentiated bliss of the Absolute. Pilgrimages helped to ameliorate the problem. Later it would be the anticipation of his disciples coming that provided the chief "desire."

To intensify the spiritual atmosphere of the shrines themselves was another factor motivating him—to leave them more heightened with spiritual charisma than he found them. The divine presence, for certain, was everywhere in the world, but could be felt especially in places where thousands, perhaps over time millions, of pilgrims had come to pray, worship, and meditate, many of them holy individuals.

How many uncounted devotees have, by their own prayers and awe, their own spirituality, created auras of holiness in that spot in Nepal where the Bodhi Tree, before it was decimated by the pious, was said to have stood; or the Sinai desert mount where Moses, self-exiled, communed with all creation, gave voice to the Self within— "I am what I am"; or where, in the Mount Alverna apocalypse, the impaled St. Francis was transfigured; or the cave of Hera outside the dusty Meccan trading post that formed the womb for Muhammad's birth and where the voice was heard that changed the world; or the place within sight of Damascus where another voice was heard, another world changed; or that olive garden where in one long night's agony humanity redeemed itself.

Eventually the spirituality of myriads of seekers becomes condensed at such hallowed scenes, and the divine presence, leading in many cases to genuine spiritual experience, can easily be felt. Ramakrishna said later, "So, there is a special manifestation of God in these places, though He is uniformly present everywhere, like water which is easily accessible in wells, pools, or lakes, though it can be had in other places also, if one digs for there."[*] By spending some days at each shrine he would magnify its mystic ambience and make it, by that much, somewhat less necessary to dig to reach the spirit.

To gain knowledge of the religious customs and aptitudes of the people of India was another purpose served by the tours. Dakshineswar being a world unto itself, he had first-hand acquaintance only with Kamarpukur and a small section of Calcutta. Otherwise he was not too conversant with how religion was actually practiced in his country, and before he could function as teacher for his age he would have to know more of the character of his audience than he did. He admitted that before he went to Benares he thought everyone there

---

[*] *Great Master* 558.

would be plunged in samadhi in reverent adoration of Shiva and that in Vrindavan everyone would be lost in ecstatic love for Krishna, and was surprised to find that such was not the case at all. No doubt he had much else to discover.

His travels through the shrine country brought him into contact with many wandering monks and fakirs of different sects, which always fascinated him. He loved to talk to them, to study and compare them, as he had begun to do among their counterparts drifting through Dakshineswar, drawn there by Mathur's largesse undiminished since Rani Rasmani's time. Whenever he passed near someone reputed to be a yogi he took pains to track him down and spend time with him. These *sadhus* and ascetics offered him new windows into the mystic country he had made his own—rather, recalled early stages of his own spiritual path, and each was relived as he met some sannyasin embodying that single phase with his entire life.

One such encounter was at Benares with a celebrated monk, Trailanga Swami, pursuing a vow of silence. The master scrutinized him closely, felt his body, made certain gestures, announced him to be a man of knowledge in a high state of realization, completely lacking body-consciousness. On a return visit he fed the monk cooked rice with his own hand. By signs they managed to discuss philosophy. The master, like a teacher catechizing a brilliant student, asked him whether God was one or many. In the depths of samadhi he was One, replied the swami, but after the return to the phenomenal world, with its essential characteristic of diversity, he was many.

But Ramakrishna, like Buddha and Christ before him, had achieved a state far beyond this—namely, the One *as* the Many, the Many *as* the One. To the man of Nirvana, as Buddha called this state, or of Brahman-Consciousness as we have been calling it, the One was experienced at all times whether in samadhi or not because the faculty that *perceived* diversity—the ego—had been dissolved in the supernal light. Trailanga Swami, who had achieved total conquest of the body, was far from this realization, as the vow of silence—like Tota Puri's nakedness— might suggest: a human device, an act of resolve, to collect new forces of spiritual energy into the will in order to drive the mind, in more powerful contemplations, into its innermost recesses.

An ancient and often effective asceticism, whose limitations, however, we have seen. The likelihood is that in Trailanga Swami the master was dealing with another expression of greatness and rigidity mixed in one individual. It had taken Tota Puri eleven months to discover what his spiritual life was lacking. The Benares swami—who in summer slept on burning sands and felt no pain—may have learned his lesson in the few silent visits Ramakrishna made to him.

Another renowned saint, a woman, Gangamata by name, about sixty years of age, also attracted his attention when he was in Nidhuvan, to such an extent that he seriously considered foregoing everything in order to remain with her—not only the rest of the tour but the return to Dakshineswar. This woman, a combination of austerity and intoxicated love for the divine pair, Radha and Krishna, saw, by the power of her long *tapas*, his extraordinary state and at once considered him an incarnation of her beloved Radha, feeling her life blessed and fulfilled beyond her dreams. Ramakrishna, captivated by her, lived with her for a time in her hermitage, the two of them together, forgetting everything else. Mathur and Hriday had much difficulty persuading him to leave and return home, which he agreed to do only when he realized he would be abandoning his aged mother at Dakshineswar. "Who would take care of her?"—Once that thought arose he found it impossible to remain there any longer in a tranquil state.

Ramakrishna was in an intense devotional mood, the so-called "great mood," or *Mahabhava,* [*] when he and Gangamata met, the mood of worship of the Personal Goddess and of all living forms where the divine charisma was particularly manifest: in saints like Gangamata. In her he felt the presence of the deity he worshipped in samadhi and was overwhelmed by the realization. The thought of living close to her day after day excited him: ecstatic to contemplate emerging from the realm of the Formless to see in the female form in front of him the same divine being he had worshipped in secret. The feminine nature with its sweetness, delicacy, maternal love, intuitive sympathy, its spiritual beauty, was irresistible to him as he experienced it in the saint. There was undoubtedly, in addition, a swift empathy of temperament and

---

* These "moods," comparable to electronic wavelengths in the atmosphere, are *inner* frequencies, channels in the *mind*, which contains hundreds of such, as does the atmosphere hundreds of different wavelengths, each intact, each functioning independently. So with the mind. Each spiritual mood is its own reality, its own world. When we are absorbed in each we *are* that, have no other reality, know nothing else, just as each electronic channel excludes knowledge of any other reality but its own.

similarity of spiritual orientation that made him talk to her from the first minutes as though they had known each other all their lives.

Perhaps they had. For what he came to "know" now was not the body or the creatureliness of the woman but the spirit within, her essential being, as their minds opened at once to each other upon the recognition of spiritual kinship, of being part of the same spiritual family or grouping of souls who immediately feel a part of the each other's reality—that reality being their own, the larger soul-consciousness they have in common. Therefore when two such people meet—those destined to be lovers, to be disciples of a master, to be spiritually companioned in this lifetime—we say it is "as though" they had always known each other, for in truth they had. The soul, the inner presence, the spiritual temperament they had known, and *been—themselves*, in others words—was only meeting them now in another form. Literally they were encountering themselves. Hence with such difficulty Ramakrishna left Gangamata.

But sexual polarity made a strong contribution too. *We do not find him acting this way with male saints.* We find him, like any idealistic, truth-seeking man, unable to resist the feminine presence at its most loving and sensitive, feeling whole in a new way just by being with her, unable to remain complete unto himself without close proximity to, and spiritual union with, a feminine counterpart of himself.

From which we might conclude—at least if we see his life in its impersonal truth for modern man—that this feeling that all male aspirants have is not to be renounced or combated as a dangerous thing (the attitude that *used* to prevail) but to be regarded as a manifestation of that same divine whose presence we feel so radiantly penetrating from the feminine form before us.

Such would be the ideal mood for approaching the practice of Tantra. Success would almost be assured, since at the outset—ecstasy mingled with profound adoration of the divine nature of the woman beside us—we have been graced with the Truth. So armed, so sensitized, we may discover that the lion of lust can easily be neutralized and the gate to mutual bliss be opened.

Sarada, meanwhile, was slowly approaching puberty, the ripening of her beauty, and the readiness of time. In the passage of the months Ramakrishna's mind revolved all the experiences and insights of the past years as he prepared himself, given his preternatural sense of the coming of events, for the momentous arrival of his girl-wife ... though soon enough to be a woman, to test him quite as much as to learn from him, in still new fires of discipline the Designer had made ready in the eternal matrix that feeds the soul-life of all mystics.

In 1871 Mathur died, the most prominent of several individuals who, Ramakrishna declared enigmatically, had been appointed to be supplier of all his needs during his lifetime. Others would follow in the fifteen years remaining to his life. Whatever Mathur's shortcomings, there is no doubt the master loved and appreciated him and wept when he died, as Jesus had wept for Lazarus. For us, tears might be superfluous. But at least we can acknowledge that without him life for Ramakrishna would have been very different indeed, much more difficult and hazardous. From the first time he came to Dakshineswar Mathur gave him full protection and support, and for the next fifteen years. For that we can be grateful.

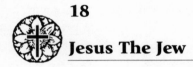

18
Jesus The Jew

JESUS HAD NO MATHUR but during the scenes recorded in the biblical narrative, at least, he does not seem to have suffered actual want. "Foxes have holes," he says, "and birds of the air have nests;" adding that "the Son of man hath nowhere to lay his head" (Luke 9: 58), but we do not find him sleeping out of doors very often. On the contrary, we gain a strong impression that he and his disciples are able to find food and shelter in their wanderings. Jesus' putative membership in the Essene movement, long assumed in esoteric circles, would explain this, since some of the Essenes did not live permanently in sequestered communes but in accessible households. In Bethany he habitually stayed with Mary and Martha and their brother Lazarus, and there were other houses open to him and his followers.

More than sufficient money was available also. When Jesus rests at the well in Samaria after a long day's journey, his disciples go into the town to buy food. Their group seems to have possessed enough money to need a treasurer (the luckless Judas), and donations from sympathizers would have supplied their needs—Joseph of Arimathea among the chief donors:

> When the evening was come, there came a rich man of Arimathea, named Joseph, who also himself was Jesus' disciple. He went to Pilate, and begged the body of Jesus.... And when Joseph had taken the body, he wrapped it in a clean linen cloth. And laid it in his own new tomb, which he had hewn out in the rock; and he rolled a great stone to the door of the sepulcher and departed.
>
> (Matthew 27: 57-60)

The work of hewing a tomb out of rock and rolling the massive stone in front of the sepulcher required labor and expense he evidently could afford. Matthew's acknowledgment of his wealth is significant, since most similar touches, conflicting with Jesus' image of a man of poverty and his teachings as supportive of that image, are excluded. Perhaps he felt he couldn't ignore entirely his financial role and had at least to hint at it. If Joseph of Arimathea, a man of position, was willing to risk exposing himself to ridicule and enmity by identification as the man who begged Jesus' body from Pilate, he must have been an active contributor when he could do so in secret.

As there were saints and scholars in his own time who considered Ramakrishna an avatar, so Jesus had his share of eminent men besides Joseph of Arimathea who—if privately—believed him to be the messiah:

> Nevertheless among the chief rulers also many believed on him; but because of the Pharisees they did not confess him, lest they should be put out of the synagogue.
>
> (John 12: 42)

Of whom Nicodemus, a strong sympathizer, he who assisted Joseph in preparing Christ's body for burial (John 19: 39-40), is the most unmistakable:

> There was a man of the Pharisees named Nicodemus, a ruler of
> the Jews. The same came to Jesus by night, and said unto him,
> Rabbi, we know that thou art a teacher come from God: for no
> man can do these miracles ... except God be with him.
>
> (John 3: 1-2)

We note the ingenuous assumption that miraculous feats constitute
divinity in the doer, a belief shared by seemingly everyone in the pages
of the gospels. [*]

Ramakrishna is always aware of the vast spiritual tradition of India
behind him. His life of superconscious experience becomes a laboratory
to test the truth of the sacred texts. His fervent belief in them is matched
by Jesus' analogous respect and veneration for the Hebrew scriptures. "I
came not to destroy but to fulfill" (Matthew 5: 17) is a theme equally
applicable to both.

Jesus constantly quotes the ancient books, the Psalms especially, in
which his mind was congenially immersed both for its psychology and
imagery. His most pathetic utterance— "My God, my God, why hast
thou forsaken me?"—is drawn from the first line of Psalm 22: in his
darkest hour his mind by instinct has recourse to phrases long since
memorized. (He may have been David in a previous embodiment, with
a precognitive awareness of his coming destiny.) He is thus consciously placing himself in the spirit-line of mystics who have established the
Hebrew religious tradition.

He never allows himself or others to forget that he is an avatar—
of the Jews. In his identification with the Hebrew prophets he sanctions
their words, augments the prestige they will enjoy in succeeding ages.
In the same way Krishna, the divine teacher of the *Bhagavad-Gita*, often
answers the questions posed to him by long verbatim citations from the
Upanishads, the archetypal scripture of India. Jesus in many passages is
as apt to quote from the Old Testament, or refer to it, as he is to set
forth his own teaching. His allusions to Moses, David, Elias, and Isaiah
are numerous and always made in a spirit of reverence and implicit
acceptance, an attitude enshrined in the Transfiguration experience
where Moses and Elias, shining in their visionary garments, acknowledge his own prophetic role in the tradition.

---

* Not excepting even the mystical John—e.g.: "But though he had done so
many miracles before them, yet they believed not on him" (12: 37).

He fully realizes the revolutionary impact of his teaching of love and of the indwelling divinity in man, the necessity of nonviolence and loving one's enemies, but this *new* testament is not presented as contravening the Mosaic Law, rather as perfecting it: "I came not to destroy but to fulfill." The earlier, ethical law is to be obeyed to the letter; then, with the lower nature subdued and controlled, the higher impulses may awaken, the spirit may discover a habitation fit for entering. Moses' doctrines are oriented to an ethnic mass of unruly souls who have to be intrigued and intimidated into compliance with morality. He gives them a religion of commandment and taboo—*Thou shalt not*—just as Allah's messenger gives a similar kind of people in the sixth century a similar moral code.

In Islam the higher religion is later discovered by Sufi mystics: the religion of inwardness, of direct vision, of divine immanence. In Judaism the higher path is discovered by the Hebrew prophets (outsiders to Jews as a whole) and, more fully, by Jesus, whose religion is an earlier version of Sufism, both being versions of the one universal, eternal religion which, as St. Augustine remarks, has always existed and which, he says, about the time of Jesus began to be called Christianity. About the time of Krishna it began to be called Hinduism and about the time of Buddha, Buddhism.

Jesus thinks the Jews are ready for the Higher Teaching: the knowledge that the individual soul and the Supreme Soul are one—knowledge to be gained not by "knowing" but by direct and immediate intuition, organic apprehension. This is the truth, we recall Jesus saying, that is to free us. We are to experience the oneness of the soul and the Supreme Being, discovering—for all our ignorance—that they have been united eternally. And in that knowledge we are instantly free from bondage.

Jesus has come to give this truth to the Jews.

For nearly six centuries prior to his birth the Near East, the Hellenic world generally, had been inseminated with the insights and vibrations of saints, mystics, adepts of varying degrees of Knowledge, so that by the time of Jesus the sullen, unappeased tribes among whom he found himself—the People of the Book—had been, or should have been, tempered by the preceding ages of gathering atmospheric influence. Their most illustrious philosopher, Philo of Alexandria, living a few years before

Christ, was preaching a mystical doctrine of the Logos remarkably similar to what we find in John's gospel and in Jesus' own proclamations. He, in turn, had caught much of his own thought from the Platonic tradition, then at its height, Plato himself one of the master-sages of the pre-Christian period, and still more so his guru, the peerless Socrates, a Christ figure for mankind during that era. And before him, influencing him also, the seer Pythagoras, supreme pre-Socratic mystic, founder of the mystery cult that served as a model to many others throughout the Mediterranean world.

There were the continuing mystery religions themselves, their source dim in the shadows of Hellenic and Egyptian antiquity, brought to Greece from India, as many thought, by the fabled Orpheus, their influence difficult to calibrate, yet certainly by the time of Jesus the seeds of their higher teaching—the characteristic mystical element in their doctrines—had been sown broadcast through the Mediterranean skies, filtering down into the soil of minds ready for their germination.

Quickened by the pervasive winds of the radical new Gnosticism, the essene and therapeutae sects of mystic Jews, flourishing contemporary with Jesus, were a particularly promising aspect of the age. He could not but have wondered how many such there were, potentially at least, in the orthodox bastions of Jewry, where he betook himself after his decade of hidden apprenticeship among such communes around the Dead Sea region or, more likely, in Egypt, the nurse of Moses, with its powerful mystery-cult tradition reaching back a millennium and a half—to the renowned Akhenaton,[*] at least: perhaps, as some have surmised, traveling all the way to Persia and India. During those same six centuries both these exotic environments, besides their far-flung and celebrated mystery communes, had produced an ongoing succession of *illuminati*, notably Zoroaster and the mighty Buddha, whose missionaries, after his passing, became a part of the mystique enveloping the Middle Eastern shores, penetrating deep into that world with strange new doctrines of a oneness of life and of charity toward all its manifestations. Then there was the ubiquitous presence of

---

[*] The enlightened young pharaoh, himself a mystic, who had inscribed on the Egyptian temples where the mystery religion was practiced the words *Nuk pu Nuk* ("I am what I am"), which would later appear in Moses' communion with the deity of Sinai: Moses, brought up in the royal household, was heir to all the Egyptian esoteric wisdom.

Apollonius of Tyana, the storied magus of Jesus' own generation, though the two never met, a later inheritor of the mantle of Pythagoras, fabled for his wisdom and supernatural powers.

Against the slow mounting ferment of these diverse but onflowing influences the Jews maintained themselves behind their barricade of Law and Prophet, but if they were ever to be ready for redemption the time was now, the savior at hand. Not for centuries would there be again so auspicious a moment.

Jesus' incarnation among the Jews was brought about by a number of motives which intermix, reinforce, at times seem to mutually exclude, each other: all of them together, in the mystery of divine intention, constitute the providential motivation.

The mysterious being who, beyond race and nationality, incarnated as Jesus of Nazareth, chose the Hebrew nation for his embodiment because, first of all, it had sustained the longest outward religious tradition in the Western half of the world and would provide him with the organized focus, the psychological impact, he needed for the dissemination of a new faith. Because he could preach, partly at least, in terms of celebrated prophets who had preceded him, he could present himself and his doctrine as essentially a development, if a radical one, of what had gone before him.

But because this being thirsted to sacrifice himself for a benighted, spiritually lethargic human race, and to offer his life as an atonement for their election of bondage over freedom, he came into incarnation as a Jew because, inheriting at least some of the Jewish characteristics generally, to some degree karmically, he would thereby experience humanity at its most contentious and egocentric—traits in the overcoming of which he would feel, most acutely, what it actually is to be a human resistant to the light, and thus would experience, at a fundamental level, the peculiarly perverse texture of human nature itself ... as it is possible that Ramakrishna, at least as a Hindu, never came to know so well.

In other words, Jesus becomes a Jew to find out what human nature truly is.

While humanity in its perpetual self-bondage is the object of his mercy, he functions as essentially *the Jewish savior* and to the end remains oriented to his Hebrew background and cast of thought. The vicarious atonement is not for *Adam's* sin—it is *for the Jews'*. Enlightened by his mystic attainment about the origin of the world and the nature of mankind's slow descent into materiality, he would have found the Eden fable an instructive allegory, but the only atonement he could achieve would be for the people with whom he had long identified, the unchanging Hebrew race, full of colossal self-righteousness and an anti-spiritual psychology—a contumacious self-will—for two millennia.[*] To give this people one more chance at redemption he rejoins them once again—and for the last time—with a heart bursting with sorrow and love. The sight of their golden city fills him with yearning to embrace all Jews in his sacrificial ardor, his pity:

> O Jerusalem, Jerusalem, thou that killest the prophets, and stonest them which are sent unto thee, how often would I have gathered thy children together, even as a hen gathereth her chickens under her wings, and ye would not!
> (Matthew 23: 37)

At times—many times—his impatience breaks out unmistakably: "O faithless and perverse generation, how long shall I be with you? How long shall I suffer you?" (Matthew 17: 17) But his vexation is an aspect of his love: "And when he was come near, he beheld the city, and wept over it" (Luke 19: 41).

Many Jews believed Moses had reincarnated as David and might still come in another form as the messiah. By his close identification with David, so that in his last hours the Psalmist's very phrases are on his lips, we conjecture that the same great soul—Jesus, that is—may well

---

[*]The exasperated cries of the Hebrew prophets in dozens of passages are the most dramatic reminder of this. In the New Testament St. Paul, himself a "Hebrew of the Hebrews," offers many others: "For I bear them record that they have a zeal of God, but not according to knowledge. For they, being ignorant of God's righteousness, and going about to establish their own, have not submitted themselves unto the righteousness of God..... To Israel Isaiah saith, All day long I have stretched forth my hands unto a disobedient and gainsaying people" (Rom. 10: 2-3, 21) and "Their minds were blinded: for until this day remaineth the same veil untaken away in the reading of the old testament.... Even unto this day, when Moses is read, the veil is upon their heart" (2 Cor. 3: 14-15). In Acts (7: 51-52) Luke reports Stephen's defiant words to the Jerusalem council of elders just before he is stoned to death: "Ye stiffnecked ... ye do always resist the Holy Ghost: as your fathers did, so do ye. Which of the prophets have not your fathers persecuted?"

have been David—four hundred years and perhaps as many spiritual epiphanies after Moses; may have been Isaiah also, three hundred years following David; may, indeed, have been the dominant prophet, beginning with Moses, in each of Judaism's historic ages. Finally appearing as Jesus of Nazareth, spiritually far in advance of his predecessors and become an avatar. As each of them he had been, in varying degrees, embroiled in dimensions of personality and politics, as well, mingling hours of limited enlightenment with secular passions. As the Christ he had *become* the experience, had received a new I-consciousness born of the experience, and it was the experience itself—not the man or mind he had been—that spoke through him—as with Moses and the others, it was spoken *of:* "I am the Way, the Truth, and the Life."

With a full grasp of man's divine nature, of the urgency of communicating to his fellow Jews—*once again*—the highest truth he has received, and feeling the time is ripe at last for the highest truth—*The kingdom of heaven is within you—Know ye not that ye are gods—Be ye therefore perfect*—he incarnates once more and this time offers his life for the salvation of his people, which is to say, humanity at its most egocentric, most willful, most bound—even as he knows they will reject his offer and his teaching. But it must be done. The drama must be played out. They must know, and the world must know, what was made available. Writes Isaiah—conceivably Jesus himself in an earlier incarnation—in the famous prophecy:

> He is despised and rejected of men; a man of sorrows, and acquainted with grief: and we hid as it were our faces from him; he was despised, and we esteemed him not....Surely he hath borne our griefs....
>
> But he was wounded for our transgressions, he was bruised for our iniquities: the chastisement of our peace was upon him; and with his stripes we are healed.
>
> All we like sheep have gone astray; we have turned every one to his own way; and the Lord hath laid on him the iniquity of us all.
>
> He was oppressed, and he was afflicted, yet he opened not his mouth: he is brought as a lamb to the slaughter, and as a sheep before her shearers is dumb, so he openeth not his mouth.... For the transgression of my people was he stricken.

(Isaiah 53: 3-8) [*]

So deeply are the Hebrews mired in the coils of an ancient intransi-
gence that he is willing to go this far to save them, to shock them out
of themselves. It is the Jews more than humanity itself he comes to
save.

Nor does he require personal homage. By accepting him they
would discover not simply another leader but a radical code of *living*
which, in the process of being followed, would *transform* them.
Salvation was to come by *change*—change from what they had been. The
teachings—*the way itself*—was to accomplish it. On the rudimentary
level Moses' code had served to train. The time had come to transform.

For another, completely different reason he chose the vehicle of
Judaism because, given the Jews' traditional rejection of prophets,
beginning with the long-continued resistance to Moses himself during
the forty years' wandering, their "stiff-necked" opposition to new ideas,
their legalistic love of Book and Statute, it was inevitable that they
would reject him and in so doing would furnish the budding religion a
powerful thrust forward into history. For their rejection would neces-
sitate his execution and martyrdom, presenting his followers with a
deathless symbol under which to raise the banner of the fledgling
movement and with an incomparable incentive to exert their energies,
at the cost of their lives, to advance its progress.

His allusions to an inevitable arrest and death-sentence are many.
Yet he must act as though the Jews are free to choose him, so that the
record will reveal the scope of their tragic decision. He must show genuine compassion toward them and their doomed city, must be seen lift-
ing his arms out in protective embrace if they would but open their
eyes. Even as he knows they cannot. Their role, based on their nature,
decreed by providence, is fixed: "It must needs be that offenses come"—
with the ominous warning— "but woe unto them by whom the offense
cometh" (Matthew 18:7). One proof he was an avatar is the degree of

---

[*] The passage really describes the role of *any* saintly figure in the divine design
whereby the enlightenment of one leads by a process of spiritual chemistry to the
salvation of many. Only a "once-born" understanding could have assumed the passage refers to Christ alone, though there is no doubt his life implements the profound, subtle content of the "prophecy" with special power.

suffering the Jews have had to endure for rejecting and crucifying him. The effect—the negative karma—has been immense (though perhaps now fully atoned) but not greater, as no effect can be, than the cause which generated it.

For Judas, it had been better had he never been born. But someone had to betray the Christ, someone crucial to the plot, someone of such a nature as the unfortunate disciple.* It is clear that Jesus knew not only that he would be betrayed but by whom—he who had been delegated for the role. Yet there is no hint he singled him out in any way— a depth of compassionate forbearance, sustained over many months, attesting to his divine nature far more significantly than the miracles. He treated him exactly as he treated the others, with the same concern and love—perhaps more so, since the hapless Judas, himself unaware of his ordained fate, would, by force of circumstances meshing with the tendencies of his own waywardness, be driven to the act that would stigmatize his name throughout the earth. That Jesus showed him no less affection than the others is demonstrated at the Last Supper when, the subject of his betrayal introduced, they turn amazed to one another, asking "Who is it?"

As he knew the fate of Judas, and his own, so he knew the overall script in which each man had his appointed lines to read, acts to perform. For him, as for the evangelists to whom he made the matter crystal clear, the Old Testament in passage after passage prefigures the New—that is, the life and death of Christ. Therefore his reverence for the scriptures of the past is not entirely because of their content of spiritual truth—it is more because of their anticipation of himself as the end for which they were written, the culmination of all their centuries: Before *Abraham was, I am.* "Search the scriptures," he says, "—they testify of me"** (John 5: 39). And he goes on:

---

* Among the other disciples there were varying degrees of potentiality, at least, for betrayal. Thomas' misgivings, Peter's thrice-repeated denial of any knowledge of Jesus after his arrest, and the disappearance of all his followers except John (and the women, of course) during the crucifixion, suggest that Judas' motives were shared to some extent by others. His apostasy, in other words, was not totally unique.

** "And beginning at Moses and all the prophets, he expounded unto them in all the Scriptures the things concerning himself.... And he said unto them, These are the words which I spoke unto you, while I was yet with you, that all things must be fulfilled which were written in the law of Moses, and in the prophets, and in the psalms, concerning me" (Luke 24: 27,44).

Do not think that I will accuse you to the Father: there is one that accuseth you, even Moses, in whom ye trust. For had ye believed Moses, ye would have believed me: for he wrote of me. But if ye believe not his writings, how shall ye believe my words?

(John 5: 45-46)

Yet he is always conscious of where and why he transcends the limits of the Old Testament religion, just as the Father in Heaven he gave to the West so far transcends the anthropomorphic Jehovah, made in the image and likeness of fearful worshippers: "The law and the prophets were [in effect] until John: since that time the kingdom of God is preached" (Luke 16: 16)—John being the Baptist of course, the precursor. The old Mosaic code concerned itself with forms, appearances, a material morality; Jesus' doctrine focuses exclusively on the inward life:

Ye have heard that it was said by them of old time, Thou shalt not kill.... But I say unto you, that whosoever is angry with his brother ... shall be in danger of the judgment....

Ye have heard that it was said by them of old time, Thou shalt not commit adultery. But I say unto you, That whosoever looketh on a woman to lust after her hath committed adultery with her already in his heart....

Ye have heard that it hath been said, An eye for an eye, and a tooth for a tooth. But I say unto you, That ye resist not evil: but whosoever shall smite thee on thy right cheek turn to him the other also....

Ye have heard that it hath been said, Thou shalt love thy neighbor, and hate thine enemy. But I say unto you, Love your enemies, bless them that curse you, do good to them that hate you, and pray for them which despitefully use you, and persecute you....

Be ye therefore perfect, even as your Father in heaven is perfect.

(Matthew 5: 21-48)

Only those with God as their nature could be presumed to become perfect as he is. Those without an inward perfection already present (though hidden) could never be. Those with such a perfection latent could.

A new commandment I give you—that ye love one another: because of the divine presence, the divine nature, of your neighbor. A startling mandate for the law-shackled Jews. This was Ramakrishna's epochal discovery also, grounded in the transformative fact of his realization of Brahman: all *is* one, all *is* God, all *are* divine. And he added that ye love not only one another but one another's religion, for they are all pathways (though pathways only) to the same Truth, the same God.

Jesus makes one final attempt to free the Jews from their long, self-strangling yoke. Failing, he becomes the model for thousands of spiritual Christians to follow, and his teaching becomes recognized everywhere as a divine utterance. Significantly, it was the Sermon on the Mount—with its persistent emphasis on selfless love toward all, on the necessity of nonviolence in word, thought and action—that exercised over the mind of Gandhi the strongest influence, and thus indirectly—*almost* directly—led to the liberation of an India whose consciousness of worth, of innate spirituality, of unquenchable greatness as a people, had been revived by the words and life of Ramakrishna—and by the singular product of his life, his disciple Vivekananda, the St. Paul of this *yuga.*

Thus in Mahatma Gandhi, Jesus and Ramakrishna meet, and the teachings which, in their rejection by one people, result in nineteen centuries of pogrom and ghetto, in their acceptance by another, though strangers to the man who first uttered them, result in their liberation.

But Jesus had incarnated as a Jew for another, hidden reason: for his own sake. *It is finished,* uttered on the cross in the last moments, could not refer to the mere termination of a physical life he had taken such pains to ignore, but to the end of an ages-long travail of mind, will, and soul in the service of an ultimate enlightenment and of his efforts to redeem the strange race whose welfare over the course of fifteen centuries he had assumed.

Henceforth, in future incarnations, undertaken perhaps incognito —as St. Francis, for example, or as Ramakrishna, or as both—certainly in other scenes, with the Jewish struggle expiring then and there, and with it the Jewish elements of his psyche, there would be found in his character a simplicity, evenness, and self-effacement we do not find, on balance, in his advent in Palestine. Displays of miraculous power would vanish. There would be no attempt to found a religion or to save the world, for no man need think he is necessary for mankind's salvation—rather, mankind is necessary for his. There would be no attempt to present oneself as the way, the truth, and life—even if we understand these sentiments in their purely mystical sense—for fear of seeming to separate himself from the equally divine potential for spiritual enlightenment in his fellows. There would be a shrinking from attention being called to himself, an abhorrence of the dramatic action, the memorable gesture—things we associate with Jesus' behavior among men in that embodiment. There would be no anger, no impatience, no rebuke toward anyone, for all would seem as reflections of oneself, and as manifestations of the One. There would be no sense of diversity in one's perception, rather a sense of perceiving the One at all times. There would be no foes and friends, but co-actors in the same divine drama. There would be no need to seek the violence of crucifixion and torture for attaining the higher realization: pure contemplation, austerity, and silence—as they did with Ramakrishna, with St. Francis and Buddha—would suffice then.

He came as a Jew to pluck out of his psyche the last vestige of his Jewishness and, equally, the final seed of any influence of environment.*

He had to enter into an absolute condition—become the Father, as well as the Son ... *truly* become the Truth, forgetting it sometimes among the provocations and abuse of men. For this the Passion and Crucifixion awaited him: he wished to drink the cup of humiliation to the uttermost—the way to *his* perfection.

He wished to test his will supremely for those everlasting hours on the cross—an eternity of willing, perfecting a part of his nature—the last part—that could be perfected no other way ... the way, also, to humble and counterbalance an overdeveloped femininity, that part of him which in life, somewhat too much, had called attention to his person.

---

* To conquer the powerful self-will of the Jewish mind with a still more powerful spiritual will to selflessness the Crucifixion was necessary. Thus the Pharisees, representing the self-centered, worldly elements in the Hebrew constitution, deadly adversaries of the man who represents the soul of the same race, become the necessary means for his ultimate elevation and perfection: on the cross. Likewise, the gross, self-willed elements in our individual psyche, combating to the death the emergence of our spiritual consciousness, become, by their resisting force, the means for our own enlightenment.

By the excruciating rigors of the cross the masculine half of his being would strike the balance, attain consummate equipoise. And with a mind so elevated by the agony, so established by the heights achieved, he might become the savior of mankind.

During his life he does not forgive his enemies for insulting him but on the cross forgives them for killing him. He is *different* then. The serenity, majesty, grace of his last days show him in a new radiance, and only on the cross is the light more blinding. Indeed, when he overcomes the hesitations of Gethsemane the Transformation is well under way, is in essence accomplished. Here he is far from the miracle-worker, the denouncer of critics. Golgotha will be the Pentecost that consumes the lingering dross of his personality, leaving only the fire of a purified will, a liberated consciousness, a divine being—his acts, words, sacrifice, perfection branded forever in the human imagination.

As Ramakrishna after *his* highest experience had come to love his relatives, so Jesus in the midst of his own apocalypse came to "forgive" his mother ... to see *her also* as the divine, the universal feminine. She is to be the mother of John— "Woman, behold thy son"—and by implication the mother of all: is to become a true spiritual, a universal mother, rather than the mere nature-womb she has been. But she has always been this potentially. Has she changed? *It is he who has changed.* It is he who sees the truth in her: the pure spiritual maternalism. With the last vestige of ego burned away in the immolation of his being—the cross his sacrificial fire—so is destroyed also the seeds of perceiving differences (where in reality none exist), distinctions (where in reality there is only the One). The last vortex of his awareness of "others" is the family, where differences between spirit and nature, so acutely "seen" by the ego, are magnified as nowhere else. Now that stronghold has been overcome. His earth family rejoins his spiritual. John, his archetypal disciple, the purest of his followers (that is, the one who most discerned his message) is the representative of his spiritual kin, she of his natural. In that scene (Matthew 12: 46-50) where, while she and his brothers awaited his acknowledgment outside, he had declared, with arms in a gesture of embracing his disciples, that his true mother and brothers are those who do the will of God, the occasion had clearly distinguished between the two families. Now they are joined—because joined within his own consciousness. Differences have vanished in the crucible of his final ordeal, and truth is experienced on the deepest level he has known—and not in that life only.

Thus he makes peace with his mother at the ultimate moment of his life and when he has returned to earth in a nonmaterial form he makes peace with Magdalene, the other feminine principle of his existence. In not only rescuing her from sin and ruin but in appearing first to her at the "resurrection" he surrenders to her, symbolically, the fruit of his labors. In order to be fully united with the divine, we must first be able to offer our lives up to its surrogate on earth, Woman.

This is far from the entrenched masculine mentality of the Hebrew tradition of which he had been an intimate part—so many centuries, as we surmise. He is no longer a Jew on Calvary but has achieved self-transcendence. Jesus is dead before the heart stops beating. In the death of Jesus the Jew the birth of the Christ appears in its glory of humility, self-effacement, self-annihilation, nothingness.

All this he had foreseen before the life began ("my hour is not yet come"). Though the other reasons we have studied were necessary to the unfoldment of the drama, coming into incarnation as a Jew for his own sake, this last time, was clearly the most significant. Thereby he transcended karma, race, nationality, the past, limitations of any and every kind, and passed into that stage of total freedom and oneness with the universe which is the dream and memory of us who labor still in the subterranean dens of our own becoming.

 19

The Marriage of Ramakrishna

IN MARCH 1872, A few months after her eighteenth birthday and one month after her husband's thirty-sixth, Saradamani prevailed on her father to agree to her going to Dakshineswar and to accompany her, joined by several others from her village of Jayrambati.

Ramakrishna had given no sign that she should come; indeed she had not heard from him since their memorable contact of a few weeks in 1867. But in the bloom of youth, blessed with beauty and virtue in equal proportions, a model Hindu girl, pure, selfless, spiritual, noble in character, she felt the summons of destiny, of God, of Nature, all commingled in her brooding sequestered soul—patiently, like a flower, growing, breathing, waiting, longing there in her unknown hamlet ... pushing her mind irresistibly toward the strange man with the divine smile and the gaze that, though gently, was like a light penetrating the hidden places in her secret life, the man who was her husband but who acted like a brother, father, friend, teacher, mother, by turns, and in whose company she had felt, as she said, as though a jar of bliss was pouring constantly in her heart. The thought of him in the intervening four years had renewed the bliss, the longing that made her feel, though in truth she had to confess she did not know him yet all that well, that she could give up everything for him, that she was ready to lay down her life at his feet if he should ask for it. The bond was already stronger than anything she felt with her dear family or her beloved father, who had such solicitude toward her on the long foot journey—as though it was an eternal bond, one that had always existed, always would. Such puzzling trains of thought came to her in those four gestating years in Jayrambati. He was like a god to her—almost like a real god, and she living a part in a miracle play, like a fable she may have read about. She did not know if she would ever see him again but she knew, all the same, that she was his forever—that without him she had no life of her own.

The village gossip that he was mad—the old rumor that never died out—confused and saddened her. She couldn't believe it, but as the years passed and no word from him came—which some suggested was itself a sign of his mental derangement—her misgivings began to affect her more and more. She resolved to go to him directly as the only way to solve the problem and convince herself one way or another.

But these tales of his madness—the wandering about naked, repeating the name of Allah among Hindu temples, dressing as a woman—turned out, really, to have made little impact on her love-nourished mind. The moment she had put Jayrambati behind and started the long trek to Dakshineswar she felt free, happy, and her father and the others in the little caravan caught the spirit of her happiness and all moved forward in a singing, carefree rhythm mile after mile.

Gradually, however, the arduous journey told on her reserves of energy. She fell ill and contracted a high fever. The march stopped, encamped at an inn. In view of the steep ledges of consciousness that awaited her, her illness is not surprising. On the unconscious level, where her psyche may have intuited what was imminent, there was likely conflict—desire mixed with fear, spiritual ardor with rustic creatureliness, the new with the old.

While she lay delirious one night a very dark, beautiful woman suddenly appeared and sat down next to her, comforting her, appearing to know all about Dakshineswar and the man she was going to meet there. She ran her hand over Sarada's face and body and soon the fever abated. Who was she? Visions received in delirium are suspect. The abatement of the fever could have been self-willed, given the *faith* that the vision was real. That it returned before the destination was reached suggests that the experience may have been hallucinatory.

Ramakrishna was delighted to see her, welcoming her with warmth, courtesy, concern. In a moment she realized, even in her unwell condition, that all the rumors of his madness were, again, baseless. Her father, coming to the same conclusion, was soon able to leave her in her husband's care, setting out again for Jayrambati with a mind at rest. Ramakrishna nursed her back to health, supervised her diet and medicines, keeping her in his own room for a few days. When she had recovered, he arranged for her to stay in a nearby room with his mother, and soon began to instruct her.

This was his wife—and his first disciple. His most important one. Through her—and through their relationship—he would articulate to modern man (and woman) a new wisdom as vital, as necessary as anything he conveyed through the searing eloquence of Vivekananda.

Just as Rani Rasmani had been taken away from the scene immediately prior to the Brahmani's advent in 1861, so Mathur—the previous summer—had been removed on the eve of Saradamani's coming. And just as the relationship between Yogeswari and Ramakrishna, offering her no precedents in social custom, would have been too much for the Rani's struggling intelligence to grasp, so the visibly perceived, unquestionably married state of the Master might have been—probably would have been—too strong a challenge to the conventional Mathur's preconceptions of a holy man. He had, it is true, witnessed in Ramakrishna innumerable deviations from the most liberal norms of spiritual behavior, but the fact of the Master not only married but living and sleeping with his wife in the same room month after month would likely have been beyond his powers of assimilation. To preserve his untempered faith and to spare the Kali Temple the reverberations of his shocked dismay, he was carried off.

Six or eight months would also pass to allow the new manager—Mathur's son—time to fall under Ramakrishna's influence sufficiently so that when Saradamani appeared the temple setting would once again be serene, orderly—in providential condition. It is also worth noting that at the death of Mathur in July 1871 it had been fifteen years since Gadai had first come to Dakshineswar; it would be another fifteen years more before his own death-month. With Mathur's passing the era of Ramkumar, Rani, Mathur himself, Yogeswari, Tota Puri ended and a new era arrived, to be dominated by Saradamani, Keshab Chandra Sen, and Swami Vivekananda.

Why didn't Ramakrishna himself call for his wife? Why require her to take the initiative by making, unsolicited, the long overland trek from Jayrambati? Would he not have assumed she was waiting all that time, through the more than four years, for his summons?

The answer undoubtedly is that by now he could initiate *nothing* on his own—not to speak of so momentous an act as calling his wife to his side at last. "Live in the world like a dead leaf," he would later tell his disciples. At every phase of his relations with Saradamani it had been the same. Marriage had first been proposed to *him*, by others. He had concurred, but made no effort to find the bride—only suggesting she had been "prepared" for him long before, five-year-old though she was. At their next contact years later, in 1867, he had been enjoying his stay in Kamarpukur for weeks before she brought herself to join him there, after waiting a decent interval for some overture. He delighted so much in her presence that Yogeswari had feared for his continence, but, again, he had made no move to *bring* her to him.

Further, as the very idea of marriage was so singular, so difficult to reconcile with his entire life, it becomes clear that it was a special dispensation of the Divine, and hence there was no need for him to *do* anything, merely to respond to events positively when they had bearing on this particular matter, which he could do without constraint, since he could see his wife with a degree of visionary insight that perhaps no man since Christ has brought to womanhood—could see her, indeed, as a direct manifestation of that Goddess he worshipped in the Kali Temple: see her as the Divine Mother, having transformed itself into a woman, visiting him as his own wife.

In which event Sarada, too, becomes an incarnation of the Divine—if he himself was.

He may not have been. But if the Divine *did* incarnate as a man, his personality and life would offer it an irresistible temptation, a matrix to pour into it more of its essences than into almost any other. When acknowledged incarnations, such as Jesus and Buddha, do not excel him, may fall short of him in some respects, what other conclusion can we come to?

A little over a year after her arrival he carried out a formal ritual worship of her as the living embodiment of the Universal Feminine— when the mood of their relationship had become richly woven with spiritual truth sufficiently to warrant so portentous an act, and when the consciousness of his disciple-wife had been elevated to a level where its significance and uniqueness could be absorbed.

But he had known from the moment of her arrival that their months together would culminate in that sacred symbolism, and during the year leading up to it he perceived her in the light that flowed into his mind from the fountain of his spirit—as a divine helpmate, his feminine soul, his eternal love, so ready for their meeting that in the space of a year he led her rapidly to the heights of samadhi: a feat unparalleled—he himself, years before, having scarcely equalled it.

She came to him full of something like total reverence and awe and saw *him*, we know, as divine, as truly a god—later, indeed, as the divine itself, incarnate. From the outset he guided her step by step towards not only samadhi but to the realization of the same truths he had known, including the wondrous discovery that the two were eternal companions, soul mates of ages, personifications of the divine feminine and masculine principles, divided only for the purpose of experience and the gathering of wisdom, and the exemplifying of truth to others, but in reality undivided, inseparable, one, through all eternity.

He not only trained her in spiritual matters, in the disciplines of devotional meditation and mind-control, leading to the superconscious state; not only in scriptural study, his text being his prodigious memory of the scriptures; but in many matters of practical application: how to treat different male members of a family, who to serve first in a group, how to estimate a person's character from his behavior, how to trim a lamp. He also showed her ways she could serve him personally—like massaging his feet—and his mother, too. Gradually she learned his tastes in food and began to cook for him each day....

Day after day they are together. A few months after her arrival, once she has grown accustomed to his presence, she is sharing his bed. Night after night, month after month. For nearly a year. Every night he enters into samadhi, she fearful lest she disturb him, lest he not return to consciousness, wondering sometimes if he was actually dead, so motionless he lay. The atmosphere in the room was electric, charged with a power palpable, like heat. Many nights she could not sleep at all. Sometimes he lay in the superconscious state through most of the night, his body rigid as a corpse, his eyes partly open, fixed inward, his expression shining. He could not control himself: it was a pure and new ecstasy for him. Beside him lay not only a beautiful woman but his soul's companion. Was she more goddess, or more woman? Even as woman she intoxicated him—a pure, guileless girl, free of lust, of carnal attitudes.

Desire she could not but feel, but it was sublimated by something stronger—her devotion to him as a god-man, and her worship of the Divine Mother as her protectress at all times—protectress of them both. Thus desire was converted into more potent spirituality—the Tantric ideal. Indeed theirs became a Tantric marriage—the perfect one. Not sexual union, but spiritual union—the object of Tantric rites. A fusion of identities in the ardor of mutual devotion, like Adam and Eve before the fall.

The sexual power of Ramakrishna had long since been converted into spiritual power; what remained was the chance to test his continence in a far more tempting circumstance than he had known during the Tantric disciplines. Then, the women brought to him were unknown, he had related to them in a purely ritualistic, symbolic manner, there was no tie of karma, no covenant, no providential design. Now it was far more difficult. He *himself* was involved. Bound to the beautiful, love-struck Sarada by vow, by providence, he also rejoiced in her—her presence, her spirituality, her guileless youth. It was not a matter of *bracing* himself against a potential threat to his continence or remaining uninvolved in the ritual intimacy, but of uniting with her in a completely spiritual, sublimated manner so that the physical element in *her*—that in him having been purged and transmuted—did not awaken in its purely sexual channel. In this he succeeded—they both succeeded. For it was her daily, at times almost her constant prayer that she be freed from any taint of lust, that she remain as a sister-daughter-mother to her god-spouse, and not for a moment tempt him to thoughts of bodily intercourse—or tempt herself: the prayer being answered, according to both their reports.

During his instruction and her questions and their endless surveys of the spiritual path, in which she flowered so rapidly, one knows there often were hushed moments, a divine closeness, as he looked at her, gazed into her eyes, brown pools of liquid flame gently but implacably enveloping him in their shimmering still depths. Among seductive women brought to him in the arduous Tantric rituals to tempt him he could, by exercise of will or surrender of will to the Divine, cope with the threat they posed and neutralize their power. But what if the partner shares your outlook totally, wants what you want—continence, purity, God-consciousness—and approaches you only with virginal serenity—what insidious desire might then take possession of the soul, when no struggle was needed, no resistance called for, and only inevitable harmony of two kindred spirits seemed the reality? Would this not constitute a challenge beyond what he had encountered in the Tantric labyrinth? For years he had sat fearless among ghosts and serpents in the nearby jungle, had fought with and overcome the red-eyed, black-hued Satan in his blood. But the eyes of Saradamani drowned him, calling for renewed efforts, more prayer, more yoga, more meditation, until—little by little, getting larger each week—the margin of safety grew.

Buddha declared the uprooting of lust was the most difficult task he had faced—the reason being that his experience of desire had been intermingled with great love for his Yasodhara. He had known sexual experience, in other words, at its most irresistible, not as something degrading, humiliating, weakening. Hence his agonized struggle. It was similar with Ramakrishna. We noted how, with women skilled in the seduction arts, his sexual organ at first onset of temptation had, by reflex, like the tortoise's limbs, retreated into itself—his body but a register of mind, of transformed will. But now the temptation was not from without, an alien menace in voluptuous guise. It was from within, his Sarada an aspect of himself, his own soul externalized, the divine realizations of woman he had known come to radiant life. She was the internal goddess perceived as living before him; she was the world of inner beauty that secretly intoxicated him, manifested in glorious form and color, sitting before him, massaging his feet, sharing his bed, occupying his dreams. Here was temptation like nothing he had known.

But with both their minds united in a common effort—self-control, continence, spiritual union only—and fervently, prayerfully attuned to the same objective, the temptation—neutralized, circumvented—provided, in its power, its quiet but overwhelming intensity, energy to feed the spiritual wholeness created between them which every day deepened until it seemed to encompass the universe—the two of them together conjoined in a divine unity of power, blessedness, and truth that seemed to have existed eternally.

One night, as she slept, he was awake, gazing at her, feeling her purity pour into him like an aroma of heaven, strengthening him, elevating him, but also making him tremble as before some new mystery, some sacred portal of the universe being opened to him as he lay there, propped on an elbow, noting the rise and fall of her breathing, her eyes closed like the petals of a lotus at dusk—some new annunciation of the Great Mother which he was to receive, assimilate, and make his own.

It was a warm night. As she lay next to him, the outline of her limbs and body visible in the moonlight, the stillness was absolute, unbroken, except for the faint movement of the Ganges in the distance, and the occasional whisper of a breeze.

Night after night, testing himself: O mind, this is a female body. It is the prize of worldly life. Men live for it, die for it. Do you want it? If you take it, you will lose what you have. If you think of it as an object of enjoyment you will be deprived of your spirituality, will sink to the level of flesh, and become sensualized. It is the great alternative that this world affords to what you have, but you cannot have both. If you regard the dweller in that form as your true wife, your companion, your disciple, with whom you can relate without carnal enjoyment and with whom you cannot relate *with* carnal enjoyment, then you will know the peace and bliss and ecstasy you now have. If you ask her for her flesh you will know bodily pleasure only for a few short moments, unlike the ecstasy and joy you both share and which is unending. What do you want, mind? Make your decision.

His mind responded to the question with the self-ravishment of samadhi—lasting through the night, well into the next day. He had given Sarada a number of mantrams—sacred sounds—to whisper into his ear if a particular samadhi was prolonged. But this time they had little effect.

It might be conceded that the extraordinary pair had known a beatitude rarely encountered but in their mutual continence had missed the joy of sexual climax—the earth's keenest delight. The mystique of Tantra declares, utterly to the contrary, that those who practice a continent sexuality experience all the joy of earthly lovers and much more besides, that it is that very *current of joy itself*—a spiritual joy—which they seek to experience and which, when controlled and maintained in its own proper channel, leads the individuals to ever higher raptures, ardors more intense, each protecting, guiding, fostering each other on the delicate inward and upward path toward not only erotic bliss but the ecstasy of something close to divine realization.

Ramakrishna and Sarada bypassed the stages of love-play leading from the sexual through the erotic on to the higher, spiritual joy, and went directly to the latter by virtue of their rare self-control and elevated state to begin with. There were doubtless affectionate, loving embraces but they sought no vital middle-ground of the erotic, where others would normally dwell through the entire love-encounter and only slowly moved upward, in time, to the level where divine joy—the essence of pure joy itself—might be known.

He gave her full credit—they shared in the triumph equally. In one sense she deserves more praise, since, in the ripeness of her first youth and beauty, a stranger to high revelation and to yoga and its disciplines, not dreaming of the experiences that for so long had inundated her husband, she kept pace with him on the delicate swaying bridge they negotiated together. "Who knows what would have happened," he remarked years later, looking back, as his disciples sat raptly attentive, "if she had not had self-control. Mine might have broken down and body-consciousness arisen." We cannot doubt that in that sensuous bloom of her youth she knew desire but what she was finding as a substitute for gratification was so much greater, generating so much more bliss, enlarging every day, that it was, perhaps, actually not too difficult for her to turn from desire to what had displaced it.

Once, while massaging his feet, she asked him: "How do you look on me?" Without a moment's hesitation came the reply: she whom he worshipped in the temple as Mother Kali, and she who was his earthly mother living in the music room, was the same one now massaging his feet. "Truly, I always look upon you as a form of the blissful divine Mother."

The time had come to solemnize this conception—the new-moon night towards the end of May fourteen months after her arrival, the occasion of the annual worship of the Goddess in the Kali Temple, where his presence was expected as the chief element in the celebration.

Seventeen years before, in that very temple, he had had his first vision of the power behind life—a vision of pure energy, joy, beauty— that power he called Kali, which he had worshipped in so intensely a personal sense—as Christ did—that he called it his Mother, as Christ called it his Father, entering into so close a relation with Life and its All-Creative Power-Source—that he functioned as its son, its child, and that Power had brought him everything and everyone he needed almost as soon as he needed them, included the latest in its bounty: a feminine soul to match his own for this and for every life. A gift all the more remarkable because this time, it appeared, she had come with the gift, had *become* the gift—at any rate had entered into it in so subtle a manner that it was impossible to separate the two.

From the beginning we noted Gadai's close study of womanhood, his early identification with women, and their pronounced response of affection and tribute for his strong affinity with them, which continued on into manhood. Was it karma—answering the call of desire, as well as the cumulative power of many hidden actions—that had brought him a woman for his first teacher, with whom he had immediately entered into an intimate relationship that lasted for several years? Or was it even then the Divine Feminine answering the cry in his heart for the love of a beautiful, virtuous woman who would unveil to him the secrets not only of the spiritual path but of the way leading into the forbidden country of woman herself—Tantra? Then there was the gravitational inevitability of his advent at one of the most consecrated temples of Kali worship in Bengal (though worship of the Goddess had not been domi-nant in his life) and his instinctive, rapid, almost overnight acceptance of her as his ideal. And, not least, the unprecedented appearance of his mother at the scene of his struggles, coming to spend the rest of her days there: we search in vain for a similar occurrence in the career of other prophets or yogis.

The purpose of it all seemed to be: surround this soul with the Feminine in every possible guise, so that it is borne in upon him, and upon the consciousness of those who study his life, what the unique role of Woman is to be in the modern world and what a spiritual man's relation to her must henceforth be.

Nor should we overlook the poignant and unique drama with the saintly Gangamata at Vrindavan a few years before. How strongly she had affected him: to the extent of being willing to abandon everything for the chance to live in the same hermitage with the holy woman. How he had longed not only for the Universal, the Unmanifest Feminine but for the Feminine *Manifested*, desiring not only the *spirit* of woman but the ineffable beauty which combined spirit and form in human incarnation.

And if Gangamata, pure soul though she was, had produced such a response and rapport, what must it have been like with Saradamani, who brought into his life not only the potent spiritual and psychological combination that had inebriated him in Yogeswari and Gangamata but also the immense, undergirding power of fate, providing him with the feminine mirror image of himself in this girl who had been, as he so well knew, "marked out" for him from the moment of her birth, equipping him with the means to discover his own full being as an incarnated entity: brought into his life, in answer to his magnetic soul's cry for womanhood all his own, as the Goddess herself—in her supreme masterstroke—coming as his own spouse ... with perhaps a hidden aspect of it in the idea, which he himself more and more was to recognize, that if his life was to set an example the same might happen to other men if they were sufficiently devoted to the universal, mysterious, ever-enthralling Feminine Principle: sufficiently devoted to God and to Woman.

But great and urgent themes, universally applicable, call for symbolic enactments. Man's need of sacrifice for his salvation required the Crucifixion—which, in turn, as we saw, required some majestic soul who needed the Crucifixion for the annihilation of his lower will. So the gathering forces behind Ramakrishna's lifelong adoration of

Woman prepared him for a dramatic ritualizing of this love in such a way that would not only formally bind his soul to Sarada's in the nexus of an eternal nuptial, in which he was both Bridegroom and Priest, but leave etched in the astonished consciousness of others an image radiant with living truth and reverberant with implications for the centuries to come.

On that new-moon evening, as the day darkened rapidly after sunset, preparations went ahead for worship of the Goddess in the Temple. This year he sent word he would not attend but would perform the service privately in his own quarters. Hriday was asked to assist them at the temple, leaving him alone with Saradamani.

At nine in the evening the worship commenced, whereby a man's spouse was formally annunciated as the embodiment of divinity in the husband's life, the giver of bliss and all auspicious treasures, the feminine principle of the cosmos incarnate, to be adored by him as though the Universal Mother herself had taken form in her. An empty, freshly-painted chair was always reserved for the Deity at this particular service, in the hope that she would honor the worshipper by occupying it—just as in Jewish household observances an empty chair is placed at the head of the table in the event the messiah might choose that gathering for his expected return.

Incense had been burned, sacred lights illumined the indoor scene, the bridegroom intoned certain traditional mantrams, then with a sign motioned Sarada to occupy the empty goddess-seat, which she did, moving in a semi-trance, already, like him, in a partial state of divine inebriation. Continuing the familiar rite, he sprinkled water over her repeatedly, at the same time praying, in an invocation to the Goddess, that the Supreme Feminine manifest herself in Sarada, purifying her in mind and body, bringing her to perfection. Then he worshipped her—now become Sarada *Devi*, the Blessed—as the Goddess herself, offering her food, holding it to her mouth with his hand, at which point the woman-become-goddess passed into full samadhi, as did her bridegroom-god. Meeting in that superconscious realm, their souls merged and united, becoming one. First, the divine realization—then their souls embrace *as* the divine. The union of Shiva and Shakti, the fusion of male and female essence, the crown of man's eternal dream.

It was Tantra in its purest perfection: doubtless rarely achieved before in the two millennia of its history. Approached, glimpsed—

bringing incomparable bliss to the male-female experience conjointly shared—but seldom attained before that night. We cannot say *never* attained, in view of Christ's life of unknown disciplines and our intuition of the cardinal influence of Woman on his psyche.* But in the light of Ramakrishna's career of relevance for contemporary man, the symbolic truth of that night's ceremony seems meant to be conveyed to misery-bound moderns in a manner more explicit than humanity ever before experienced it.

Returning to a semi-conscious level *hours later*, he offered himself up to the Devi—not to Sarada as she had been but as she was perceived to be, namely, the Goddess herself—offered up his experiences, the fruit of his struggle, his years of sadhana, his monumental revelations. He gave away everything to his goddess-wife. The bliss of her presence, her devotion, her union, her heart, was equal to everything he had attained. Marriage with her was the height of his life, the fulfillment of a lifetime of longing for the feminine, for the soul of woman, an experience to rank as equal to his months in the nirvikalpa realm itself. Then he had discovered the truth of being, now the truth of creation: the unmanifested, the manifested; the Absolute, the Cosmos. Nothing had been hid from him. In total, inebriated surrender to the Power behind Life, the Reality whose essence is Love and Beauty and Truth, he eagerly gave away what, in any case, was not his to hold as an individual: "*Thine* is the Kingdom and the Power and the Glory."

So men, to the women in their lives, offer up their treasures, their substance, their accomplishments, instinctively doing this, intuitively feeling its rightness, but never before has it been made so understandable. Now we know *why*.

Let us remind ourselves: Ramakrishna's first love is God, not his wife. But he sees more of God in her than in anyone—as she sees more of God in him. So they adored each other as a new species of humanity: as God-Man, God-Woman. We are invited to attempt the same. Even the *attempt* will transfigure us, and utterly transform our relations with

---

* And there was Krishna and Radha, Francis of Assisi and Clare, John of the Cross and Teresa, Francis de Sales and Jeanne de Chantal ... the rites of *agape* in early Christian times, the mysteries of the medieval courtly love cult, the many in the Hindu and Buddhist Tantric traditions ... all these having left only their influence, not their names.

the other sex.

The Tantric ideal, in short, is a simplified version of the Ramakrishna experience. It recognizes that an evolved, sensitive man sees more of the divine in a woman—especially a spiritual woman—than anywhere else. On that basis it builds its philosophy and practice, which Ramakrishna came to recommend to contemporary man, tormented by so many things—not least, the tempest of his sexuality.

Ramakrishna married to test his spirituality, to prove the validity of the spiritual knowledge he had gained. He married, also, to set an example to modern seekers about to enter upon the age of sensuality; to dramatize the truth of the marital relation: namely, marriage is for Divine Knowledge, not for Pleasure. Marriage is holy: sensual indulgence robs it of its true character.

And he married to make it overwhelmingly clear to male spiritual aspirants that they must somehow wed their spirit to the feminine before the gates of transcendental knowledge will open for them. Woman is the key.

Das Ewig-Weibliche zieht uns hinan. [*]

Finally, he married because he *wished* to—because of his adoration of Woman with all her beauties, mysteries, and divine graces. And because She was awaiting *him,* her greatest champion since Nazareth.

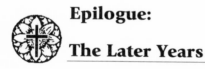

Epilogue:
The Later Years

AFTER THEIR LABORS IN the innermost caves of being, Ramakrishna and Sarada rested for a time, each absorbing the shared apocalypse. The vast infusions of grace shed on her from beyond, and from her husband-god directly, had stretched Sarada's nerves to their limit. She needed time in an environment utterly different in which to assimilate the momentous

---

* Goethe: "The eternal feminine draws us on."

tidings of immortality that had been brought to her. Especially she found his presence nightly in the same bed more difficult to cope with, since his long samadhis did not abate—but seemed to grow more profound. Many nights she hardly slept, in a period when her physical being was crying for respite and recovery. After a time Ramakrishna suggested she repair to Jayrambati for an indefinite stay, until her soul had renewed itself on every level. In October 1873, two months before her twentieth birthday, more illumined than Ramakrishna himself at that age, she returned to her home village.

In the next dozen years a similar pattern was followed. For long intervals she would remain with him, alternating with periods equally long in Jayrambati. One significant difference appeared in Dakshineswar: a room with a kitchen attached was prepared for her in a small thatched house close to where he slept, and thereafter that became her nightly quarters and, when his disciples began to appear, her retreat. Daily she served him in various ways, but they always met alone. They represented the soul to each other. The presence even of kindred spirits blurred the sacred image they had found in one another. In each other's presence they felt the wholeness of spiritual reality itself; with others, a social reality obtruded.

When she first parted that October she had been eighteen months with him, leaving him changed even beyond his previous transformation, merged for all time with the feminine principle: a condition of consciousness which must irresistibly bring his soul into immediate awareness of the other shining knight of Woman of whom we have record, the other master who had scaled the heights of mystic knowledge that now was his.

He had immediate spiritual experience of every divinity within his knowledge, including lesser manifestations of the divine such as Muhammad—but not of Jesus and Buddha.

Though he lacked the benefit of instruction in Buddhism from a qualified teacher, there being so few available in India then, he never seems to have questioned the divine nature of the Tathagata. He always thought of him as an *avatar*, without having actually experienced his character in a vision: other avenues of spiritual perception—direct mystical intuition—were open to him. To someone's suggestion that Buddha was an agnostic, since he never discussed God, he replied:

"Why should you say that? He had an experience that was indescribable, and simply chose not to talk about it." When Girish Chandra Ghosh, the Bengal dramatist and later a fervent householder devotee of Ramakrishna, wrote a play about the life of Buddha, the Master, escorted by disciples, visited the Star Theatre in Calcutta to attend a performance. At the dramatic moment when the young Gautama decides to renounce the world in order to search for the secret of life, he was so overpowered with divine ardor that his mind plunged into the state of samadhi and he was unable to watch anything else.

As for the experience of Christ, we can discover no reason why it had remained closed to him until we reflect that only after attaining the degree of intimacy he now had with the Universal Feminine would her earlier devotee come to him in mystical union. In 1874, a few months after Sarada Devi had left him with the burden and glory of his new wisdom, the time had arrived.

One of his first householder devotees, Sambhu Mallick by name, had, early in the year, begun to read him the story of Jesus' life from the New Testament and he had listened enthralled. We, reading it in the West with the numbed minds we bring to scripture-study, can only envy him this experience of the narrative as a fresh, unspoiled document: how powerful the impact must have been to discover not only the life dramatized there but the marvelous utterance, memorable beyond compare. He must have been astonished to find such beauty, power, mystery, eloquence, divine truth, and force of personality delineated on every page. Coming particularly after the somber gravity and dense profusions of the Koran (the other non-Hindu scripture read to him some years before), the high literary and spiritual grandeur, alike, of the Testament would have created, upon a mind uniquely fit to grasp its every subtlety, an overwhelming impression.

Slowly, steadily, the emanations of Jesus' life—radiantly solitary, like his own, like Buddha's—poured into the recesses of his mind, gradually magnetizing it away from familiar devotions. One day he was sitting alone in the house of a Dakshineswar acquaintance not far from the temple, intently gazing at a Madonna and Child of the Italian school, and in the fixity of his gaze the painting seemed to come to life, emitting rays of bright effulgence from the eyes of mother and child, which entered and possessed him utterly.[*] For three days after this experience

---

[*] One need not believe there was actually light in the oils, rather that the light (cont.)

he completely forgot about his Kali devotions as he wandered trance-like about the temple compound, his whole being immersed in the thought of the Galilean master, whose life, for him, had become vividly contemporary, the past abolished. Once again he had demonstrated his unique ability to concentrate all his powers on a single idea to the exclusion, for days together, of his most cherished conceptions. Which confirmed a central truth of Vedanta—that the Self, the Soul, is independent of *every* image, every devotional concept, however sacred, and is indeed the only sacred entity in the world—that the most hallowed trains of thought are but incidental to its autonomous, self-authenticating processes. In his total absorption in the wonder of Christ's life, forgotten was Kali, Krishna, Rama, and Shiva, as each of these had displaced each other at various times as well, and as—soon enough—each in turn would displace the image of Jesus.

This brief period of Christ-intoxication climaxed one afternoon in the Panchavati as he was walking by himself: he saw, coming toward him, he later recounted, a blue-robed, god-like individual of surpassing beauty and serenity, looking intently at him. Enthralled by the divine expression on his face, he wondered who he was, and as the stranger drew still nearer he heard a voice[*] declaring: "Behold Jesus Christ, the Master Yogi, Divine Love Incarnate, who gave his life for the sins of mankind." Then the figure of Christ embraced him, turned into a spiritual form, and merged with Ramakrishna, whose mind plunged into deepest samadhi, giving him realization of his identity with Christ, and

---

was in him and that when he concentrated the powers of his mind, or when for some reason or other they were collected for him, so to speak, by intense interest in some object engaging his attention, he would have found, and obviously did find, light in everything, even in stones. The phenomenon recalls Wordsworth's paean (in the *Immortality Ode*) to the mystic innocence of childhood—

—when meadow, grove, and stream,
The earth, and every common sight,
To me did seem
Apparelled in celestial light...

—a time of effortless concentration and absorptive wonder in the young child's soul, comparable to—though of course a state far more diffused and errant than— Ramakrishna's blazing one-pointedness of all his faculties.

[*] Rising from within, for the experience was intended for no one else (similar to Jesus' baptism by John when a voice—audible to Jesus and John only—was heard from the inner heaven).

the two eternally with Brahman.*

The experience revealed two more truths he had not known before to the same degree: Christianity was divinely inspired, a genuine path to God-consciousness, and Jesus himself was a divine incarnation. For the rest of his life Ramakrishna worshipped him thus, kept a picture of him in his room, adorned daily with flowers, and always spoke of him with special reverence.

This was his last breakthrough into the higher mystical regions. He was thirty-eight. There were to be no more paramount new experiences, though there would be samadhi several times a day (that state to reach which once in a lifetime is considered enlightenment) for the next twelve years. There were no further revelations from beyond.

His life of personal spiritual illumination had reached its apogee. Heaven could teach him nothing more.

In 1876 Chandramani passed away at eighty-five, her last years overcast by senility. She would warn her son about certain people who were trying to harm him. She had fixed ideas about food and would not eat on days when the whistle of a nearby jute mill did not blow; she insisted it was a conch horn calling devotees to worship. To the end she was the woman we have seen her to be. One looks, in any period of her life, for some action or observation that reflects not a saintly but even an unusual mentality, and finds none.

The last decade is of less interest to us than what preceded, it being chiefly a period of disseminating among his fifteen or twenty closest disciples, some of whom were householders, the fruits of his supernal insights, of moulding the characters of those who would propagate his message of the indwelling God to be realized, of the universal truth of all religions, of the necessity of serving mankind as vehicles of the Supreme. The dominant figure in those last ten years, for whom Ramakrishna waited so long, is the famous Swami Vivekananda, the peerless expounder of Vedanta philosophy to the West, and equally unrivaled as the awakener of his countrymen to a renewed sense of

---

* A few years before there had been the spiritual union with Chaitanya, who had possessed him in a similar fashion. Yogeswari, we recall, had identified him with Rama during their first meeting; Gangamata had seen him as Radha incarnate. One is led to wonder who he actually was.

their spiritual heritage and the glorious destiny that he felt still awaited India as the reservoir of the world's mystical tradition: the most eloquent religious genius since St. Paul.[*] To this disciple Ramakrishna gave away all his powers,^{**} his knowledge, training him with meticulous care and watchfulness over a period of five years, remarking that by his spiritual and intellectual endowment he would "shake the world to its foundations." But their association is fairly well known, and biographies of Vivekananda himself exist. After traversing the special terrain we have chosen for this study, it does not seem necessary to explore in depth a relationship more than adequately treated elsewhere.

Besides his monastic and householder disciples, scores of others of every philosophical and religious persuasion visited Ramakrishna at the temple grounds in the last decade, and had been doing so for longer than that. While outwardly they seemed to be paying their respects to the "holy man of Dakshineswar" and he seemed to be courteously responding as a genial, compassionate teacher, he was quietly inculcating into their minds the essence of mystical discoveries made over two decades. He knew that many of his visitors would, in their turn, influence hundreds and thousands of others, carrying into untold lives the seeds of his teachings. Some were religious leaders with followings of their own; many were wandering monks and sadhus who, in the course of months, would sow far and wide the essentials of his thought. Often enough both groups might present the ideas as original with them, but in any case the ideas themselves would spread.

He was aware that a life like his own had rarely, perhaps never been seen before in India, at least none that had been recounted. "My experiences have gone much beyond those recorded in the Vedas and the Vedanta," he told his disciples. And therefore the truths that had issued directly out of those experiences had gone much beyond what

---

* Mahatma Gandhi in his thirties and forties read the complete works of the Swami and generously conceded that it was the inspired writings and addresses of Vivekananda, even more than his own pioneer efforts, that laid the foundation of modern India. And yet there is no doubt that the fountainhead of Vivekananda's genius was Ramakrishna himself. (Which Gandhi is not likely to have questioned: "The life of Ramakrishna enables us to see God face to face," he wrote.)

** Quite literally. In an extraordinary exchange, during which both realized the state of samadhi, Ramakrishna transferred to him all his supernatural powers, of which, it is true, he had made little use himself.

had been discovered or promulgated in the past—in India or the West. He had come at a time when India was being seduced by Western materialism and atheistic philosophies, causing its brightest youth to wonder if the long religious obsession of Hindus was only a standing illusion.* This development, so ominous for India, was reflected in the stream of visitors to Dakshineswar, so that Ramakrishna in his temple garden retreat knew that the reality of life around him was very different from what was taking place in Calcutta, the seedbed of these disruptive ideas.

By various means—through the innumerable contacts made at Dakshineswar, later through the far-reaching influence of the mature Vivekananda, as well as that of his other disciples, most of all through the intangible effect of his own mystic contemplations—he was to be the chief power, in life and in death, to bring India back to a renewal of ancient spiritual ideals and to offer to everyone, not Hindus only, a truly universal conception of religion such as we do not find in any prophet or philosopher of the past—one which, since him, has become increasingly an integral part of the thinking of advanced men and women in all religious communions.

In his relationship with Keshab Chandra Sen, in particular, we see dramatized his view of himself and the role he felt he had to fill in these later years—so different from the earlier, when he had no teaching, no disciples, no wife, no role: only his naked hunger for the Absolute.

Keshab Sen, the leader of the Hindu reform sect, the Brahmo Samaj, had come into his orbit for the first time in 1875, the year after his Christ experience, and, though outwardly as different as two individuals could be, they became fast friends almost at once. (All the momentous relationships of his life, with each serving very different purposes in the overall scheme of his unfoldment, had that trait in common: those with Sarada Devi, Vivekananda, Yogeswari, Tota Puri). Keshab was married, the father of children, for whose welfare and marriage prospects he felt an active concern, a religious leader who found Christ an attractive alternative to the various Hindu deities whose existence, under the influence of his Western education, he tended to interpret symbolically. He had traveled to England, had been received by Queen Victoria, lectured on

---

* Vivekananda in his late teens had agonized over this problem and only resolved it after meeting Ramakrishna.

the "new Hinduism" coming to birth in India, everywhere impressed his listeners by his oratory, intelligence, magnetic handsomeness, and quiet, simple nature. At the same time, his worldly interests were a match for his religious passion and he seemed able to harmonize the two worlds in one personality. He knew no Sanskrit, had no guru, had never been formally initiated. Despite these unorthodox tendencies and his skeptical view of much of traditional Hinduism, Ramakrishna felt drawn to him by an overpowering attraction and Keshab responded mutually: disciples of each were astonished at the strength and endurance of their friendship.

During their nine years of close association Ramakrishna gradually led Keshab to see the injustice and shallowness of his views of Hinduism—in particular his scorn of images, traditional rituals, and a belief in a personal deity, and Keshab in turn, always giving full credit to the master, passed on his insights to his own Brahmo Samaj followers, many of whom in time became admirers of Ramakrishna themselves. Undoubtedly the master's extraordinary reverence for Christ, which had so impressed Keshab, was a powerful factor in deepening their rapport. Eventually Keshab, while retaining his partiality toward Christ as his personal ideal, became a devotee of Mother Kali and often accompanied Ramakrishna, both at Dakshineswar and at his own residence in Calcutta, in fervent devotional songs and dances, to the amazement of many. In converting Keshab, the idol of numerous intellectuals in Bengal committed to his "New Dispensation," as he called it, Ramakrishna helped stem the tide of religious skepticism and secularism sweeping the country and to turn it, to a considerable degree, back into a spiritual channel. The similar influence he had on other religious leaders and social reformers resembling the early Keshab in one degree or another was not, however, matched by the love and esteem he felt toward the Brahmo leader.

The master's affection for Keshab Sen, so unexpected a follower, so different from his own personal protégés, demonstrated again his power to respond to experience freely, independently. Nor did his affection wane with time. When Keshab died in 1884 at the age of forty-six, though Ramakrishna was then surrounded by all his disciples, for whose coming—not for Vivekananda alone—he had so long waited, he was paralyzed by grief, could not move from bed for three days, spoke to no one, and said that he felt as though his body had been sawn in half.

• • •

As one ponders the steady emergence and widespread acceptance
of his three central ideas—the universality of religious truth; the
indwelling divinity in all men, the spiritual oneness of existence; and
the special divine nature of woman—one is possessed by a singular intuition that the unique intensity of his thousands of samadhi experiences[*]
has imprinted upon the medium of the collective psyche the pattern of
his superconscious visions, providing the minds of modern men with a
model from which the most significant insights and essential tendencies
would arise to advance their spiritual evolution. The specific thematic
content of his mystical ecstasies, in other words, has engraved itself
indelibly on the race-mind of the contemporary world. The result has
been—or may well be—that humanity in the last century has been
enacting *his* visions on *its* level, while thinking the ideas are its own.

The 1860s was the decade of his greatest experiences, with the
1856-74 period, from the first vision of Kali in the Temple to the final
vision of Christ in the Panchavati, covering the totality of his spiritual
conquests. Before those years the vital ideas that have taken possession
of our century, with increasing sway, were largely unknown.[**] Most
of what is significant in the modern soul was first glimpsed and pro-
claimed by Ramakrishna—All is One. The Soul is All. Truth is
Universal. Every Faith is a Path to that Truth. Woman is the Divine in
Life, to be Worshipped by Man—These commanding themes form the
pith and marrow of today's spiritual psychology, include every major
dimension of religious philosophy, and all were discovered—possibly
engendered—by Ramakrishna as a result of his unparalleled victories in
the mystical realm.

He has given the product of his spiritual visions—the inner form—
to mankind; they are to fill it with *their* experiences, inner and outer,

---

[*] Most monks and contemplative nuns, for example, do not experience this state
even *once*. After a quarter century of seclusion Thomas Merton did not—hence his
sanguine searching in Zen Buddhism for an answer. Patanjali, the legendary yogi,
considered it the crown of spiritual aspiration, attainable, after much difficulty, by
a selected few.

[**] Carlyle, Emerson, and others—the Transcendental school, notably—"knew"
them, but theoretically: not experientially, not on their pulses; knew them only
as they "knew" many other ideas. The *degree* of their knowing did not free them,
as Christ promised that the Truth, if *truly* known, *would* free us.

and the end-result, impressed into the fabric of their lives, for the purpose of *their* movement toward truth, will be the distillation of his insights.

An avatar, a divine personality, is necessary *before history can take place*. History exists for the world's creator, not its creatures. It is *his* pageant. It takes place in Him first, then in humanity. Life is to be lived *ad majorem gloriam dei*. So many prophetic words remind us of this eternal truth and we go on thinking the earth is here for our benefit. It is an illusion, born of familiar human vanity and ignorance, to believe that we have been put here primarily to develop our potentialities *per se*—for our own sakes. Since we are here by a divine Will, we are here also for *its* pleasure. *Thine* is the Kingdom.... We could not be left free to make history ourselves, for it is certain we would make it badly. With the divine goading and coaxing us at every step and living out its own history through us we almost scuttle the creation anyway.

It is the thoughts and experiences of the divine itself that become the history of man—including modern man. To implement this design it periodically seizes on one individual and overwhelms him with its truth, as Ramakrishna, from the moment he arrived at the Kali temple at the age of twenty, was overwhelmed. Then he becomes the mould in which, unknown to itself, and though he also remain unknown, the thinking of an age is to be shaped.

Visualize a band of travelers lost in a vast dark forest, seeking a path to freedom. For a long time they wander gropingly, in desperate circlings, beginning to lose hope of ever finding a way out. At last they find a man-made clearing, then a man-made path. They follow *that*, although at first with some reluctance, because it takes them miles from where, by heeding their instincts, they had been intending to go. After another long interval the path leads them out of the forest. Once free, they declare what they have achieved, tell the story of their struggles and wandering, their endurance, their courage, and their final victory. *But it was the path they found that made it all possible.* Adhering to that path, they discover another fate, another history, from the one they would have known by yielding to their own impulses.

Likewise there are pathways in the collective psyche of man, leading him through the vast forests of the subconscious mind, impressed there by saints and yogis, who in turn received *their* guidance from some master-yogi, some avatar, some Christ or Ramakrishna, known or unknown, whose mystic intuitions, divine insights, and very thoughts become the attitudes, goals, and dreams of the entire world in the generations following. Thus each of these shaping souls—the supermystics—lives the history of mankind quite literally in themselves. For the psychic pathways cannot *not* be followed—since what they communicate to the discriminating, decision-forming faculty of the individual mind seems his own innermost impulses—seems his very self. The following of the pathways is man's history, the pathmaker the begetter of that history, the shaper of the world. The *Zeitgeist* itself is his creation.

Each level of mankind will react to the impress of his thought in its own way. Whether literally, symbolically or howsoever, the main thrust of his message will be communicated. In the sphere of a revolutionary sexuality, for example, higher types of men will begin to live a Tantric relationship with the feminine power in their lives, gaining in the process, among so many things, a spirituality denied to them before. Lower types, responding to the same ideas, will indulge—for a time, more than ever—in brazen sensuality—which, though self-defeating, yet manifests, through the fog of lust, an undoubted worship of the female. On all social levels there will be a sexual upheaval, prelude to the still hidden, millennial revelation, reflecting—beyond the visible convulsions—Ramakrishna's discovery, made under Yogeswari's tutelage, that sex is divine, is a gateway to the transcendental. Not, truly, as common men indulge in it; nevertheless they blindly carry out what superior men are more knowingly attempting—it is all they can yet do, but the meaning, to those able to read the signs, is similar on both levels.

Militant feminists, though showing the feminine in its least attractive light and least genuine aspect, are also reflecting his enthronement of the feminine principle. Beneath the sound and fury of their crusades one dominant theme emerged for those who could intuit it: woman must be respected, there must be a new relationship between man and woman. In their abrasive way they have called attention to the reality of womanhood and made a necessary contribution to society as a whole. Though discriminating men did not require this service, ignorant men, making up the majority, did.

The exploitation of the female form in our time has a significance beyond the obviously sensual one: the true beauty of woman, her divine allure and mystery, discoverable in the yoga of Tantra and then

in mystical experience itself, is graphically imposed on the consciousness of modern men in a shamelessly provocative manner, to make
them aware of woman over and over—again there is the same principle
at work—far more than they would have been without this naked
appeal to the senses. *

On every level the message is coming through, and Ramakrishna's
Panchavati hours are being translated into universal realities which all
may understand and in which all may participate, though the understanding may not yet be conscious, the participation not yet enlightened.

Let us take, then, the pathways already grooved out for us. There
is perhaps no good way to resist them. Let us carry out the promptings
of our heart once generated there by Christ, then by St. Francis, in our
time by Ramakrishna. Certainly, if left to ourselves, and to *our* promptings, we know that *we* would not care to worship woman, love our
neighbor, admire his religion, or think of the Supreme as our very own.
When Ramakrishna's mind became totally fused with the Universal
Mind, every individual mind became but an inlet to that, namely, to
his. Our freedom is marginal. No evolved man of this age has the motivation, and surely not the need, to resist the depth and power of
Ramakrishna's vision, and the existential truths—to be applied by us—
that have emerged from it.

It is *his* tendencies we feel ennobling our best hours, though we
think of them as ours—*his* teachings that have made us wise, tolerant,
and universal—*his* worship of woman that is transforming our human
loves. Whether we know him as the source, matters not. It is the teachings that matter, the ideas, the worship, the tendencies that matter.
    ... It is the Truth that matters, the truth that liberates, the truth
that saves. Not Christ, not Ramakrishna. The soul in each of us, the
soul in them. The soul of all.

In the spring of 1885, not many months after the death of Keshab
Sen, who was only two years younger, Ramakrishna contracted a sore
throat which rapidly turned into something far more serious: cancer. A
little more than a year later it proved fatal.

---

* This idea was suggested in an important article by Swami Nityabodhananda,
"The Ascent of Woman," December 1972 issue of the Ramakrishna Order publi-
cation, *Prabuddha Bharata.*

It was urged upon him to remove the disease by his yoga power but he replied that he had long since offered up his body to the Supreme and could not now, to preserve his physical life, ask for it back. Life and death, he said, were matters for which the divine, not man, was responsible. When it was wondered how a man of such a pure life should have to suffer so painful and repellent a disease as cancer, he said it was the result of the sins—the negative karma—of his disciples, which he was assuming on their behalf. As Christ had assumed the sins of *his*.

Further, the manner of Christ's death was repeated with many of his disciples and in the three centuries of the Christian persecution multitudes died, as he had, a martyr's death, similar in essentials to that of their master. That is, he had lived the future in his own flesh. Even in the long age that followed Christianity's ascendancy, many individuals suffered death and torture at the hands of the Church—first Catholic, later Protestant, which in each case enacted the role of the ancient Pharisees. Thus, both in life, inspiring saintly votaries in every century—and in death, captivating more intransigent ones—Christ has prefigured the course of Western history, imprinting upon the psyche of Christians both the splendor of his spiritual principles and the solemnity of his self-sacrifice as the way, when necessary, to uphold them.

Likewise, as the thought and life-experience of Ramakrishna are steadily conquering the psyches of men in a post-Christian era, so the manner of his death has become the way that millions are dying: by cancer. Whether they will accept the cross of that malignancy in the same spirit as he may be doubted, but at least the example is there, the instruction,* and the realization that if one cannot attain enlightenment, to die by cancer may not be the worst thing that can happen to us, but the most auspicious: a present-day version of death on a cross.

And just as none of us is yet a Christ, but in meeting death as he did countless others served, like him, an unknown humanity—so none of us is yet a Ramakrishna but may also, in our cancer, or some similar affliction, be taking upon our shoulders the sins of *our* disciples—relatives, friends, children, spouse, looking secretly to us for their salvation, their strength, their hope of illumination. By bearing the disease when

---

* Intimated long ago in the Brihadaranyaka Upanishad (V. xi.3): "The supreme austerity is indeed that [which] a man suffers when he is ill." *The Upanishads*, trans. Swami Nikhilananda, (New York, 1956) v. III, 334.

it comes, in a spirit of enduring reconciliation with our fate, we overcome the evil of egoism and of body-consciousness and in the strength uncovered by this acceptance we become large and deep and humble enough to enable divine grace, finding in our liberated minds an avenue for its presence, to free *others* from what is obstructing *their* movement toward the divine. So that the prophecy of Isaiah 53, traditionally identified with Christ alone—

> Surely he hath borne our griefs, and carried our sorrows....
> He was wounded for our transgressions, bruised for our iniquities: the chastisement of our peace was upon him; and with his stripes we are healed.... The Lord hath laid on him the iniquity of us all.
> He was oppressed, and he was afflicted, yet he opened not his mouth.... For the transgression of my people was he stricken.

—becomes a description of what, that year, Ramakrishna suffered, and of what anyone may who has had the vision to perceive that no man is an island, that all *are* one, and that the heroism of every man and every woman in their hour of affliction becomes a wave of power enabling others too to find their way to the shore of redemption.

 # Appendix:

Psychological Considerations

SINCE THE WESTERN DISCOVERY of the Oriental guru-disciple relationship, one hears of numerous yogis and swamis being hailed as a special manifestation of divinity. With the slightest encouragement by the guru, often with none, his sect proclaims him an incarnation of God. The phenomenon stems from an intrinsic weakness in the human mind, organically riven into the mind-stuff at an extremely deep level, whereby to continue effectively on our path we *must* feel that the leader of our sect, the saint of our persuasion, or the prophet of our tradition, is a Messenger, Avatar, or God-man beyond compare.

Christians stress the uniqueness of Christ and a hundred Christian sects the merit of their own interpretations of him, though granting that other spiritual leaders were "good men" or "ethical teachers," which is what Buddhists concede after first declaring the transcendent glory of the Buddha, the identical process pursued by Muslims for whom Muhammad is a name like no other. The Sufi mystics of Islam, placing less emphasis on the person of the Prophet, assert that Sufism is another word for Truth. Modern Hindus seem to reflect a larger outlook, declaring (after Ramakrishna) that all religions are divinely inspired, and they appear to be an exception to the rule, but *their* savior is Krishna: "There are many divine incarnations but Krishna is God himself."

The phenomenon represents a serious structural infirmity, testifying to an early stage of man's psychological development. Recorded civilized history regresses six thousand years, seemingly ancient from the standpoint of a single lifetime, in fact but a beginning in an area so complex and unyielding, in which little progress has been made, and those who should know better as culpable as the most obtuse.

Religion is not the cause, only the exacerbator. The cause is innate, part of our natal egoism, and foreordained ignorance: that delusion which Buddha declared *was* the state of being embodied. In politics, the other major sphere where egocentrism rules, we see the tendency equally widespread: my leader, my group, my nation, my principles. Exclusivism is its name. We need not point to its appearance in social organization where it is the lifeblood of society.

In religion it disappoints more. We keep thinking that, in spite of meager evidence, religious influence will make men balanced, clear-seeing. Individuals do change, and saints do appear, but even they are usually flawed by this congenital defect of the human psyche. Mighty in devotion, selfless in service, they are often no less narrow—save for the grand exceptions, confessedly—than the most bigoted of the orthodox. Devotion unharnessed to experiential knowledge and psychic balance will not free us. It will give us holiness, as William Blake complained, but not understanding.

Of all men of whom we have record Ramakrishna seems most to have had that understanding, that universalism we have dreamed of, that freedom from the separatist mentality, which at this stage of history may be said to characterize mankind as a whole. It is one of the chief attractions in his personality. When we come to his followers we might expect less egregious manifestations of the malady we have noted, something of the same all-accepting genius that marks their idol. But here also the disease is rife. In many it is curbed but extirpated in few, since the nature of the disease renders it unthinkable that one is afflicted to begin with.

We are not surprised to find reports of prodigies, though relatively muted, attending the birth of Ramakrishna; it is usually the case with men who attain spiritual celebrity. Their followers in mythopoeic reminiscence recall certain narratives, or intimations dropped by the master; or credulous villagers, their lives pervaded by animistic totems, by inbred belief in the magical and the interposition by celestials in terrestrial schemes, recall that the great man's mother, or father, or both, were visited by annunciating spirits, and solemn prophecies invoked in dreams. This does not mean that with the advent of the genuine world-savior such wonders may not arise, but that the plethora of background magic around the birth of religious heroes tends to leave us unconvinced by even authentic signs.

Nor is wish-fulfilling remembrance confined to spiritual luminaries: the secular have their legends. Plato was called, for centuries, divine, and his begetting attributed to transcendental influence. It was rumored that his mother had been visited by Apollo before her marriage and after his death his memory was venerated on the birthday of the god. His disciples could not believe that a man of ordinary parentage had manifested so incandescent an intellect. Alexander's mother, the fierce Olympias, a mystery cultist, propagated throughout her wild existence the idea that she had been impregnated by Zeus himself in the form of a thunderbolt, thus accounting, together with her own barbaric origins, for her offspring's invincibility.*

The circumstances surrounding Jesus' nativity seem a composite

---

* Other sons of Apollo were the Emperor Augustus and the famous mystic Pythagoras, the latter believed to have been sent to earth as a human manifestation of the god to enable mankind to receive the ancient teaching. Likewise Apollonius of Tyana and Simon Magus, both contemporaries of Jesus, had followings convinced of their divinity.

of the chief features in the birth-epics of celebrated predecessors. Buddha's advent was heralded widely long before it occurred, nature agonized in convulsion at his birth, which was brought forth by a virgin, and worshipping soothsayers gravitated to his cradle prophesying future glory. The coming of Krishna, India's archetypal prophet, was announced by a star in heaven; his father was the god Vishnu. At his birth—in a prison—nature was shaken. A wicked king, Kansa, apprized of the infant's future sovereignty, schemed to have all male babies slain, though Krishna and his guardians, assisted by an intervening angel, escaped from the prison in the nick of time.

The truth is that these events first take place in the mythology of the heart—then in our histories. As such they have their own reality which need not be, and cannot be, estimated in terms of historicity alone.

But the historical facts are potent:

St. Paul *makes not a single reference* to the virgin birth, evidently interpreting the rumor as symbolic. That is, the birth of the Christ-consciousness into the world, the supreme event of earth-life, takes place without benefit of any parentage except the divine: it is self-generated—a virgin birth. "The first man is of the earth, earthy; the second man is the Lord from Heaven." (1 Cor. 15: 47). Mark and John, as well, pass over the idea in silence, and when Matthew and Luke introduce it they do so awkwardly: each painstakingly traces the genealogy of Joseph the carpenter back to Jesse, the father of David (since the promised messiah had to be an issue of the tree of Jesse), and then undercuts his pains by postulating a virgin birth for the new hero. Each wants it both ways—a virgin birth that can be vouched for genealogically! Such a transparent sophistry would explain why Mark, who repeats almost everything Matthew says, neglects so sensational an occurrence. John's refusal to include it would reflect his mystical conception of the Master from the beginning (similar to Paul's): "That was the true Light, which lighteth every man that cometh into the world" (1: 9)—the light of the soul, which in every spiritual birth *is* virginally conceived.

If Christians could quietly disregard the virgin-birth dogma as an imposition, unnecessary and antiquated, their religion would rest more lightly on their consciences, and those who have rejected Christianity for its untenable mythologies might be disposed to search for the spiritual power still present in the religion Christ founded. By abjuring merely this one obstacle to credibility much gain would result in other respects. We would, for example, be able to accept the fact that Mary his mother quite naturally had borne the other children twice referred to in the gospels but hardly ever mentioned in orthodox circles and, when so mentioned, usually fabricated into "cousins." (See Matthew 13: 54-56 and Mark 6: 3-4.)

By forcing the virgin birth on us we then conclude that the children were all Joseph's by a previous, unspecified marriage, though such a marriage, when it easily could have been, is nowhere indicated in any of the gospels, where a simple, clear-cut reference to Joseph's state (widower and father) when he married Mary would have been a welcome convenience.

Most of all, of course, the theory of virgin conception has inculcated the idea that sex is sinful, an idea saddling with its dire consequences the psyches of millions even today ... though not one to be imputed to the uncondemning Nazarene, nor to Ramakrishna, with his momentous vindication of Tantra as the medicine for our sexual ills.

INDEX

INDEX

210

ABOUT THE AUTHOR

Paul Hourihan, mystic and teacher, was born and educated in Boston, earning a doctorate in English literature. For 15 years he taught many courses and gave innumerable lectures on the subject of great mystics and mysticism, in Ontario, Canada. For almost all of his adult years he was a close student of India's Vedantic philosophy and the teachings of her greatest seers, such as Ramakrishna.

In the closing period of his life he began at long last to publish a dozen brilliantly written books, which touch on mysticism at their core, of which, this is the first.

He lived with his wife in Northern California, where she continues to carry on his work.

Vedantic Shores Press is dedicated to publishing the written works of Paul Hourihan. Its purpose is to help readers reach new shores of spiritual consciousness.

Our creative biographies, novels and non-fiction books, which incorporate Dr. Hourihan's insights from many years of meditative practice, give a clear vision and practical understanding of spirituality and mysticism based on the ancient Indian philosophy of Vedanta.

If you'd like to comment on *Ramakrishna and Christ, The Supermystics* or would like more information on upcoming books, please contact us at:

Vedantic Shores Press
P.O. Box 493100
Redding, CA 96049
Tel: 530/549-4757
Fax: 530/549-5743
Toll-free: 866/549-4757 (U.S. only)
E-mail: vedanticshores@shasta.com